# Life Is Like a Line

# Life Is Like a Line

## A Memoir of Moods, Medication, and Mania

Cynthia M. Sabotka

Foreword by Barbara Henike, M.D.

Silver Lining Publishing
St. Clair, Michigan

Published by Silver Lining Publishing
P.O. Box 399
St. Clair, MI 48079-0399
www.silverliningpublishing.com

Publisher's Cataloging-in-Publication Data
Sabotka, Cynthia M.

Life is like a line : a memoir of moods, medication and mania / Cynthia M. Sabotka. — St. Clair, MI : Silver Lining Pub., 2008.

p. ; cm.
ISBN: 978-0-9797792-0-6

1. Manic-depressive illness. 2. Manic-depressive persons. 3. Mania. I. Title.

RC516 .S23 2008
616.89/5—dc22                2007931878

Dust jacket design by Chris Rhoads and Yvonne Roehler
Interior design by Debbie Sidman
Project coordination by Jenkins Group, Inc
www.BookPublishing.com

Printed in the United States of America
12 11 10 09 08 • 5 4 3 2 1

# *Dedication*

To my mother, my father, my sister, and my brother, without whom these lessons of life and love would have not been learned.

# Contents

# *Foreword*

My psychiatric practice of twenty-eight years has been an enlightening and often an emotionally intense journey. In spite of its ups and downs I have always felt privileged to sit in the therapist's chair. I have had the opportunity to know many individuals who have shown incredible courage, tenacity, fortitude, and humor in the face of struggle and adversity.

My patients' victories are often invisible to others but represent to me a kind of personal heroism that I have come to respect. The author of this incredible memoir is one of those invisible heroes. We have traveled a four-year journey together and I feel fortunate to have been the co-pilot.

—Barbara Henike, M.D.

# Acknowledgments

To my dearest husband Ron, who is loving and constant and true. Never wavering throughout my episodes, you encouraged me, critiqued my manuscript unselfishly without complaint, and stood beside me especially when symptoms arose.

To my daughters Jennifer and Elizabeth, whose love and inspiration complete me. Jennifer, so willing to assist me, spent numerous hours editing the early text. Her life over twelve hundred miles away did not silence her love nor prevent our communication. Elizabeth will never know how her satirical sense of humor saves me and how her love on my most critical of days keeps me from falling.

Thank you Brian, Matthew, and Sherry for your acceptance of me and for wonderful memories that we share. Rich with joy, my grandchildren give me no greater gift than their love and their preciousness. Born of innocence, they are pure and generous with their affection and they have given to me more happiness than I have ever known.

To my Aunt Anne, a woman who is warm and loving and wise. When the girls were small, your regular visits every Saturday with goodies and good humor lifted me in ways that you will never know. It is easy to admire you, you are easy to love.

Dr. Barbara Henike, brilliant psychiatrist, masterful decoder of my mind's complexities…my book took flight because of you. Fate brought me to these crossroads but fortune brought me to you. As my mental professor, trainer, and confidant, you are deserving of my unending praise.

To my friend Ann, who called me often "just to be sure I was okay." She is my friend, and her lighthearted approach to life continues to encourage me.

I would like to express my appreciation to the gifted associates at the Jenkins Group, Inc., in Traverse City, Michigan. Each member, experts in their field, moved the manuscript slowly through production until it became my masterpiece. Dedicated to my success, they were giving of their talent and gracious with their time. Rebecca Chown, my editor, kept me upwardly mobile and on task, encouraging me when I didn't believe it was possible, and Marlene Y. Satter was my proofreader extraordinaire. All under the direction of Jerry Jenkins…Thanks for a "stellar" ensemble production.

# *Introduction*

During my days of writing, I found myself filled with thoughts and moods and desires flowing from my pessimistic self. While the words came to me instantly, there was uneasiness about them. In my inability to suppress this uneasiness, it became clear that a state of flux was happening to me for some specific reason all over again.

Beginning somewhere in my ancestry, it has followed the bloodline all the way down. Genetics, I suppose, unavoidable genetics. My ancestry holds the answers to questions I will never think to ask.

I am the caboose, and the power of the conflict has been my steam. Perhaps my birth was saved for last to absorb the family spills, but my personal growth has been born out of the reflections of a child. Some say it's all in my mind, and after many years of discussion with a mental trainer, I now concur.

Memories, as you might expect, are the nucleus of our existence, and mine are based on the unintended unsuspecting events of family and the consequences of their actions. This is a story of mood and temperament, suspicion and pain, familial homophobia, coping and forgiveness. Consequently, this is a recounting of typical and atypical behaviors under specific circumstances and how their effects ultimately brought my obscurity to light.

Thoughts, moods, and temperaments are like breath. Normally a naturally occurring phenomenon, each is evidence of the mind's handiwork. Expressive and powerful, often running haywire, flawlessly cosmic, comedic by nature or not—the greatest creation is the mind as it controls senses that are the connection of the body and the life of the soul.

As my pace accelerated, my mind's eye began to see things…in darkness and in a different light. What was once breathtaking heightened to exhilaration, and then exhaustion became senselessness and finally hopelessness. Under my distorted mental command I began to change, and in my elation, poetry began to swirl unrestrained, driven by my vacillating moodiness and the high spirits of each occurring moment.

They say that everyone has a book inside of them, and mine, journal-like in style, is a collection born at conception that lay dormant for forty-eight years. The simple union of a man and woman brought the circumstances and the results I now inscribe. And they, the very circumstances that have given me pause, have driven my enthusiasm. I have written this book under the powerful force of two minds and in doing so I have endured all of the joy and all of the joylessness my life has ever known.

I do not believe my cast of characters represents anything more than earthly souls yearning, searching, and striving for their desires, battling their demons, and amending their existence to stay alive, but in doing so, each has affected the lives of the others.

# CHAPTER 1

# *Intensity and Pattern*

I feel like I have been running all my life. At full speed. Running away from something I didn't even know existed. My father ran from it. My mother ran from it. My brother has been caught, and my sister, well, I am not certain about my sister.

Where it began, I cannot say for sure. Based on what I know, it probably started at least a generation before my parents, but few people talked about those things back then. When they did speak, it was in hushed terms about someone so ill that only the treatment gained during incapacitation would bring them back to sanity. More typically, suffering individuals were said to be "moody" or were thought to have a "coping" mechanism. If you admitted you had a mental problem or worse yet lived in denial, you could be admitted to an institution, often against your will. People were said to be in a "fit" of depression, but fit they were not.

## Life Is Like a Line

Patients in state hospitals, often called insane asylums, were subjected to the uncharted territory of experimental treatments. They usually shared their mental maladies with dementia patients or those with syphilis, which was a common psychiatric disorder and completely devastating during the nineteenth century.

As the roots trace back generations, not all of those afflicted have stopped running from the ghosts of their past. Rather than face incapacitation, my family members clenched hands with their demons and ran. For most of my life, I followed their path. But as fast as I went, my demons still caught up with me. Finally, I just stopped running. Actually, I take that back. I didn't stop, really. My difficulties finally stopped me.

I know now that you can't run from yourself. You cannot escape what is inside of you. All anyone can do is look back to try to understand and look forward to learn how to live through and with it. I cannot say with any assurance at what point my parents were caught and to what degree they were affected. There is no proof of their psychological condition but history has a way of repeating itself. I have firsthand knowledge of the persistence of wavering moods that frighten with experience and I know that denial, at any level, will be brief. Often seen in childhood are warning signs, patterns of mood and temperament. Many people can probably recount tales of instability, fear, and anger in their childhoods, but I suspect most are afraid to look back and face them. In doing so, I have learned that my current state of being was created by a churning of chemicals and circumstance. But even with a lifetime of fluctuating moods, I would never have predicted what I now recognize is mine.

By design, the uniqueness of man and the meticulous creation of his mind are like the stars in the sky. No two are alike, and the complexity and depth are incomprehensible. Even though my emotional temperature has given me more profound highs and lows, I have managed to fly just below the radar.

Dr. Kay Redfield Jamison, author of *Touched with Fire: Manic-Depressive Illness and the Artistic Temperament*, says that "Cycles of fluctuating moods and energy levels serve as a background to constantly changing thoughts, behaviors, and feelings. Thinking can range from florid psychosis, or 'madness,' to patterns of unusually clear, fast and creative associations, to retardation so profound that no meaningful mental activity can occur. Behavior can be frenzied, expansive, bizarre, and seductive or it can be reclusive, sluggish, and dangerously suicidal. Moods may swing erratically between euphoria and despair or irritability and desperation. The rapid oscillations and combinations of such extremes result in an intricately textured clinical picture." Dr. Jamison explains perfectly the fluctuation of the manic-depressive mood. What appears to be normal transforms over time and as symptoms become rapidly intertwined, they are "an intricately textured clinical picture."

The more stressful my life became, the more demanding my moods were. After all, I experienced a constant flow of clever ideas, inventions, and great inspirations that kept me moving at a speed not even I could keep up with. But the cleverness turned into confusion, the inventions into frustration, and the inspirations eventually into irritation. While not particularly faceless, my difficulty remained nameless for many years. It didn't deserve a name, not from me, at least not up until now. But lack of knowledge does not nullify the force of genetics and it is apparent that some facet of our heredity exists in me. Astonished and affected to my core, I am pale with its disorderly conduct.

To understand my current state of being, which at times is limited to sheer existence, you have to know where I came from.

# CHAPTER 2

# The Past Brings Presence...Ours

Whationat I know begins with my mother Sophia, a very colorful and contributing character to say the least. She was born on September 9, 1918, in a wonderful neighborhood in Detroit, the eldest daughter of three children born to Polish-Austrian-Russian immigrants.

At a very young age, she learned that her life would be filled with countless responsibilities, which was not uncommon for children in those days. Her father owned several butcher shops in the metropolitan Detroit area and he was so successful that, as a teenager, my mother was forced to leave her education behind to work in his stores.

When she was a young child, the family resided in old Dearborn, where her father owned a very well-known smokehouse. His smoked sausages and hams were much in demand and his sales were great, but his system of credit and collections were out of sync. He was everything to the business and the business was everything to him, but it wore him ragged too soon.

Tough times and a too-generous heart forced a loss, then closure, and a move to Detroit, where the next smokehouse was born. They lived above the store because tough times returned. Their next move was out to the country, to a place they called the suburbs. Each time, the enterprise began as a success.

The family rarely escaped the smells and sounds of the animals that were their livelihood. Long hours were spent preparing chickens for market and my mother, still so young, had many tasks to perform. For a wage of fifty cents per week, she would walk several miles to purchase supplies. Upon her return, she would restock the shelves and ready the poultry for market by chopping off their heads. There were days when the chickens ran around headless, slamming into each other until their hearts ceased to beat. What a horrible image this has always presented to me, to her.

Beyond the long hours she put into the family business, my mother was charged with the supervision of her younger brother and caring for her ailing younger sister Genevieve. Genevieve was only five and a half when she was stricken with the deadly disease diphtheria, which eagerly ravaged her body. One day while under my mother's care and with her body temperature rising out of control, Genevieve's breathing became more difficult.

Surrounded by the sounds of death, my mother watched her sister pass away. Heartsick at her passing, her spirit would be darkened forevermore by this devastating loss and the ensuing guilt that haunted her. To this day, she questions with anger the lack of attention her mother gave her dying baby sister.

This family crisis did not preclude the cruelty of her father or the mental and physical abuse he imposed upon her. Often, the men who frequented the butcher shop were there for reasons besides the purchasing of meat for the family table. Not surprisingly for the time, my grandfather was a bookmaker and a gambler who was in the numbers racket.

The corruption my mother was exposed to crossed many lines, as she was also expected to sell parimutuels, a form of paper gambling. Many men visited their store and many men found her appealing.

She had not a defender for her honor. She was young and demure and her purity was enticing. Of all the experiences she was threatened by, she wrestles most with the memories of her father's relentless cruelty, his horrific temper, and his vulgarities. Too many nights drowning in his own intoxication and rage, my mother and her mother were abused by his beatings and verbal abuse. With her hair pulled as his method of waking her, he would sit atop her and begin to slap her. Calling her filthy names and making degrading sexual remarks, he was a monster.

She is now eighty-eight years old and cannot speak of him. But she remembers all too well her experiences with him, and when I look into her eyes, I hate him as well.

Alcoholism was the infirmity that ended his life at age forty-two, and while my grandmother struggled with his unpaid debts, she moved the family back to Detroit. My mother exposed, she became vulnerable in the world too soon.

She grew to be an introvert with a rather nervous temperament. Headstrong and hypersensitive, she could be difficult. Remarkably, she was able to overcome some of the heartbreak of her youth and discover a new sense of herself. In Detroit, she found a closeness with her brother and a comfort in friends she had never known before. Just after her twentieth birthday, she was encouraged to audition for a singing engagement at The Harmony Bar, where her best friend knew someone who needed a singer.

The combination of her beautiful voice and spirited temperament made her the perfect candidate for the audition. Her professional rendition of the song she chose was devoid of any shyness. She was effervescent with theatrical presentation and excited at the promise of a blossoming new career. She also desperately needed the change.

A torch singer, her musical expression was similar to Billie Holiday or Lena Horne but her intensity, strong emotion, and quivering voice put her in the same class as Judy Garland. Each night her best friend would accompany her to The Harmony and afterwards they would enjoy conversation and cocktails with friends before returning home.

My mother's tuxedo-clothed pianist was quite talented as well, and they were beginning to turn heads. Their success was short-lived, however, as she quickly became disenchanted with show business. She was asked to appear in a downtown Detroit club that would have been a major venue for her talent and was told what she was expected to do in return.

My mother was not about to show her gratitude in this way, to compromise her virginity for a chance to swing on a star. In the era of racketeering, she had seen enough and she was sickened by the overtones and unwanted sexual advances, sick enough to turn her back on this dangerous territory. On the night of her last appearance, she told her friend that she would never return, and once she walked out the door, she never looked back.

My father's youth was far easier than my mother's. Whether it was his gender or his circumstance, John was not exposed to the same hardships, even though he was born just a few months after my mother. He was raised in Manchester, New Hampshire, a town that housed the largest cotton textile mill in the world. Manchester sat along the Merrimack River, twenty miles from the Massachusetts border, fifty-eight miles from Boston.

He was the second of six children born into a warm-hearted family of Greek immigrants. Employed at a very young age, my father's days were filled with the responsibilities of working and studying, and then there were the extracurricular activities. He was a clever boy and learned to improvise. On one of the snowiest days of the season, he made his own skis out of barrel slats found behind the house. He waxed the skis and took to the snow, teaching himself as he went along, typical behavior for him.

As he grew older, he became more involved in school activities and received many accolades for his work. He was not only the star quarterback of the Manchester High School football team but an up-and-coming amateur wrestler known as "The Great Chuck Montana." With many opportunities to win the prize, his unwillingness to fall for the prevailing champ eventually took him out.

Unfortunately, his youthful spirit took a hard blow when the depression hit and everything he once knew suddenly changed. The future of the town teetered upon the bankrupt textile mill. As the largest employer in Manchester, the nine-month strike only fragmented the already crumbling economy. With a gentle push from his parents, he and his siblings were forced to leave home. With optimism under one arm and his clothing under the other, he left for the industrial state of Michigan, where his sister lived with her husband. The difficulties caused by the Great Depression made his arrival more than inconvenient for his sister, so he found meager accommodations in a gas station nearby.

After a time, he was able to move into his sister's home, but the situation was bad for both of them. The only room available was at the top of the stairway in the unfinished attic. A suitcase, a mattress, and a hopeful heart separated him from failure. As if that weren't bad enough, my father was forced to hide from his sister's overbearing father-in-law who lived there, too. Whenever the old man was home, my father was forced to stay hidden in the attic.

Weekdays were spent working in his sister's sodette to pay off his room and board, and evenings were spent learning about the life insurance business, soon to be his new career. The completion of his studies came quickly, and with his qualifications in place, he could finally begin his new career.

Every morning, with borrowed satchel in hand, he would leave his sister's home and follow the streets and avenues to his assigned territory in the neighborhoods he called home. His rather shy but friendly demeanor was reassuring to most and doors easily opened to him.

Sometime in late November of 1940, he came upon a well-cared-for bungalow on Detroit's east side and knocked on the door. While mentally preparing for this sales call, he caught the silhouette of a young woman standing in the doorway nearby, but as he attempted to get a better look at her, she disappeared from sight. Fortunately for my father, he was befriended by her brother and began visiting in the evenings to play cards. Curious about him too, the young lady made herself visible to him and soon my father knew he was in love. He proposed within six months of their introduction and my mother quickly accepted.

In the meantime, the insurance game was moving too slowly for him and he wasn't so sure it was his calling. He enjoyed working in his sister's sweet shop, so he went to his brother-in-law and asked for a loan. This would be the financial backing he needed so that he and his bride-to-be could open their own sodette.

While his sister and brother-in-law were agreeable to my father's proposal, they were concerned about the repayment of their loan and reminded him that difficult times did not preclude him from fulfilling his obligation. He was warned that this was no family partnership; this was a loan. Likewise, upon hearing the news of his rather sudden engagement, they congratulated him.

With money in hand, the Nortown Sodette became his and my father became a familiar face in the neighborhood. Charming and rather flirtatious, he liked to have a good time and he began to have visitors. Many times, women came into the sodette just to visit him. My mother found them to be a constant source of irritation and they took up valuable space, so she began charging them thirty-five cents to occupy a stool at the counter. Talk if you want, but pay you shall, and on this day she became a financial partner.

However, she did not like her fiancé's new pals or new habits and she felt deprived of his attention. Aware of her anger but unwilling to comply with her demands, my father continued to carouse and play cards and he occasionally disappeared for days on end without revealing his whereabouts. Upon his return, she would rant and rave in a fit of anger, convinced this disappearing act included sexual adventures with other women. If women were paying thirty-five cents just to be near him, it was easy to imagine what might follow. In spite of her anger, his comings and goings continued.

My mother should have been alarmed at his behavior; instead, her volatile temperament frightened him so much that he called the wedding off one week before the ceremony. Her promise to be good was enough for him, and their marriage took place the following Saturday, which just happened to be one of the hottest days of the summer. In fact, it was so hot their best man passed out during the ceremony and hit his head on the altar. Since he was dazed but uninjured, the Catholic ceremony continued for almost a full hour more.

Marital bliss was quickly interrupted when my father enlisted in the United States Navy to answer his patriotic call. At the designated time, he left his war bride and his customers and headed for Georgia to begin his studies at the Navy's communication school. He loved education and believed it was important; he thoroughly enjoyed being back at school. But the end of classes meant graduation, and this chief radioman would be shipping out soon. With money in hand, he sent a telegram to my mother asking that she come to Georgia for some rest and relaxation stateside. Excited but apprehensive, she headed for the train station bound for Georgia, knowing that she would soon be in his arms.

He was very excited to see his new wife and as nervous as a bridegroom. They took pleasure in each other's company, shared thoughts and feelings, and knew they would always be together. The instability of the sodette was forgotten; it was full speed ahead. Their weekend was quite memorable, but they would not know just how fruitful until January of the following year.

The labor and delivery went smoothly and their infant son enjoyed the adoration of both his mother and maternal grandmother, who lived together during the war, shared all the household responsibilities and infant care, and encircled this baby boy with so much of themselves that there could be no separation.

The news of the birth radiated all the way back to Brazil where the U.S.S. *Memphis* awaited her orders. It was confirmed by telegram that the twenty-three-year-old radioman was now a father, but Brazil was very far away and while the new father was absent, one of his brothers and his wife's only brother took turns "borrowing" money from the sodette. The cash register did not ring full but was never quite empty; they took just enough to pay off their gambling debts, but they took and took until the money was all gone. Since there wasn't enough coming in to keep the business going, my mother was forced to close the sodette. Then the balance of the loan came due and soon all was exhausted, especially my mother.

It was now the end of the war and my father returned home. It had been three long years, but he had enjoyed the exhilaration at every port, the women glancing, the children chasing and yelling his name. They thought he was an American movie star, and for a time he was.

## Life Is Like a Line

My father returned home with a dream, but relatives would quash any hope for success. A restaurant, the Tally-Ho, closed as quickly as it opened, as relatives continued to empty the cash register for their own use. To avoid further confrontation, my father found employment in the manufacturing industry, leaving his meager insurance residuals behind. His best decision was to do what he enjoyed. He was a born salesman. Full of vitality, he was effervescent and ready for the trade. It was his skill and expertise the company wanted in exchange for a healthy salary and bonuses. But his transition to life stateside was clumsy and he had many problems adjusting to living in the family way.

He'd had three demanding years on board ship and had been idolized whenever in port. With so much time away, he'd begun to feel estranged from his wife and young son. The truth was, he had become accustomed to living a rather unattached life.

At the same time, his rambunctious little boy did not care for the intrusion of this stranger, and many times my father felt like he was on the outside looking in. The unfamiliar kinship was not so easily penetrated, so my father chose the path of least resistance. On weekends he began leaving my mother "to play cards with the boys." This was a repeat of their earlier days, and she would not know his whereabouts until his return on Monday morning. Angered, another conflict would develop, and again he was reintroduced to her temper.

This scene was repeated over and over again and greatly affected their relationship. The more condemning she became, the less he was captivated by her. This war of words and feelings was the beginning of broken promises and ushered in an air of resentment and a breakdown in their marriage. As her dedication began to wane for her husband, it deepened for her little boy, and the relationship of mother and son continued to develop without him.

My father very much wanted to have another child, but my mother was adamant about maintaining her current status. She was not having any more children, at least not now. In her uncertainty, she was not sure she could accept the dependency of another child, and after all, she already had her little boy. Despite her intentions and desires, "Daddy's little girl" arrived exactly one year after his return from the service.

This perfect little girl should not have been a threat to anyone, but her innocence and sweet demeanor were not enough to capture our mother's heart. She didn't care to share her husband's attention, in or out of their home. Feeling detached from her life, she was frightened and apprehensive and found it impossible to care for her new infant or her young son. Someone should have realized the magnitude of her despair and her desire for solitude as it began to envelop her and she began to withdraw. My mother was moving into unfamiliar territory on a path headed for dire consequences.

Though her mother was able to leave her world to join theirs, before they even realized it, my mother's darkness paralyzed her and it was confirmed that she was sliding into a deep depression. Her symptoms were likely a postpartum or peripartum depression, which was not a recognizable ill in the 1940s. The *Diagnostic and Statistical Manual of Mental Disorders* (DSM-IV) was not published by the American Psychiatric Association until 1952. This guide for communicating mental health conditions helps clinicians share various aspects of illnesses and reach consensus on which symptoms define which disorders. Plagued by a lifetime of taxing conditions and in the absence of established medical criteria similar to the DSM-IV, my mother's darkness prevailed.

It is currently recognized that women who have bipolar disorder or other psychiatric problems have a higher risk of developing postpartum psychosis, which includes symptoms of sleep disturbances, obsessive thoughts about the baby, and rapid mood swings from depression to irritability to euphoria. But based on the medical standard of the day, my mother was treated with sedatives and psychotherapy, her mother became her caregiver, her husband remained the breadwinner, and she fought her demons back to better health.

Soon my father was offered a transfer that took them to a small town near the state capital. During this relocation, he began to travel more and was home less. They rented a beautiful home and my mother was given the one and only responsibility of raising the children and managing the household, but he was doing it again. That son of a bitch was doing it all over again. He moved her here and left her and she was bewildered. Her annoyance was visible, vocal, and penetrating and there was good reason for her anger and hurt.

He would leave her in the wee hours every Monday morning with briefcase, coat, hat, and bag in hand. He would return to her late Friday, worn out, needing rest, wanting her embrace. But there would be no embrace, no affection, no union. She was not about to forgive his conscious absence. This time, as her anger mounted, her bitterness and resentment made her turn away from him as he had from her so many times before. Her feelings resulted in blame, depression, irritation, and criticism, and often that combination would cause flying dishes and the hell of the spirit all over again.

For his part, it was not unusual for him to voice his disgust and disapproval in an insensitive and cruel way. What he continued to do was unforgivable. His elated ego helped to build the very career that was a torment to her, and while they were beginning to be able to afford more, their marriage was receiving much less from him.

He was generous and brought her gifts. He wanted to make love, and then something happened: He told her to get out of his bed and she did, for most of the remaining years of their marriage.

Such angst continued to create the circumstances that caused her fury, but imagine what life might have been like if he had kept his promises. This was the beginning of the exposure the children would always remember. They lived on the floor of battle. They should not have heard the angry words of jealousy and they should not have felt the commotion.

There was no Monday morning escape for them, no hat, no coat, no bag; they were the sponges. They absorbed. At this point, any memories of a healthy marriage were long forgotten. No talking, no eating, no sleeping together. There was too much resentment in a pressure cooker of desires. So she saw the lawyer, the papers were drafted and servable, she called him, but she couldn't do it. She should have done it, for she had so many grounds. This was for *her* sanity, but she lost her nerve. She lost her nerve two more times until the lawyer told her, "Forget it; you'll never do it."

Reminiscence can be a dangerous enterprise when it, rather than reality, determines the future. Perhaps the intensity of their relationship was addicting or the fear of being alone made her stay. The consequences of her decision weren't surprising, but rather resulted in the culmination of all her worst fears: he resumed the tendencies she had tried to end. He remained unpredictable; she continued to be nervous and anxious. He was verbally abusive and self-centered; she was intense. He was strong and independent and she was anything but.

Dependence with alliance can be harmonious. Dependence without alliance is destructive. Not much time passed before this truth would prove to be devastating for her, and although the devastation was predictable when it hit, it came not with the force of a backhanded slap but with a bolt of lightening. It was the numbing effect of a million electrical volts of darkness. The signs of her delicate emotional condition were disregarded until she finally became so weak from their battles and the relentless persistence of her mental ruin that her condition could no longer be ignored. It was determined; her present state was the culmination of just ten letters written on the doctor's chart: depression, severe persistent depression. Simple letters. Unobtrusive, harmless little beasts of the alphabet arranged in such a way that explain entirely to the reader the condition of her soul. This diagnosis would universally proclaim her suffering, disclose her anguish and reclusive desires, and verify the infestation that torment has on the human spirit.

She was given Secobarbital (Seconal), which belongs to the class of medications called barbiturates. Used for the treatment of insomnia and as a sedative to relieve the symptoms of anxiety or tension, it works by slowing down the nervous system.

Fortunately, my mother was able to rely upon her mother for help and support once again. Somewhat surprisingly, my grandmother was partial to my father. She cooked his favorite meals and often played cards with him when the children went to bed. A widow for many years, she had finally found a man to appreciate her. She was the ultimate Polish mother-in-law; she would not bear the brunt of any blame or comic tale. Adorned with a perpetual apron and rather overweight herself, she cooked and baked and spoiled them with all the family favorites while managing to sneak a beer and a smoke every now and then.

My grandmother even defended my father. She was proud of him and would declare her unsolicited belief to "Be nice to him; he is a good man, Sophie," but they were empty words to mother, who replied, "I hate him even more."

Finally, when my mother's apparent recovery was made, my grandmother packed up her things and went home. The days and weeks that followed would find my father actively traveling again, but when invited to join fraternal organizations, he thoughtfully and surprisingly declined. For once, his focus was on Mother. These were days and nights of his own nervousness and apprehension and the constant struggle with their home life began to affect him. They both wanted to move back home to Detroit, where their families lived.

Just in time, a favorable circumstance occurred. A lateral business opportunity within his company would bring them back home. No more long days without him, no more seclusion or trying to fit in; they were going home. She would be better once they were home; this was her wellness move. No more loneliness, just familiarity.

She began to improve greatly, and for several years they mutually enjoyed a better frame of mind. What once were extreme highs and lows were tempered as they focused on their young family, their neighborhood, and their friends.

Now there were picnics and travels back home to Manchester to visit family and to swim at the beach. This period provided a healthy atmosphere, and with medication as liberator, a new atmosphere developed and was maintained.

As the breadwinner, my father felt great pressure, and the expectations that lay upon him were enormous. He left the old territory to expand the new one, which included the cultivation of a new office staff. He was to assemble and educate a top-notch sales team while maintaining timetables and expense accounts.

He proved to be an exemplary manager, giving one hundred ten percent through personal sacrifice, but the home office wanted more. Weeks turned into months of developing, creating, designing, and coordinating. He was good at what he did, he had plenty of enthusiasm, he couldn't sleep, and he lived for Monday through Friday, sometimes arriving at four in the morning to prepare for the day.

But his boss was a relentless taskmaster and a frightened bully. He feared my dad's enthusiasm, and with unbridled jealousy attempted to drive him into the ground. Regrettably, he was successful in many ways, and my father began feeling the effects of an old enemy of his own. He fought his anxiety and had a few more drinks and a few more cigarettes, went out with his customers, and caroused with the salesmen. That led to more dinner meetings, more drinks, more distractions, more late nights, three packs a day, more distractions, and then questions, answers, accusations, and confrontations. Running, nope…run no more…*I gotcha*.

Unable to stop these escalating effects, he fell into a depression of his own and suffered a complete nervous breakdown. But his psychiatrist was mother's, and he did not feel that hospitalization was necessary. Dad would have fought any notion of incapacitation anyway. He was not the "out of action" kind and this whole ordeal was to be kept a secret.

In the library of his psychiatrist's home, confidential conversations were held and over the course of his treatment there grew an eventual harmony and common ground between my parents as my father came to better understand the entanglement of his boss. As was customary in those days, he was given a tranquilizing drug known as Milltown (Meprobamate) to settle him down, and that seemed to do the trick.

Meprobamate is a bitter white powder used as a tranquilizer, a muscle relaxant, and an anticonvulsant. Launched in 1955 in Milltown, New Jersey, it became a best-seller and was known in the popular media as "Happy Pills." By 1970, it was listed as a controlled substance after it was discovered to cause physical and psychological dependence. For Dad, it was just what the doctor ordered, just what he needed, just what they needed, just in time.

By no means did their relationship suffer persistently, but maintaining their marriage was an uphill struggle. My father enjoyed doing things and my mother was a homebody. The more he persisted, the stronger she resisted.

## Life Is Like a Line

She was uncomfortable mingling with strangers and knew nothing of making small talk, nor did she wish to learn. Small talk was very different from her love of the nightclub. Singing was personal, not interactive, and self-expression through singing was an escape from the mundane existence she had known, as well as the opportunity for the interpretation of her soul.

My father, on the other hand, loved conversation and practically wrote the book on small talk. He considered my mother's attitude to be a rejection of him.

In spite of their great differences, the seasons came and went many times before the churning in her stomach and her feelings of anger returned, but small problems eventually worsened and her exasperation grew out of proportion. He was gone again; he was traveling still, home now, leaving on Monday. Somehow he didn't get the picture, or didn't want to. She couldn't stop it; she just couldn't replace the bad thoughts with good. Her emotions started to run high and because of her nature, that melancholy layer just beneath the surface began to brew.

It was not her fault; there was something inescapable about it. She was often difficult to please and her moods were erratic, but it was something that just was. For reasons not then understood, the cycle would repeat over and over. My mother was all too obsessive and completely compulsive. Their arguments were cutting; they spanned many years. The expression "Don't sweat the small stuff" could have been a breath of new life had they followed its mandate. For decades my mother relied on that red glycerin capsule for her relief. The Seconal and the psychiatrist were visited with great regularity but neither would temper her moods or lighten her load. In the scheme of things my mother was a breeding ground for commotion due to her unrepressed anger and it was sad to see her so volcanic all the time. She continued to rely on Seconal for mental management but it was obvious, at least to me, that it never really addressed her symptoms or altered what was necessary.

My mother's next major depressive episode occurred shortly after my sister's seventh birthday. She was just a child, my brother not quite a teen. They were fragile children and had been through a great deal already. The stress of getting through each day was great and our mother's feelings of sadness and jealousy were too apparent. My father became concerned and so did she as her mood swings worsened. There were just too many negative feelings. They were not containable and they were persistent; they meant depression. It was obvious that she was beginning to suffer the devastation that only a complete nervous breakdown could bring and she reluctantly agreed to be hospitalized. A method of treating patients affected with psychiatric disorders involves passing an electric current through the brain. It is not for the weak or the weak at heart; she agreed and succumbed to these shock treatments and never speak of them.

Her recovery took place in a beautiful rest home about one hour from the family. She spent several months there recuperating. While there, she made a friend and my father visited, but he worried about their children and the impact this would have on them.

For their part, my brother and sister experienced the heartache that children should never feel, and although they were well cared for by our grandmother, they were much too young to understand the reason for their separation from their mother. They just felt it. The first-born war baby began to seek out friendships for comfort, gratification, and companionship. The baby boomer in blond ringlets was given Phenobarbital, a barbiturate used to control seizures and as a sedative to relieve anxiety, to help her sleep.

As my mother recovered, my father continued to work on a major undertaking. He was the founder of the largest football team on the east side of Detroit and his leadership brought about an enormous change in the community. This was volunteerism, something my father never feared. Juggling his schedule between work and the ball club, he thrived. He was effervescent on the field and as it spilled over, other members followed his charge.

Organizing this club brought a common interest to my parents and achieving something together helped provide harmony again. The necessary healing took place. Eventually, my mother took over the cheerleading squad while my father remained active on the board of directors. Fifteen years later, the club was nearly one thousand strong and still supporting the principle of "good sportsmanship" that was my father's founding belief.

## Life Is Like a Line

With autumn's arrival in 1952, the children returned to school. My mother was doing well and my grandmother was confident she could again return home. Soon the wintry glow of the season surrounded them and the harmonious atmosphere was cause for jubilation. Just remembering the holidays would be an underestimation compared to the gift that would be delivered the following fall. Once her physician learned of their surprise, he became furious. He felt it was happening too soon and he feared for my mother's delicate condition. This was the very occurrence that could jeopardize her health and perhaps drive her back into a myriad of mental complications.

Medications and shock treatments aside, this period would be more challenging than any she had ever known. The womb was too delicate a place after such turmoil, and stripped of her medications, without even an aspirin for relief, there were days and nights when she climbed the walls. But all was just a memory eventually; their gift, by accident or heaven's plan, would be the continuation of our family tree. Born the proverbial baby of the family, I was the second daughter, the third child, another sibling, a sister, and unknowingly perhaps the cusp of some grand scheme.

CHAPTER 3

# Through the Eyes
# of a Child

I was born September 18, 1953, in Harper Hospital in Detroit. My mother reports that I must have been anxious for my arrival because her easy forceps delivery went well, which was a blessing for her, given that she was thirty-five when I arrived. In those days, any pregnant woman over thirty was considered "up in age" and became an eyebrow raiser. My father always told me I was a "beautiful baby" and our family photographs prove him right. "But in fact," he would add in later years, "all of our children were beautiful."

Fortunately, my birth brought change to the family without a repeat of the previous turmoil and the transition was as smooth as if planned. The hospital was a short distance from home, straight up Gratiot Avenue just miles to downtown Detroit. Obviously, I have no recollection of arriving home, but I imagine a triumphant first meeting between my brother, my sister, my grandma, and me. I suspect there was some sibling uncertainty about my arrival, and based on what I know of them as adults, I would imagine they exchanged words about me. My brother might have said "What a treasure" with my sister replying, "When do we bury it?"

An old joke, yes, but this might have been the most candid reflection of the feelings that were evident even then. Pink and lively, I was a cheerful seven-plus-pound brand-new sister with a noted good disposition. Still, they saw me for all I was worth: baby bottles, diaper changes, and a smiling, attention-taking, spit-drooling nighttime interrupter.

In time, there would be no escaping the knowledge they couldn't share with me then. The storyline would follow: three children brought together by design, in the course of a twist and turn of life. Three very impressionable children circumstantially lacking hopefulness while sharing an environment filled with unhealthy parental behaviors.

Childhood, huh? They say the mind never forgets, and yet I remember little of my childhood, so I have cautiously used the information of others to fill in the blanks. As the years have unfolded, the truth has been revealed to expose the vivid dramatic situations that played out.

Lack of memory may be a good thing. While I sum up the early days with details that are loose, lost, or unpleasant, I am not all that anxious to open up this psychiatric Pandora's Box. But the upside for me is the thought of my father and his camera, film, bulbs, and our poses.

He was able to capture the split seconds of life on black-and-white glossies now stored in a box, and they have become my picture window of insight into our world. What my father exposed through nostalgia quietly enlightens me and gives me comfort.

It is relatively easy to distinguish me from the others in our family. I am the youngest girl and I have a deep set of dimples, one in each cheek, and I'm having a good time. I know this because I'm smiling from ear to ear. Even so, I get frustrated with the vagueness of the photos because I want to know more about the who, what, when, where, why, and how of them. I wonder about the turmoil. If I'm really at point B but it feels like Z, how in the hell did I get past A?

Contemplating the little girl in the photos is a senseless game; the only way I will ever know the scope of her is to be patient. There is no mirror's reflection that can reveal the tale of her life or the feelings that lie within her core. My parents, the birth of my siblings, and the life of my family came before me and I have a lot of catching up to do. My purpose now is to lay down some tracks in an attempt to stay in front of the speeding train. For now, I am just the caboose, a wobbly, rocking, movement-filled sign of what came after everything else. Am I still at the end? Perhaps. Will their motion cause me to derail?

This is my beginning. It is about distinguishing my line.

> *I am anxious to tell you about myself. This is my sequence of events. In other words, how a newborn lands in adulthood and how adults land in a child. It happens every so many decades, for the good and bad of it. And, well, it's just not that easy.*

Actually, you and me, we've experienced a steady stream of life's events that have shaped us, disappointed us, and rearranged us. Perhaps you've been enlightened and brightened, maybe. Changes, they've rocked my world, and the transformation has been drastic enough to bring me to my knees. My feeling is that anything called "reality" must be approached very carefully and not without sufficient armor. Now that I know exactly what is involved, I would prefer to have nothing to do with it, for this reality has brought me to an unlikely crossroads, leaving me to manage, with assistance, a part of me that is greatly exposed.

Living with a sensitive disposition can lead you where no man should have to go, with feelings and driving emotions that have many variables. My mother has such a disposition and I believe I began heading in that direction many years ago. Symptoms of varying degrees have run a marathon in my life, sharing the seductive and addictive behaviors that make me both reluctant and enthusiastic to expose myself in this way. For all the reasons to maintain my secrecy, there are more reasons to share. Just maybe, if it's good enough, something in here will help someone else along the way.

When you're a kid, your days and nights often seem boring, but not mine. It seemed as though every night was filled with an explosion of colorful fireworks and we always had a ringside seat at the fights. I remember being approximately seven years old.

*I love the spring, the summer, and the fall; I like the winter least. One of my favorite things to do is ride my bike. I have been doing it for years now; the bike came after my pushpedal ice cream truck. My father taught me to ride my bike. He ran alongside me and I never fell. There's not a day that goes by that I'm not riding it up and down our street, at least in good weather. But I even ride it in the rain! I can't go all the way around the block alone yet because the block is too big for me, but I don't mind really; end to end is far enough for now.*

*We have the Lutheran church at one end of our street and a baseball park with swings at the other and our house is in the middle. I can see the park from our house; it is about eight houses down and I can go there if someone else is with me. I like the new Yogi Bear Slide and the swings and the monkey bars. That's our house right there, the one with the big tree in front. We have those five giant trees along the side of our driveway and there are trees all the way down the street. Every house has a giant tree in front of it and each one hangs over the street and over the sidewalks and when you look from here it's like a tunnel all the way down.*

*I think the trees look like statues carrying umbrellas, one after another after another, side by side, kind of droopy and blocking the sun. The trunks are big and round with rough heavy bark and they are usually holding a million birds and a zillion leaves. My dad and I rake them in the fall and I jump in them before he burns them in the street. All the neighbors do the same thing and you can see the piles of leaves on fire. The smoke slowly drifts all the way down our block, and if you're in the way it burns your eyes.*

*There aren't too many kids on our block and it's kind of lonely, but I always find things to do by myself. We don't have a dog or a cat or a fish but I'd like one. My mother says "No animals!" and she means it so I just hang around and do stuff and that's okay.*

*I spend time imagining a lot. I make up stories and scenes and sometimes I daydream. Sometimes my dreams are nightmares and those become my memories because they're hard to forget. My nighttime ideas are in color; these dreams are complicated stories that are often frightening and usually unfamiliar to me. Sometimes I can't remember my dreams but when I wake up I'm really scared.*

*I don't understand my dreams. They usually have my family in them and my memories do too. They play with my mind for my mind's sake and all it takes is a break in sleep to make them die away.*

*But my memories...whoa. They have attached themselves to me. They don't die away. They may fade, but they never die away. Memories, what I remember of something that happened to me, something I have seen with my own eyes, tasted with my own mouth, touched with my own hands; these are my memories. Sometimes it's easy to confuse memories with dreams and dreams with memories. It's hard to keep them straight.*

*My memories include times when my brother and sister torture me when my parents are gone. I get hysterical when they chase me around the house and make me go outside. I'm sure that's why I hate winter. They don't mind leaving me outside, standing in the snow without my shoes or coat or gloves, and once I started to freeze and cry and my brother was about to let me back in.*

*"Aha, now you're in trouble; our parents are pulling into the driveway." The mere sight of our parents gets me into the house quickly and my siblings get in trouble.*

*Another day while my grandmother was babysitting, my sister chased me around the house and forced me outside again. The weather was nice but I didn't like to be out there like that and I was so mad that I yelled and screamed at her and then I decided to take action. She was holding the screen door closed and I was pulling and pulling on the handle. Somehow, frantically trying to get in, I pushed when I should have pulled and smash, there was blood all over me. Miserable memories.*

*The problem wasn't smashing through the glass; it was the skin dangling from inside my wrist that caused the problem. I felt pale and lightheaded. Scrape going in and slash coming out. As the smash broke the glass into many jagged pieces, I bled all over my clothes and onto the floor. I was afraid of what was happening and my grandmother fell to her instincts and began to tug on something that ended up being either skin or a tendon.*

**Life Is Like a Line**


I remember being hot and sweaty and dizzy and needing to lie down on the landing. Trying to stop the blood and unable to reach my parents, my grandmother wrapped my wrist and tried to console me. I was crying; there was too much of it. The bluish liquid spilling out of me was actually red, bright runny red.

With the help of the Lord, my parents came home early. Twenty stitches later, my sister was about to be burned at the stake. Home and comforted, I smiled. I also learned something from this experience: if I'm ever pressed far enough to want it, if the days of great desire overwhelm me, my demise, my suicide, will have nothing to do with the wrist. Too much history, too many memories, too messy.

> *Right now is one of the times when I really don't want to tell you something private but this is as good a time as any. I don't like talking about this because it makes me feel bad, but you'll understand more about me if you know this. There is arguing in our house. My father calls it "turmoil." To me, it feels like a tornado twisting inside our house.*
>
> *Most of the twisting comes from my parents, some from my brother and sister, none from me, but mostly from my mom. My parents really don't get along very well, and the older I get, the worse it seems to be. My brother and my sister have grown up with this too and still hear it since they live here. I don't know if other families have this problem but when it happens here, it feels terrible.*
>
> *Otherwise, life isn't really all that bad. Sometimes my parents (one or the other) take me to the ice cream parlor and sometimes I get ice cream right in front of our house from the Good Humor man. His ice cream bars and ice cream cups are great and my favorite food at home is scrambled egg sandwiches that my dad makes and the flat pancakes that are my mom's specialty. And when they cook them everything feels normal to me. I especially love being with my grandmother when we are at her house; it's so nice to be with her and she feels really soft and she lets me sit on her lap and she gives me big bear hugs.*
>
> *During the summer my dad barbecues in the back yard and in August we go to the state fair and have corn dogs and I go on some of the rides while my parents watch. We take my girlfriend who lives across the street*

*so I have someone to be with. These are the fun days filled with laughing and food and everyone getting along.*

There were many days and nights when I didn't know what was going on but I heard them and I felt the vibration of them and at my tender age it was extremely upsetting. There were no fingers capable of preventing my ears from hearing their arguments and I was obsessed with listening to every word. With every unsuccessful effort to back away, my disobliging mind bound me for eternity.

Most kids are inquisitive, and I certainly was. At the time I didn't know the origin of their fights, but it didn't matter. When Mother was angry, my father fought back, and their resentment for each other and her feelings of insignificance left the door open day after night after week after month after year for more of their hostile fire. As they fought face to face, face to face, face to face they never looked away, never looked down, never looked down at me.

*Because I am the youngest, I know the least about what's going on. There's always something scary between my mother and my father and when there is a special tone in her voice we all scatter. When they start to have a talk everything seems okay until one of them says something mean; then I know what's coming. There is loud talking and then shouting and pushing and shoving and I get so upset and I beg them to stop. They never really get along. Well, maybe they do sometimes but the bad feels more normal than the good. I don't think they even like each other most of the time. They are always yelling and screaming and being nasty and I don't like hearing them and even though they are in the kitchen together, our house is small and you would think they are everywhere.*

*This whole thing is bad, really bad, and I'm not lying—it's all true, every bit of it. We look happy on the outside but inside we are all unhappy. I try to keep busy and stay out of the way for my mom and everyone comes and goes quite a lot anyway and there is so much I don't understand that all I can do is pick up the bits and pieces of what I think is happening along the way. The weekdays are fine because my dad is working during the day but I worry about what will happen when he comes home. My mom picks me up for lunch sometimes and buys me a Top Hat or a White Castle hamburger and I really love that.*

*School is not great. There are many classes that are too hard for me and sometimes I don't know what is going on. In gym class we are climbing the rope and some of the girls can go way up but once I grab onto the rope and look up I think, "Oh, I will never be able to climb up there; it's too far" and so I go a bit more and then I slide down, which is not too smart because it really hurts my hands. They call it "rope burn."*

*During recess we play kickball and jump rope, which I am good at, and if it rains we might go into the auditorium. I have a class that's called "Auditorium" and we act in plays and I usually work the lights or set up the furniture but this time I was in the play and I remembered the lines and it was so fun.*

*I have a girlfriend who sometimes sits next to me and we take turns tickling the top of each other's hand, which feels so good I could fall asleep. My mom picks me up from school and once I come home I change my clothes and have a snack and then ride my bike or do homework or something else.*

*If we need food my mother and I go to Food Fair and pick things up. I always ask for chocolate ice cream. We have a basketball net in the back yard and I play sometimes. There are days when I'm invited over to the neighbor's house. Whenever she sees me in our yard she invites me over and she lives right next door so I don't have to cross the street to get there. Their names are Mr. and Mrs. Sauer and they are from Germany and they speak differently and I have a hard time understanding her when she speaks to me. I have no problem understanding Mr. Sauer because he just smiles at me and he barely speaks at all but he nods his head. Whenever I go over there she gives me tiny paper baskets with little handles that she makes by hand and she puts candy in them for me. When I bring them home they smell like her house, which smells, my mother says, like moth balls.*

*It's great to visit because she has a cuckoo clock in her kitchen and almost every time I'm over there I hear that clock chime and then the bird comes out and makes the "cuckoo cuckoo cuckoo" sound and after that the people dressed in German clothes come out of the clock and dance around* in circles and the "tick tick tick" sound of the clock is very loud and there is so much to watch you really don't know what to watch first.

Mrs. Sauer is very nice to me and I think that she hears the fights from over our fence and inside our house. I'm not really sure but sometimes she asks me how I am and looks at me for a long time with a funny look on her face.

Going over there really makes me happy. She usually gives me a snack to take home and I thank her and leave until the next time. If she knows about the fights then she knows that whenever my mother is yelling at my father who is mad at my brother who is mad at my sister the fireworks have started. I have been begging them not to fight and I have screamed at them so many times this week and they are upsetting me too much. I need them to stop it right now. I don't care if my mother calls Mrs. Sauer a "busybody." I like her just the same.

I have a place where I go when I want to be by myself. It's in the alley just a few houses from ours at the end of our street. What is this place? It's a tree. There are branches low enough for me to climb and once I get onto that branch I can go as high as I want. But I really don't go that high. I'm about even with the garage right behind it. You can see things when you are up in that tree and you hear the nothing of everything like birds and cars and people talking from far away and kids laughing and playing. There are also soft sounds from the leaves shaking in the breeze and the sound they make is a happy sound. There are times when I sit for a long while in that tree. There are times when I just don't want to go home. I'm scared at home, and I love that tree.

It's my "all by myself" place. When I want to hear nothing and be quiet I climb up my tree to be alone. It's just a short walk and I'm right there. Sometimes I'm sad there all by myself but in my sadness, that is my home.

I have two girlfriends who live on our block; they are both older than me. One girl lives next door but I don't like her very much. Her grandmother is mean and barks at you when you call at her door. I say, "Cathy, Cathy" and the most awful old witch answers and sends you away even if my girlfriend is home. She is a Polish lady, short and pudgy, and her lips sink *in because she has no teeth. I usually run across the grass, scared to death, and head for our front porch and wait a while until my friend comes out or I just run inside our house.*

*The other girl lives farther down the street, almost to the end, and she is my friend, too. She is Italian and her grandmother lives with them because her mother works all the time. Her grandmother is kind of unfriendly and a little scary too and I think she is getting a beard. My girlfriend taught me how to ask her grandmother for a glass of water and it goes like this: "Me a wani una begetti aqua."*

*I know it sounds weird but it works. I say it and her grandmother brings me a glass of water and then she says things quietly and sounds grouchy as she walks back to the kitchen, but I don't know. When no one is home I ride my bike for a while and then I go into the house and watch TV.*

*Tomorrow is the rec department's painting class at the park and I'll ask my mother if I can go. It costs twenty-five cents so I'll get it from my mom so I can buy a small statue to paint. Noon at the park, crafts, the swings, the drinking fountain, and the Yogi Bear slide. I'm sure they'll let me go.*

My parents kept me busy with extracurricular activities so I could interact with girls my own age. Whether by plan or surprise, the activities were often diverse enough to help me forget about the friction at home. In addition to the summer projects through the City of Detroit Recreation Department, I was a member of the local Girl Scout troop where work and fun were a pleasant collision, so much that I remember two memories vividly. The first was, we went to Camp Holly on a weekend Girl Scout trip and it rained every day. It was damp and cold and we were almost all the way home before I realized I'd left my favorite red rubber boots back at the cabin and when I got home I cried.

My other memory is that, while working toward a "cut your finger off at the knuckle" badge, with knife in hand I whittled my way toward a bloody mess, became ill at the sight of my own blood, and decided that was enough for me.

Once I began outgrowing my uniform and my sash was full of badges, I felt that anything having to do with blood, knives, and selling cookies had lost its luster. Overall, it was confidence I lacked, and although I tried to make friends, I was often shy. I may have tried too hard. In any event, there was something missing. In the game of fame, I wasn't ever in the clique.

> *My bedroom faces the front of the house and on the other side of that wall is the attic. We get into the attic from the hallway through a tiny door that is just a bit taller than me. The attic is really large and has a wooden floor down the center and my mom puts all her extra carpets over the wood. There is also a window in the peak of the house that brings light into the attic in the daytime and my father wired lights with a switch for the night. Usually we store our extra this and that in the attic like clothes and lamps and rugs and winter coats and other stuff.*
>
> *We also have mice in our house and they have been in my room (they were scratching at my chocolate kisses I had in a bowl), so my father set traps to catch them and when I lie in my bed at night I can hear the "snap snap snap" of them and the noise of them flipping the traps over as they are caught. Gross. In the morning my dad says what he usually says, "Well, we got the whole family," and within minutes he sweeps them off the trap, feet first into the trash. And then he resets the same dried old bloody traps, ugh, for another night. That gives me the creeps. I just hate it.*
>
> *On the other side of that wall are the footsteps and the howling and the breathing of the ghosts and the bats that flutter through our rooms. One time my dad said the bat he "got rid of" came back as Dracula and knocked on our front door. I am sure he is kidding. I'm thinking and I'm hearing and I'm scared and I'm sure they're there; I SENSE them. When I grow up, I'm never having an attic. I hate that attic.*

I'm not sure when the nightmares started but once they did, I just couldn't shake them; they were attached to my vivid imagination. I remember the continuousness of them, and although they varied in length and obscurity, it was as if there was no escape.

I was usually terrified. I would see myself running and I would keep running, keep running, don't stop, don't look back, what is it, right behind me, catching up, running still, I'm running, and now I'm bending down and grabbing the green grass under me, one hand in front of the other to help me run faster. I need to go faster, faster, and farther away. I have no idea what my terror is, but I am afraid to sleep night after night after night and when my shattering screams wake me, they also wake my mother, who sleeps in the bedroom next door. I know they will never leave me. They are manufactured especially for me.

They are often masterpieces, so complex, in living color, always moving along quickly, repeating themselves, repeating themes, one after another. Even when I wake up to go to the bathroom, they continue where they left off. I know they are "just below the surface" thoughts and often they look familiar. They are somehow trapped inside my mind and they terrorize me. I never have dreams about mice in traps in our attic; one would think my screams alone would send them into orbit.

> *I go to Sunday school at the Lutheran Church across the street just about every Sunday but I don't go with my family. I go alone. My mother and father don't go to church even though they know the pastor very well. We don't talk about church at home or God or the Lord or Jesus or anything like that. My mother has a small round picture of the Lord hanging on her wall and I have seen a rosary there too but I have never talked to them about those things.*
>
> *Sometimes I hear the words "goddammit" or "son of a bitch" but I think some of that might be swearing, which would have nothing to do with church. The pastor of the church is a member of the football league and is responsible for the prayers at opening day and at all the banquets. I started going to this church with my girlfriend from school. She invited me and I thought we would be in the same class but we are in different classes because I'm new. I feel that church is a peaceful place where you can just sit and listen and sing along and every Sunday the pastor tells a story. When you are there, people are really nice to each other.*
>
> *We are getting prepared for the Christmas season and it is our job to sing at the children's service on Christmas Eve. I do like it there. It's calm. I like the statues and the colorful glass in the windows. It's warm and friendly; everyone is friendly. I feel something there. I don't feel alone.*

Some would say my parents had an abusive marriage. It is true, they had a mutual boiling point, and once reached, there would be hell to pay. In my eyes, my mother seemed to be the worst offender but perhaps she had legitimate reasons for her behavior. In my lifetime, there have been hundreds of instances in which my mother's temper would simmer before turning into a rolling boil. If my father spoke to her in even the slightest off tone, she would come at him with the dirtiest expletives one could imagine.

If I attempted to defend him (though he needed no defending from me), I only made matters worse. It was several years before my father's death and just after an angry episode of my mother's when my father sat with me and explained the reasons for her conduct. It was important to him that I not think ill of her and afterwards I felt that what he told me was plausible.

He simply said that my mother had lived under the thumb of an abusive father who on occasion had become physical with her. He had been a self-employed, domineering, and boastful carouser and my mother had remained under his thumb until his early death. So, in fact, my mother's resentment and hatred for her father was born out of his domineering abusive nature and he intimidated her, which led to her resentment and complete lack of self-confidence with men altogether.

*I'm going down there right now. I keep hearing things banging around and I keep imagining what's happening. I know what they are doing. I have seen them. I have peeked around the corner and then screamed at them. This is about the time I start screaming and screaming and my heart is pounding and I am biting my nails and I keep telling them to stop but they don't listen to me and then I start yelling like right NOW. "Dad, STOP, please!"*

*They are not listening; they never hear me. "STOP PLEASE STOP." Oh, my stomach aches; it feels so bad. They make me afraid and sometimes I hide and then I think that if I don't stay close something will happen. There is no end to this. Somebody's going to get hurt. My mother keeps hollering at my dad.*

*"Stop it, Dad, please oh my oh my gosh PLEASE stop. Please STOP."*

*They stopped. It's quiet. What is going on? Here she comes and she's crying and she's still swearing quietly. I'll stay in my room and peek out the door. I can't go downstairs. I'm scared now and I hate my dad for what he does; I don't want to see him. She slammed her door. It's over for tonight…I can sleep with my buzzy stomach…it's finally over.*

## Life Is Like a Line

Every day a surprise, the days of war led me to vacillate between hating one parent and then the other. Loving them both and hating them both. There was a sadness as my thoughts would turn to hatred, but then I loved them more, both of them, loved them…just loved them more. During their disagreements, I never knew the direction we were heading in and because of that I often felt fearful and anxious.

There were times when their behavior was harsh and destructive and frightening and even though I didn't know their reasons, I had an innate understanding of them. On the lighter days it was just bitterness and insults, bickering and then separation. Worried always, I was scared. They were the moving targets my cries couldn't penetrate; they didn't hear me, not my begging or my pleading or my weeping.

On those days life was a collection of all my fears rolled into one. I would have had a better chance at the O.K. Corral: me, a cowboy, one rifle shot, boom, and for me it would have been over.

I would have rejoiced in the bliss of relief, but I was never that lucky. Life was about endurance, theirs and my own. I have no idea what life was like for me as a baby, but I knew what it was like as a child, and by the age of seven or eight it already had a vicious reverberation. With marriage vows sealed on the hottest day of the year, their emotional heat never cooled and their seas never calmed. They were both hypersensitive "Type A" personalities and being with them was like permanently walking on eggshells.

Whenever with them, I found myself living old feelings. Occasionally, without encouragement, those childhood memories would come back to me. Assessing, analyzing, remembering, trying to forget, I am analyzing still, I am assessing still, I am remembering still; it is my past and it is with me now. It is the present turmoil that keeps yesterday fresh.

The difference in their personalities was nothing but a test of wills because they were the same. Everyone experienced helplessness in our home and no reason to be optimistic. It was clear that what they did to each other, they did to us, but they were clueless.

Still, their degree of mutual mistreatment was not quite as severe as it might be today. Life was generally simpler then and people were kinder all around. I wouldn't exactly say my parents were civil to each other, but today people routinely kill each other for less. Though it would not be unusual for a knife to be pulled out of the kitchen drawer, one player manic and threatening, the other defensive and threatening, the bystanders freaking out, no one was ever stabbed. But these redundant, upsetting threats of my mother's sent chills down my spine and these were the days I hated them.

I longed for the perfect mother and adored the perfect family on television shows like *The Donna Reed Show* and *Father Knows Best*. I wanted to walk to the pond with Andy of Mayberry, fishing rod in hand and a plan to visit Aunt Bea for homemade pie, but those families were part of a tale. Though I visited them in their television homes, I could only dream, but in some ways, thanks to them, my head was able to modify the disruption of home.

> *It's Saturday morning and everybody's home and I'm in the basement watching TV and it's just another Saturday around here. Dad came home late again last night and missed dinner and told my mother he ate out with his customers but even I know that he should have called. I'm scared over it and my stomach feels wobbly. When he is late and doesn't call my mother, she gets mad, and when she is mad all night she's super mad in the morning, just like this morning.*
>
> *They were arguing last night, getting it over with I guess, but I guess they weren't done because they are in a fight now. Or maybe this is about something else. I am trying not to hear them but they're in my mind.*

I remember everything about that house, and to this day I become upset when I think about aspects of living there. What I remember most is my mother retreating to her room, worn out from combat, never winning the war, trading reality for her seclusion. I always wondered what the neighbors heard and if they were hushed out of embarrassment or indifference.

With all due respect to my mother, there were days when my father was relentless. He would boast about the neighbor's business savvy while calling her "Lottie the Body" to infuriate Mom. Lottie's eighteen-year-old daughter would find it entertaining to undress herself in front of her bedroom window. With the shade drawn, you could see her quite perfect silhouette as it was illuminated not more than fifteen feet from our kitchen window. In our home breasts were to be hidden, so this intentional exhibition was new to me and upsetting, as well as reason for another battle in our house.

Another irritant for my mother was the thirty-something Spanish teacher who lived across the street. This well-dressed, well-polished charmer, unmarried and living with her mother, was sharp enough to really irritate my mother. When my father, fresh from work, engaged in lengthy conversations with her in the middle of the street, my mother would begin to steam. No sooner would he enter the front door than she would greet him with threats and cursing, and even an idiot would know what was about to happen.

When he was in one of his moods, my mother could never measure up. She didn't wear nice enough clothes, she had no career, and she was too temperamental. There would be no escape from his disparaging comments, no matter how hard she tried. This was another piece in the puzzle. Those days had a "Help yourself to your dinner" attitude. Fortunately, there was plenty in the fridge, but by that time I just couldn't eat. The cursing and the accusations stirred me but I wouldn't realize the outcome for years to come.

I do know this: if my husband treated me in this way, I would have been pissed off all the time too and divorcing him would have been too pleasant an alternative. Every time my father invited controversy, every time he was deliberate, she would understandably retaliate. She remembered her past and connected it with her present. He was just another man and she was under his thumb. There was just no escape for her; his lingering insults were like dust on a wood floor, hiding right around the corner.

*Usually I don't hear them when I'm down here in the basement except for the footsteps in the kitchen right above me; they almost always fight in the kitchen because that's where my dad sits and reads the paper. Now all of a sudden I am hearing some thuds but today they are especially loud. There is cursing and yelling and more cursing and I feel like something bad is about to happen. I start to cry. My brother is home now and he has been listening and just couldn't stand it anymore so he went up there to try to break things up and I hear my father threatening him and my father hardly ever does that, but I don't think my brother is going to stop helping my mom.*

*This is a terrible day. First the voices yelling and then the thuds and the crash and more yelling and crying, ahh. This is what I do when this happens. Small girl screaming and I'm awfully afraid and I feel really shaky and I want to throw up. Well, at least my brother is there to break things up. I hope he is always here for my mother; what will we ever do without him? All I can say is that he was great today. He really helped my mom because he kept trying to get her out of the room and he tried to put some distance between both of them. I am so afraid. I went up there too but my dad told me to go downstairs and he sounded mean and my hands were shaking from his voice.*

*My brother didn't get hurt. He never gives in and he never gives up but sometimes my dad gets physical with him but my dad ought to know that he's going to get right in there and push him away if he has to but I don't like him doing that either. I am afraid for my brother. They fight by the stairs to the basement. They are on the landing and there are many steps down to the basement. I can only imagine what is about to happen. I can't stand them right now. I get so upset at them, sometimes I even hate them. Oh, I don't feel good. I hate them right now; I hate their guts.*

My brother and sister attended the same high school together but they did not associate because their relationship was torn. I was too young to understand the words my family used to describe the situation or the ones that exposed my brother's crime, but my sister knew. She had to endure the harsh teasing in school and carry the burden of the sibling jokes that were so painful and her shyness made even the slightest embarrassment crushing.

*Time has gone by very fast and I know that my brother is planning to leave for college soon, maybe in a couple of days. He is packing. My mother and my brother are very close and I would say that he is my mother's favorite child, but that's okay. I have always known this. She will really miss him because she has said this so many times and I have seen her cry. I know my brother will miss her too. He has been protecting her for as long as I can remember and she has been protecting him, too.*

## Life Is Like a Line

*My dad and my brother still don't get along very well; there have some problems that I really don't know about but it might be because my brother helps my mother if she needs him. I remember when he had a broom broken over his back by my dad. I hated that. I screamed and I was so scared. I think my father shouldn't hurt my mother or my brother this way. No pushing, no shoving, but he says he is just fighting back.*

*I am pretty sure that no one wins in these fights because we are all really upset and what they do is break us up and make us pick sides. I know my brother is going to be happy when he gets to college because he won't have to go through any of these fights ever again. But I know one thing for sure; some of these fights are about him. He has a favorite boyfriend and my father doesn't like it and calls him names and then my mother starts a battle and then my brother defends himself saying "I'm not this" or "I'm not that." Then my mother tells him not to worry about anything and she even goes behind my father's back so anyway I hope he will be glad in his new life. I will miss him no matter what they say.*

Not only did my brother breed controversy, he delivered himself into jeopardy too many times throughout his life. Each ring of the telephone brought a plea for money, and with each entanglement came a loss of my father's affection, but his outspoken disappointment in his son only ensured him my mother's protection. She became his enabler. Her blindness destroyed many so that one might survive. In order to keep him, she had to beg on his behalf, borrow as he required, and steal the affection from our family. All is pitiable. My father, aware of the game, abhorred it. He detested the lifestyle, the preferences, and his son's masterful betrayal.

*My mother has been really upset because of my brother's absence, but that's the way it goes and anyway they keep in touch by telephone. But he lives at college now and that won't change. His college is one hour from our house but we don't see him almost ever. He doesn't call me either and he doesn't visit. He calls my mother to keep in contact and sometimes they talk about school and books and by my mother's response I know that he asks for money. Things happen to my brother a lot; I think he got into a car accident or something but I don't think it was that bad. I remember hearing my mother say something on the phone.*

*I'm not listening in, really, but it's hard not to hear since the telephone is in the hall and eventually my dad finds out about the problem, whatever it is. My mom sends him the help he needs and that upsets my dad. Whenever my mother sends him more money, they get into a big fight. They have little fights and big ones; this one was big. You just never know when a big fight is going to happen but you can feel it as soon as my dad walks in the door.*

*My father doesn't know that my mother bought my brother a car. It's a yellow doodle bug and I saw it. My brother gave me a ride in it. We met him somewhere far from our house and I had to promise not to tell anyone so it's our secret. It's a really cool car too. My sister is having problems at home now. She is going to move to my grandmother's house soon. I wish she wouldn't go. She is not getting along with Mom and says she has to leave. If my dad were home more he would help us. He would make her stay.*

*It looks as if my sister is going to move away for sure. She is spending more and more time away from us and she doesn't sleep here very much either. Dad is gone a lot and it feels lonely around here. I know my sister is really upset with Mom and everything around here feels bad and after my brother moved away to college, everything got worse. My sister and my mom get angry with each other and Mom isn't very nice to her and she says mean things to my sister that I don't like and then my sister says that she just can't live in this house so she is packing up some things and going away. At least she won't be hearing the yelling and everybody won't be mad and sad at each other. This is hard to get used to. I guess I'm going to be an only child. I'm going to be alone.*

Once my sister moved out of the house, the bedroom and the closet were mine but I still shared the bathroom with my mother. My father's habit of coming and going as he pleased persisted, which left my mother and me alone. Too young to "run the streets," I was at her side and we spent time together and I watched over her. She had lengthy periods of solitude and spent days at a time in bed and I didn't understand why and I worried about her. All I knew was that Mom was not her usual self. I would lie by her feet, compelled to watch her every move, but I was awkward at this.

I would try to engage her or please her or provide for her or just be quiet with her and as I lay next to her, she would ask me over and over again to *"Lie still!"* and I would try so hard not to move so that she wouldn't be mad at me. Once she found sleep, I was relieved just to hear her breathe, knowing that rest would come for me soon as well.

My father, recognizing her condition, would climb the stairs to her room to console her and offer nourishment or affection, but he would be thrown out, only to recoil just in time to make her angry. Tremendous feelings of loss and sadness were mine during those periods. Not even the sunshine could brighten the dimness of my heart.

> *I don't know if the Navy taught Dad about shoe polishing or if he learned that all by himself, but he has his own polishing station in our unfinished basement just over the washing machine. For him, getting ready for work means a spit shine on his wingtips, which I know how to do very well. I'm the spit and buffer; he puts on the polish and snaps the cloth.*
>
> *I have watched Dad time after time after time do this to his shoes and he has polished mine, too. He taught me how to polish shoes many years ago and he taught my sister, too. It's fun. He has a form of a foot and it hangs on the wall and his shoe slides right over it. He keeps his shiny shoes in the front hall closet right next to our front door. Dad says work is very important and he must look like a businessman.*
>
> *At night after a long day and after dinner he reads the paper and then he might go downstairs and give his shoes a "slick and a promise" and then he and I might watch TV. I like to watch TV with my dad.*
>
> *On Saturdays we do chores together. First, his shirts go to the Chinese Laundry where they press and starch them and when they are finished, the shirts practically stand up all by themselves, just like a board. They wrap them in thick brown paper and the smell of the store is really yucky and it makes me feel sick and I can only stand in there for a few seconds and then I wait for him right outside the door.*
>
> *The Chinese man is funny because he yells when we come in but I think it's because the machines are noisy. It's not like the home yelling;*

*that is different and horrible. This is like "Mr. Main, Mr. Main" really fast. That's a shortcut for our last name. I guess that tells everyone my dad is here to get his shirts and then everyone scrambles for his shirts and bows and smiles at us.*

*Next the shoe repair, where the shoeshine men are. The repair is right next to the Ramona Theatre where we go to the movies and have snacks. Today is a happy day and always is when we do things together. Next stop Heisler's Drugstore where we have to get medicine for my mother and ciga-rettes. Dad said I can get some candy and I'm going to look at the toys too and at the comic books. I like Archie. We'll buy Mom some licorice too. She loves black; that's what Dad says. After that we're going to pick her up for lunch; I love lunch.*

That was a peaceful Saturday and I thanked the Lord for those days. It didn't matter what the ratio was between the joyful days and the hell-on-Earth days as long as they were evenly spaced out. My feelings of alarm were wiped out on Saturdays when Dad and I did things together.

There were other days when I thought I was losing my mind. Crazy thoughts ran in and out, unknowingly harmful scenes where normally a child's peaceful innocence should reside. Our parents made life more dif-ficult than it had to be and the bits and pieces of happiness were so much less than I longed for.

During this period, our parents alternated between obliviousness and self-importance, which dashed my hopes for change. If earlier there had been at least a modicum of emotional nurturing for my siblings, there seemed little left for me. My father was the nurturer, but he worked Monday through Friday, often long and late, so our time together was short. My mother was needy and I provided her with the companionship she required. I loved them both, I was fearful of them both, in need of them both, angry with them both, and empty all at the same time.

When my brother left for college and my sister moved away, I was vir-tually on my own. They must have hit the door running because they kept on going and rarely looked back. My parents were undoubtedly harmful to each other and their explosive nature affected us all, but my siblings knew enough to run. They were older, seven and ten years older than me, and they could do so. It was their mechanism for survival.

As for the controversy at home, it was never out of sight. Our parents' behavior left my brother with a deep-seated nature based on extremes glazed by confabulation and untruths, which throughout the years harmfully affected our family, his career, his relationships, and his life. The alternative lifestyle he chose would prove to be devastating.

My sister, for the most part, chose to avoid the unstable environment of our family by not being drawn in. With a broad brush, she would paint herself in and out of the family portrait at will, offering no continuity, no commitment, and her rules and restrictions at every pass. During the periods when she kept away from the family, a strong foundation could not be established. Although her avoidance may have been her coping mechanism, it was very sad to have our family draped under the veil of separation and sadness. It was not until the birth of her first child that our new relationship was born.

> *I feel lonely. I hear noises down there. I don't like to be alone. I'll sit on these stairs until someone comes home and I don't care how long it takes. I am bored; there is nothing to do. I heard it. There is something there, right down there; I can feel it. I can hear something like the inside of a sea shell and it's really loud, but it's so quiet.*
>
> *Maybe ghosts are walking around the house. I'm afraid of ghosts. It's too quiet and the floor is creaking. Why is the floor creaking if no one is down there? I don't know; I'm afraid. I don't even care if they come home fighting and start pushing and shoving and swearing at each other as long as they come home, and it had better be soon.*

I hated to be alone. I was always afraid. At some point, as my feelings of desperation grew, I learned to keep them hidden from others. I just couldn't show my grief, or my weakness, or my fear. Maybe that would be giving them too much of me. I knew my dad didn't like it, didn't like weakness, but as I stood strong in my tracks, my knees knocked. With that desperation came fear: the fear of aloneness and the crush of it. It was a time when my imagination clearly ran me by hostile takeover. Unprepared for my spontaneous thoughts and grand mental images, I was swept into scenarios of immediate upcoming peril or impending doom, always frightening situations composed within the shadowy places of my mind. Simultaneously, out of the darkness and into the light, I would plan for my escape or rescue. With each story, I was the hero.

Three children living at home presented life "on the go" and through the chaos lived a sense of liveliness. When my siblings left home, I found that the intensity of our parent-sibling battles was less painful than the silence from their absence. Their departure brought a sense of great loneliness and isolation. The union that had once brought us together had separated us.

My mother contributed to the mix with the principle that everything in life is either black or white, with no room for gray; it was no surprise that my father saw black and white and gray.

My mother stayed rigid and felt no remorse in her displeasure. While she was on the offensive, he was on the defensive and vice versa. Had my mother understood the connection between her visible moods and my father's invisibility, blameless lives might have changed, but my parents were now, more than ever, fixated on fault.

When Monday through Friday exhausted my father and his moody and sensitive emotions sought weekend isolation, my irritated mother lashed out with ridicule and blame and thus the tides were turned and the cycle continued. I know that on some level she longed for something more, as did he. The connection between their moods and their marriage was a mystery to them, but it seemed crystal clear to me and it meant chaos.

Here's my definition of "chaos": a large glass of confusion with a side of stomachache. And so the final years of my childhood passed by.

*I'm biting my nails way down and if they want to know why they ought to listen to themselves from up here, but I can't tell them that. I wish I had a recorder so they could hear this. Their noise has been coming through my bedroom floor and there is no way to stop it. If I turn up my record player I can drown them out, but I know what is happening so doing that is useless. I don't know why they're fighting today. It's Sunday and it's so nice out and I think we should be doing something fun. My mom is upset because my brother called and he asked for something that my father is not going* to give him and so my mother is saying mean things about how my father feels about my brother and my father is beginning to get nasty and I guess that's just the way it goes.

I don't know why it's always about my brother, so on and so on and so on. And now Mom is saying things really loud and oops she just swore again. Whatever they are saying is said in stern voices and even though they seem to be mumbling, I know that they are fighting and drawers are slamming so I guess my mother has finished the dishes. I hope they don't start throwing things again because that just opens up my terror. I will sit right here at the top of the stairs until it's over or until I am too afraid to sit here anymore. I have tried to close my eyes and cover my ears before but it never works and even though I don't want to hear them, I just have to.

Ahh, it's too late to cover my ears. I feel it again, that whatever it is that happens to my stomach. They worry me; they worry me so much that my hands get shaky and wet and my insides get jumpy and I don't want to live feeling this way. The problem is that I don't know whose side I'm on. I love them both but I feel like I have to choose and I just can't. And worst of all, no one can help us.

I have been thinking about it all day. I just want to do something that will help but there is nothing to do. I don't know much about this, but I have to go to the psychiatrist's office with Mom today. Dad is going to drive us and then we will have lunch.

Sometimes I sit in his office and he closes the doors with the little glass windows and he asks me how I am doing and how I feel and how is school and how is this and how is that. After he asks me the questions I sit on the couch in their living room and wait for them or his wife invites me into the kitchen and I watch her cook something and sometimes she asks me to get something out of the pantry and their pantry is almost as big as our bathroom.

I do have feelings that upset me and maybe I should have told him about them but I couldn't. When these thoughts go with my imagination, my stomach feels fluttery and I start thinking some more and then I feel worried and I feel something else but I'm not sure what. The problem is that I'm afraid of things like there's something in the dark, or being alone *in the house, and there are those sounds, or there's something in the closet, something behind the door, what is at the end of the hall, please don't turn off the light, please don't leave me alone.*

*I think they know about these fears. I am frightened about many things and my parents calm me down at the time, but it only lasts a while before it starts up again.*

*When Dad is late, I'm afraid, too. It would help if he would call when he is going to be late. Then Mom wouldn't get mad and at least I wouldn't be afraid of their fights. I can't stop worrying about this or that and them. They are my parents and they are important to me. But I am afraid they won't live together or that someone is going to get killed. Killed for real. They make me afraid of that.*

*Summers are fun because we go on vacation or we go to the state fair or to the fireworks or something. In the summer we go to a resort with some of my parents' friends. My dad goes golfing and Mom stays with me and some of the other ladies and we lie around the swimming pool.*

*Dad swims with me and when he jumps off the diving board he can touch the ceiling. Sometimes I do cannonballs off the diving board but I don't feel safe in the water. I have to wear my nose plug because I'm afraid I'll try to breathe under the water. I met a boy last year and we played pool and ping pong and walked around and talked and swam in the pool and he asked me if he could kiss me and so we went over by the locker room where nobody else was and kissed a few times and then a few times more. I liked it when he kissed me and he was really nice to talk to. He sent me a letter in the mail and in the envelope was a ring for me, but my mother sent it back. My mother told me that girls twelve years of age were too young for that type of nonsense and I cried. Honest, I did not understand what she meant. All I knew was that when we were together that summer it was the best. Not only did my parents get along, but there was someone for me. I didn't have to put on the happy face; it was already on.*

There are memories of my childhood that I would prefer not to remember now that I am an adult. My parents beat each other up psychologically and that left a mental photograph not suitable for the family album. It seemed

## Life Is Like a Line

as though eternal conflict was our best-kept secret, and while I did my best to pack and push and stuff it away, I only made room for more of it.

Over the years, much of the sensation of those days has faded, but a certain vividness remains. I am not amused by the once-discarded thoughts that reappear and ooze from deep within me to recapture my days and infiltrate my soul because they change me. Those that lie in wait for me must be opposed, for if set free, they will cause me harm. In time and with any luck, the feelings of confusion and joy, sorrow and reverence, and hate and love belonging to that little girl will find their place.

*Dad called to check on us. We've been at my grandma's and I guess it's time to go home. She has a big front porch to sit on and that's where I am. I like to watch the traffic from her stairs. That's Harper Avenue over there. I like to be here but it's lonely. Today I called my girlfriend but she won't be back for another week so I kicked the ball in the yard instead, being careful of my grandmother's rose bushes. If my parents didn't fight so much we wouldn't be here for this long, but my mother said she couldn't take it. I heard something about a divorce.*

*I guess this is our other home. My grandmother lives on the corner right off the alley so we see all the stuff going on over there behind the stores. Today I saw the man with the horse and covered wagon coming our way. You could see the lamps and chairs and all the other collections piled high behind his seat and I wondered about him. He is called something like the junk man. My mother said he's probably a millionaire and I don't know what a millionaire looks like, but I love it when he comes by. His chestnut-colored horse clicks his heels, I mean hooves, when he walks by and you can hear jingling, like bells, coming from the wagon.*

*The man's skin is very dark like my girlfriend's across the street and when he comes closer you can see his white teeth and his great big smile and he sure looks happy. I wonder why they fight so much, my parents I mean. I beg them not to fight, but they just won't listen. My grandmother doesn't like it either. When they get along we go out and have nice dinners and before you know it they are mad at each other and one won't talk to the other and then there is banging and yelling and it starts over and over again.*

*I wish I could stop thinking about it, forget it, just forget it. I hear it over and over in my head. Last night my grandmother and I watched Lawrence Welk on TV and Mom was in bed and then I went to bed. Our room is upstairs and we have to walk through the attic and it is very scary to be up there. If I wake up and have to go to the bathroom I don't go because I don't want to wake up Mom so I try hard to fall back asleep. The floors creak up there and it is so dark except for the street lights from the alley through that window. I like it here but I want to go home to see Dad, to my own room and my bike and my climbing tree. I want to be with my things and since Dad said something to Mom, we are going back.*

*Saturday will be coming soon and this means we will be doing something together, Dad and I. We missed last Saturday so this one will be extra special. Mom will stay home and clean and we will run errands and go to Dad's office and have lunch and pick up some candy for Mom. My dad is really nice to me and he holds my hand and when I am upset he wipes my tears but he doesn't treat me like a baby either. He says "Ah, come on, Honey" when I am sad or frustrated or mad. Yep, that's my dad.*

*He teaches me a lot of stuff too. Sometimes when Mom doesn't feel like talking or doing anything and Dad wants to stay in his room or watch the football game in the TV room, I go and visit a girlfriend or watch TV with him. I sit on the floor leaning on a pillow with my feet under the TV, very comfy. I know that my dad cares about me and I hope my mother does too. But I just need them to care about each other and the rest of us will be happy. Even though they don't live here, they will be happy too.*

It was not until I became an adult that I realized many of my experiences as a child were something more than childlike. I also began to notice that I felt two different ways: one was the cheerful, happy way and the other was the sad, dismal way, but I was too young to be able to articulate my feelings. When good feelings were missing, I tried to create them, hoping to make myself feel better.

*Besides dance I am taking piano lessons. Dad surprised me and bought a white baby grand piano, a bench, a metronome, and lesson books and had all of it delivered to our house. It was there when I came home from school, right in the living room. I was already taking lessons so he thought this would be a great surprise and it was great, but I kept practicing and practicing and found that I was all thumbs and when I became frustrated I would cry and then I just stopped trying and then I just quit.*

*Disappointed, Dad had them pick it all up and I felt bad for a long time. My dad said it was okay and asked me about horseback riding lessons at the fairgrounds and if I liked the idea and I said yes. This is now our Saturday activity. We still have lunch and maybe stop at his office and I draw on the chalkboard or type on the typewriter and usually we stop at the Sydney Bogg store for more chocolates; my mother is addicted to chocolate.*

*I will be riding at the fairgrounds soon too. There are days when the horse I ride, High Tower, scares me. He's so huge I can barely get on his back but I have a great time. I ride English and I have the velvet hat and the coat and blouse and boots and the whole outfit. In my first competition I won a blue ribbon and a trophy for first place. Oh, and did I mention that during practice I fell off the horse and landed right on my head? They made me get back on and I did but I was not very happy. In fact, I cried.*

*My mom takes me to my dance lessons once a week. I can't wait to go with her. She usually has her cigarette in one hand and the steering wheel in the other and I'm in the front seat looking out the window. I still remember that terrible day when we were driving to the studio and we heard a loud bang and my mother came to a screeching halt realizing our car was hit by something. Just as we looked into the street we saw a little boy and we saw a bike and one was not with the other. The best we can figure is that he was racing across the street at breakneck speed and didn't see us coming down the road and since he did not see us he began to cross the road and he hit our car.*

*The speed of his bike and the force of the crash sent him into the air and he looked like he was flying. Neighbors ran out of their houses from everywhere and someone called the police and the ambulance came and took him away. I did not see him as he lay on the side of the road and when they put him in the ambulance he was covered up with a sheet. Mom wouldn't let me out of the car so I sat there perched upon the seat, watching. I remember beginning to feel worried when we heard the bang and it just got worse and worse and I began to feel sick and kind of buzzy under my skin.*

*I was really afraid for my mom because she was worried too. Even though the accident was over I could still picture him flying in the air, and I watched it over and over again in my head, him flying in the air. I didn't want him to die.*

*My mother was smoking cigarettes one after another and when she came back to the car Dad came and gave her one of her red pills. It was a good thing Mom carried a small bottle of water. I could tell the pills helped her because her hands quit shaking but I was still upset.*

*When they told us we could go, Dad went home and Mom insisted on taking me for my dance lesson so we continued down the street to the studio. My mother told me that the little boy was going to the hospital near our house to be examined. He was not hurt that badly but they were afraid he might have injured his head. My mother said the sheet was just to keep him warm. Once the ambulance men strapped him on the gurney, they took him away and we went on our way too.*

*Late for dance, they were practicing a new step and I really tried my best to learn it, but I had a problem concentrating and coming in late didn't help and I was still shaken up from the accident. But I tried my best anyway and when we went home I was glad to be there and I felt better and I learned something on that day: don't ride in the street, take a red pill when you're shaking, and whenever you have a problem, call Dad.*

*This accident did not help my mother. Nervous anyway, she became more cautious and would never drive very far from home.*

*I was the first one up the next day. Once awake, I just couldn't fall back asleep so I went downstairs to see if anyone else was up but I was the only one. I sat on the living room couch, the one that faces the street and our bay window, and waited for them to join me. It was a sunny morning and I could see the blue sky through the tree right in front of our house. I was feeling fine on this morning and I just knew that it was going to be a good day.*

*Right then I saw him sitting there looking my way and I liked him looking at me. It was his large body and red breast that gave him away; it was a robin redbreast. There he was looking and waiting and watching some more. Then whatever caught his eye put him into the air and soon he was flying but not away from me; he was coming toward me, heading right for our big bay window. I wondered, "Bird, where are you going?" and as he came closer and closer to our house he never deviated from his path. He was interested in the bird in the window, not realizing it was his own reflection and nothing more.*

*My suggestion, "Stop bird, turn!" didn't help. He was traveling at breakneck speed and he never slowed down and then it was almost too late and then it was done. I could do nothing but watch and wait for what was about to happen. It was an earth-shattering slow motion "thud" and the window's vibration astonished both of us and he dropped out of sight.*

*"Oh, help, help!" I started to scream and I kept screaming and screaming and each scream got louder and longer and I couldn't stop seeing him looking at me one minute and flying to me the next and then crashing into the window.*

*I continued to scream at the top of my lungs until my father came running to see what was the matter and then he put his arm around me but there was no immediate calm. But my dad, he came to me when he heard me cry. He came to me when he heard me cry.*

The bird, the window, and me. A twist of fate or the outcome of something else. As I watched him in that tree, without a breath of concern, he charted his fate. Rather than liberate the bird in the reflection, he fulfilled an adverse destiny.

When we went outside to assess the damage, he was lying between the bushes just under the window in the dirt and I didn't want to look at him. His beak was smashed in and it was just awful. He had been alive only moments before, flapping, flying, anxious, optimistic, chasing his own reflection or finding his mate, and now he was nothing more than a limp and lifeless memory. It was a worthless death.

I felt the same way about the little boy who hit our car. I worried that his fate was just like the bird, limp and lifeless and very dead.

CHAPTER 4

# To Perceive the
# Untouched Line

Imagine a straight line, like the horizon perhaps, something fixed horizontally. It represents the division, the thin line, between happiness and misery. Living on the line is unchanging, level, sure, and consistent. Living on the line means living in an ordinary state, a normal state if you will. Typically, this line is the partition between two drastically opposite sectors of emotion.

Becoming aware of my own mental atmosphere and the analogy of the line as it relates to my emotions describes well the theory I set forth. Devoid of my own high and low emotions, any existence other than what I have known would be stability in disarray.

As a child, I knew nothing about lines or degrees of mood. Like my parents, I had my own undercurrent of melancholy, but life was a balancing act. Children are simply expected to be happy, but at

## Life Is Like a Line

a young age I found myself teetering near but mostly somewhere below the line.

As I grew, life was a mixed bag of highs and lows. There is a fine line between each degree away from the line. If the horizon represents level emotion, above it might represent beauty, joy, warmth, happiness, pleasure, excitement, exhilaration, euphoria, ecstasy, and more. These are emotions of mental preference, emotions of desire. But like my parents, the undercurrent of the opposite filled my mood. Sadly, the farther below the line one falls the closer sadness, discouragement, loneliness, misery, and anguish become.

In childhood, the awfulness of mental manipulation is not understood and therefore cannot be dealt with in a manner that releases its sufferers from its grasp. Unfortunately, my adulthood did not differ from my child-hood. I did not recognize the situations I encountered and the degree to which they affected me. But they produced symptoms that should have been an indication, and the warning signs that went unattended provided for instability and my own self-medicating. In other words, there were periods when I used drugs as a method of self-medication, as a coping mechanism, never realizing that my mind was teetering on that fine line at the exact time. Falling below the line, which I did regularly, meant struggling with sadness, hopelessness, and a desire for isolation, any of which could mean the beginning of depression.

I have found that falling lower and lower into the well of life is an empty and worthless journey in which exhaustion quickly is felt. Lower still lay despair, panic, and sometimes even paralysis. This depression and overall sickness oblige the contemplation of suicide, albeit by despair or obsession.

Although some may argue that living below the line is occasionally cathartic, I would submit that it is a slippery slope to the underground. It may very well be a race against time to prevent the earthly silencing of one's soul.

I have apologized to my husband many times because living below the line has not only affected me; it has affected our entire family. My siblings, daughters, and I are very accustomed to parental volatility, but it takes some getting used to. Although my own upbringing lacked family unity, it was my heartfelt desire to avoid any resemblance of my past. The circle that lacked emotion, devotion, and allegiance should not have been my legacy, and my ancestors would expect no less than for me to do my best to overcome it.

It is my feeling that, exclusive of some genetic disorder or mental incapacity, children who are raised with love, even in the worst of circumstances, surrounded by a minimally positive environment, have a reasonable chance of living above the line. Hooray!

In my topsy-turvy world, the lack of nurturing, warmth, and family support invited the mayhem that was bewildering, but I survived by necessity. I learned to smile and I learned to be accommodating. This was my sustenance; it showed that my spirit was intact and it kept me from sinking.

My father encouraged me to be kindhearted. I perceived him as that and it gave me delight to mimic him. My childhood could have been worse. In every place, at every stage, I have had plentiful moments. We were a typical middle-class family. My father made a good living and as the "baby," I wanted for nothing. So mine has not been living on the foul line or the firing line, often just below the line and sometimes above the line and even when I had to draw the line and fall in line, it has not been the end of the line. Not yet.

*We've had a lot of fun times. This week we went out to dinner to one of our favorite restaurants. Dad and I usually have a steak and Mom has the lobster tails. I like to go out to dinner with them and we go out often. I like to dress up when we go out and my mother does, too. This fancy restaurant is really dark inside and when we pull up a man parks our car. My dad gives me pennies for the waterfall. You can find almost anything on their menu but Mom orders the lobster tails and Dad and I have a steak and it's the same every time. Between Dad and I, we must have eaten about a million breadsticks loaded with butter before our dinner came. We sure had a nice time and we were still smiling when we returned home.*

*I didn't really want to go home afterwards so I asked if I could go over to my girlfriend's house for awhile. She lives only three houses down across the street in a house that her dad built. We used to play in the empty lot before the house was built but now we play in their yard. Almost every night in the summer we play hide and seek on our block and sometimes we hide in the alley behind her house and it's really fun. She is one year older than me and has two sisters. She usually invites me over for dinner; in fact, she invited me over tonight but I told her we were going out.*

*Her whole family speaks Italian so sometimes I don't know what they're saying but they look friendly and when her grandmother speaks she is loud and sometimes she has an angry face, but I know she's not angry with me. I really like it over there. Everyone is busy and they are all talking and cooking and it's fun. I'm always over at their house and I'm glad they don't mind.*

*On my way home I heard the chimes of the ice cream man and I ran to my house to ask for some money and Dad came out to the truck with me while I picked something out but he wasn't happy that I was so friendly with the ice cream man and he didn't like that the ice cream man was so friendly with me so now I can't go up to the truck without one of my parents. That is silly and I don't know why they are making me do this but it's the rule.*

*Later I heard Dad say something to Mom about me talking to that man. My dad thought he was too friendly to me and said that I'm too friendly to everyone, but between Girl Scouts and Sunday school, what else should I be?*

There was a point when I stopped yelling at them. Even as the wrath that lay between them continued to grow, I wanted them to love each other but there was a problem with my thinking: it was mine alone, based on my needs and my desires, and it didn't match theirs. I loved my parents, but I was frightened of their behaviors. I was an inconsequential little girl begging for a ceasefire, hoping for it without any understanding of their history of turmoil and abject difference of opinion.

To accomplish this they would have had to have been the perfect combination emotionally as well as rational thinkers. My father would say there is a fine line between love and hate, and I believe they unknowingly crossed this line many times. They needed intense psychiatry. Blame some of their behavior on their idiosyncrasies or their peculiarities of personality, but when their aggravation turned into aggression, it was way too much for me to cope with.

If I became more involved in their twist and shout, I remembered more of the stuff that I wanted to forget. My mother was angry again, the subject matter the usual. She said he did it on purpose and he began to defend himself and when she started to storm about the kitchen, she began to lose control. Her mood was agitated and violent and at this point she was unpredictable and she began to threaten.

I saw her in that rage and it was an impressionable scene, one I should have hidden from. I entered just in time to see my father come out of left field. He had a plan. He moved toward her and proceeded to dump one half of a half-eaten watermelon over her head, seeds, juice, and all. It dripped down her clothing and onto the floor. She was shocked and she swore at him, a push and then a shove and then she was on the floor. Then there were tears, hers and mine, and screaming, just mine.

It was my photographic memory I feared, the memories that would fortuitously be mine without my conscious effort to recall them.

My parents had a penchant for the kitchen. That's where my father would land after a hard day at the office, unless he closed himself in his bedroom with the invisible "Do not disturb" sign posted on the door. But generally, once he was out of his suit and tie and into his pajamas, he would check out the fridge and then read the newspaper cover to cover. If there was going to be conflict in the kitchen and the time was right, it almost always involved food. The day the inverted bowl of chili, beans and all, came cascading down her cheeks and into her eyes and onto the floor was another alarming experience.

She was seething and storming and he was defending and another push and shove directed her to the floor. It was another screaming match, mine against theirs, begging them to stop, please stop, and then simultaneously his yelling against hers. It should have been the last straw had there been any way to control them. I was too young to have them committed and nobody really knew what was happening inside our doors. Although they shared abusive behaviors, they didn't result in physical bruising. And even in the worst of times, there were more gifts and trips to the furrier and flowers brought home by my dad to smooth things over.

My shaking-nauseous-throw-up-at-any-minute reaction, my nighttime imagination, set in motion another sleepless night until school the next morning. A little more of my own anger and a little more terror was added to the mix every single time.

In the balance I liked school, but my complaints of mild illnesses kept me home often. Mornings would find me not feeling well and not feeling well and not feeling well and I had no explanation really and no symptoms for a doctor's script. My mother was accepting of my complaints and allowed me to stay home. It was something, something...I felt it; it surrounded me, but it ran its own course. Was it physiological? Psychological? Who knew, and who made any effort to know?

Over the years, I somehow believed this hell would end and that all the energy I had used worrying and panicking and fearing would reveal a purpose. "Dad, stop, *please stop!*" It was tiring. Time after time I would beg them, but I had no leverage to use against them. The power of man, zilch. I could no more control them than I could stop the wind from becoming a tornado or change water into wine. I couldn't make them love each other in a way that would stop their behavior and I was too naïve to know that trying harder served no purpose. They were accustomed to living this way, tolerating each other's behaviors and embracing each other's emotional upheavals with animosity and their own sense of affection. Every day, I promised myself that once I was gone, this life would never be mine.

Every time I thought they would kill each other, peace would re-emerge. Whether they were going out to dinner or to the little league dances with their friends, all their blistering issues would miraculously appear to be healed.

As I grew older, occasionally Saturday mornings with me were replaced by some men from the football league stopping by for coffee and conversation with my father. My mother would serve the coffee and then excuse herself for household chores while I found my girlfriends or the television. For the moment, I felt no unusual concern. It was cartoons and cowboy movies until the visitors were gone. This was calm, perfect, fantastic.

> *I don't see my brother too much but I see my sister more often. She just got married and I was her junior bridesmaid. I had to convert from Episcopalian to Catholic but it didn't really matter to me. Maybe two religious backgrounds are better than one, especially when sometimes I need help.*

*I have some problems in school; I don't like school really and there are subjects I don't understand. Math is my problem; I just don't get any of it. My brother works in the hotel industry and moves about the country quite often. His life is an absolute mystery to most of us including my dad, although we all know that my mother knows more and admits to nothing. My brother is not married and lives with some guys. This is cause for concern and when they fight, it's not over him but about him and it is constant. It would be cool to visit him; he's either living in California or Texas and I have never been there so if we could just forget the problems for a while, we could be a family.*

There were days when I was sensitive, not knowing what was happening within me. Anger, I believe, was my underlying mood, though it was not immediately recognizable. I figured I would grow out of my upset stomach, my jumpiness, and my worry. Perhaps my feelings and sensations were based on a growth spurt, perhaps not, but during that restless period I was impatient. I didn't have many girlfriends, but I loved the boys.

The older I got, the more I kept my real self hidden. Comedic sarcasm took over and it could be cutting. It spun so easily off my tongue I could not control it, let alone explain it, and often I was privately embarrassed by my wagging tongue. On many days, I was content to be a loner, but other feelings began seeping out around the age of twelve or thirteen and I became flirtatious with the boys. I was attracted to them. They were different than the girls; they were just plain fun. I liked to smell their cologne and exchange notes with them and I was warm with their attention. I never gave them exactly what they wanted, but they liked me just the same.

I remember my mother's frustration when she barked out the words, "*I should have raised dogs,*" but I don't think a loveless master could have made them any better than us. We were just children caught up in someone else's game, unclear about the rules, unaware of our evolution. My brother caused friction between our parents, my mother resented my sister, and I was daddy's little girl. Under those circumstances, yes...she should have raised dogs.

My father continued to come and go with business meetings, dinners, and golf outings with business associates and my mother's resentment grew, though on occasion they managed business trips together. One week while they were gone, I stayed with a neighbor who lived only four houses from ours.

Midge and her family lived simply. They were unpretentious and they made me feel very comfortable but I wanted to be home. Staying with them was a pleasant change, but I missed my life terribly. Oddly enough, in spite of all the turmoil at home, I felt empty without my parents. I missed my bed, my bathroom, our habits, my mother's cooking, the essentials of my home life. Surrounded by strangers, not loved ones, I felt alone and I wanted my parents more than ever.

*Weekends are family days. Dad is usually home from work and we do stuff around the house or go for a ride or something. Today we're in the basement cleaning. Mom and Dad are cleaning the bar and arranging the glasses and looking at the bottles and they are talking to each other and having snacks.*

*I was playing my favorite game on the table over by the couches but I like sitting up here better, up here at the bar. I can see what Mom and Dad are doing when I'm up here and I can have potato chips out of the bag and my pop sipped out of a fancy glass. We even have stirrer sticks with elephants on them and I have one in my glass; it's pink.*

*Mom and Dad both smoke cigarettes and my parents are listening to music on the record player. My mother has some lady named Rusty Warren but when they play that one I have to go upstairs.*

*I feel older when I sit up here on the bar stools. You have to be careful when you sit on them because they spin when you turn them and they are easy to turn, but that's the fun of them. I can spin all of them when I am standing on the floor and they make a funny noise. Right now I am spinning around and around in circles on the stool in the corner of the bar. I was going to play a game but I can always play later; I am having too much fun spinning.*

*Mom always says "Be careful" and I am really careful but right now I'm beginning to feel a little dizzy and oops, now my stomach is feeling funny. Oh, I feel sick; I'm so diz…"Ohhhhhhhh, help, Dad…Help, Ohhhhhhhh…"*

*As soon as Dad runs over he picks the stool up off of me and says, "It's okay, honey, you're okay."*

*"It hurts, the stool hit me and ahhhhhh, my head, oh I'm sick, I'm getting sick. I don't remember…it just tipped over. I didn't mean to."*

*"I am going to be sick, Mom. I'm going to throw up. Why do you need to call the doctor, Mom? Why are you so upset?"*

*"Dad, don't go. Why are you taking my temperature? My head hurts so much. I feel really funny. Why is the doctor coming?"*

*"It's right back here by my ear; it hurts. I feel sick. I don't have any glass in my mouth. What do you mean? I didn't swallow any glass; I would know if I did."*

*"Why can't you touch that silver on the floor? What is mercury? I bit into it but I didn't mean to; it just happened. Will the doctor come down here?"*

*"Mom, what did the doctor say? Why did he leave so soon? I'm still sick; he didn't do anything."*

*"Okay, but I still have that funny feeling and I'm scared. Could I have a blanket? I know I'm going to be okay but I'm scared and I'm never sitting on those stools again."*

*"Here I go; I'm going to throw up again I think."*

After lying down on the basement couch a while longer for observation, my dad carried me upstairs to my room and my parents tucked me in bed and I stayed there for two days resting. There my meals were consumed and television viewed. On the second day I tiptoed downstairs to the kitchen but they wanted me to stay upstairs and rest. For three more days, I was just plain scared and mostly nauseous. Off and on I had hallucinations, which even today I can recall.

I remember leaping down from the landing and then floating down our stairs to our basement, my feet never touching the ground, moving one by one over each stair, hands outstretched, gently feeling the walls as I passed. I remember "seeing myself" float down those stairs over and over again, seemingly hundreds of times, before the image finally began to subside. Days after the fall, I was still afraid of these unusual sensations, fearing they would never leave me. I felt panicky and I heard sounds; it was an unexplainable condition for a youngster and I couldn't separate reality from what I was feeling and seeing.

The colors and the walls and the sounds were frightening and they were not meant to impress or invite, but they made an impact. This nervous little girl, unfamiliar with the words "normal" and "abnormal" and "thermometer" and "mercury" and "hallucinations," was naive to the fact that crashing your head onto a concrete floor can mess you up. I am told that I may have suffered a concussion or some type of closed-head injury that should have been medically pursued.

At some point after this, I began to experience horrifying mental images and sensations in which I was overcome with confusion and feelings of terror. Living mute under fear gave freedom to this state.

First I experienced absolute terror, and I knew when it was coming. Then came a mental vision with a physical sensation and what I saw with my mind's eye was nothing more than a dimensional black line. It was a vertical reverberating line, seated in the depth of me, beginning in my mind, pushing down through my body. When it was present in my consciousness, I became trapped in a state of confusion and dread and anxiety and I was afraid...terrified, simply terrified of this black line. Overwhelmed and terrified, I was fucked whenever struck by the black line.

There was nothing disingenuous about this line. There was an intensity and breadth to it that made encountering it the single most frightening feeling I have ever had. It was a relief to learn that someone else experienced a similar sensation in another way when I read Dr. Kay Redfield Jamison's words in *The Unquiet Mind*: "Sex became too intense for pleasure, and during it I would feel my mind encased by black lines of light that were terrifying to me."

Though this experience began sometime after my crash in the basement, I cannot trace it to any particular time in my life. Nonetheless, it became my enemy and it seemed to appear on my worst days throughout my life, ceasing the year of my forty-eighth birthday.

> *Since puberty started, my thoughts and feelings have changed and I am doing something that's just about me. I find myself knowing about this something in an all-of-a-sudden way. These very personal and private*

*feelings have started to occupy my mind. It's like the force of my body; it listens to my brain and I don't understand why but I do it. It's a little creepy actually, but my vibrations and feelings are strong and I have no idea where they are coming from and I can't tell anybody because they will think there is something wrong with me and I don't understand it either.*

*When I woke up that one morning it just felt like I was somebody different. In my mind I started thinking about it but I knew I shouldn't be. These ideas are coming from everywhere. I don't try to think about it; it just happens. I've never done this before and I've never wanted to do this before but it feels good.*

*I don't want to get caught. I don't think I'm supposed to do it, but it is something that makes me happy for the moment. I don't want to get in trouble, but I'll still do it anyway. It's just about me and I'm free.*

The urges of physical desire were not too difficult to comprehend. Everything about me seemed to be changing: from the morning my first menstrual cycle began (which my parents forgot to prepare me for) to the first day of desire (not a subject for the sixties), it all frightened and excited me. There was a boy who lived at the end of the block and we were pals. We played with trains in his basement, and as his mother filled my thirst with a water glass, he attempted to fill me with sexuality. Although I knew of his desires, at the time I feared the consequences, so when my curiosity reverted to "No" I stopped going to his house.

Nevertheless, by instinct alone, I learned to find a temporary pleasure carried out by my own hand that brought to me the satisfaction of orgasmic relief. However, the pleasure of this experience did not change the detached view I had of the process overall. My parents chose double beds on separate floors; therefore my point of reference for physical intimacy between two lovers was warped.

The self-absorption of my own sexuality remained throughout my youth. A degree of moodiness also lingered and remained in a familiar and demanding way. With my desires turned on, I favored satisfaction in the privacy of my own room until my mother's intrusion forced an embarrassing admission. Her angry reaction and invective retort did not prevent me from

## Life Is Like a Line

this self-arousing act, since I knew my territorial discovery was more sophisticated than her own.

As I began to mature, some of my self-exploration gave way to puppy love relationships that had the bonus of affection and refuge, and in adulthood I moved into many cozy acquaintanceships, none of which came close to nourishing my heart's desire.

> *Tomorrow is my sixteenth birthday. This is the eve of it and I am so afraid. I know I'm not to blame for any of this. I can't stop thinking this way and I feel like there's a weight inside of me. My room is closing in on me and it's hot and stuffy and I can't seem to be free of my fears. I am fifteen for God's sake; what is going on? I feel nauseated and it's like a voice in my head, a silent voice; it's a whisper that has lasted all night. But why now? Why today? Why is this happening to me?*
>
> *I am so young. How can this be happening? I haven't been that bad; I'm good actually. I'm not great, but who is? Ahh, this is horrible. This sounds so stupid, but I feel heavy and lazy and I just feel like sitting here on the floor all night and my music isn't helping me; it's too psychedelic. I feel this all around me and over me and under me and inside of me. Tonight I will die. My feelings are about my death and my death is coming and I have a strong feeling that I am going to die in my sleep tonight. I am going to be dead in the morning.*
>
> *Maybe I could have stopped it if I had told someone...They'll think I'm crazy if I tell them something like this. This is crazy, but I know this is for real. I am so sure. Just go to bed; don't close your eyes; lie there all night. That's what I'll do.*
>
> *No, I can feel it; I am going to die in here, alone. Nothing really matters; it's over. I hear my head. One side is chanting, "Going to die, going to die," and the other is saying, "That's ridiculous, that's ridiculous, go to bed, go to bed," but I feel panic and fear and I feel more panic still and my mind is running wild and I can't change my thoughts.*
>
> *I need to be free of this. How do I stop this? This will all be over soon...ahh, they will find me in the morning. It will all end tonight and I'm so sorry. I am sorry; I should have told you.*

I was shocked when I woke up the next morning. I remember so clearly how stunned I was. Grateful for the extension on my time, I was filled with joy and sorrow both. My disappointment was not that I had cheated death or that God had changed his mind; it was that my strongest thoughts were not accurate.

Nonetheless, on that night, I gave one thought enough energy to grow and multiply, and as it evolved, it affected my body. I lost control of it and lost myself amid its noise. It was the worst night I'd had in fifteen years, but it was not the worst of many that followed.

Because my siblings and I grew up exposed to a life centered on negativity, our outlook seemed likewise destined to be negative. Over the years, I have made many attempts to suppress a multitude of thoughts that come uninvited, but some persist by the fuel of my pessimistic self.

My parents were funny. Even though my father separated himself from my brother, he would speak kindly with him on the telephone and their conversation would be that of allies rather than adversaries. But once my mother took over the conversation, my father would become angry and estranged again.

Likewise, when my sister moved away, my mother mentally disconnected herself from her because of her jealousy but would speak kindly with her on the telephone and then refuse to attend any family gatherings at her house. My father, "the glue," would coerce Mom into visiting and we would briefly appear to be a family once again.

My father and I were the closest. As they aged, I attended to their needs. Devoted at a young age, my daughters looked to him as a father figure and that kept him young. My mother resented me; she once told me she knew all along that my father loved me more than he loved her.

I told her that was insane and became quite upset; that simply cannot be true. My father had enough love to go around; perhaps he was just cautious of having his heart bruised too many times by his wife.

Our parents made it easy for us to remember the violence and antagonism that flourished within steps of our malleable minds by repeating the process relentlessly as we grew. When I was old enough, I became their go-between, but there was no intermediary for me and sometimes I got stuck in the middle. The driving force for not sinking entirely was my dream that an eventual reconciliation and permanent ceasefire would come and that we would share a closeness that never, alas, was to be.

There were days in my youth when I was like a train prepared to derail, forced to weave back and forth at each unsteady turn. With a strong sense of aloneness, not even the strength of the tracks could keep me on the straight and narrow. Their battle fought on shaky ground became mine, and though the periods of smoothness helped to level out the course, I weaved and changed with every birthday. As my exposure kept changing, so my survival techniques had to change too.

As children develop, they eventually grasp the environment they live within. Once my parents' behaviors were internalized, my exposure demanded evolving survival techniques. Though the small child may hide in the closet or under the covers, the older child learns how to cover her ears and scream for help. Later, smoking pot or drinking wine becomes the answer.

Of bottle, of self. This was my father's remedy and my mother's and now it would be mine. Some of my techniques were hazy, but that is exactly where I was looking to be. Indeed, there was no escaping altogether the life that seemed to bury me.

# CHAPTER 5

# Of Bottle, of Self

For many years, my father battled mood swings. The change in his personality was easy to detect, and often the swings were problematic. Still finding relief in his anxiety medication, he continued to take his pills and at times one of my mother's red capsules as well. In our home we all drank the white medicine, the stomach medicine, the shaky sick stomach cure.

It was the bottle that got my attention. I wondered about those pills, and when I sat in just the right seat at the kitchen table, I could watch him move toward his closet, reach up to the top shelf, bring down a small prescription bottle labeled with his name, twist off the cap, and swallow.

I didn't know what they were or exactly why he took them, but it was obvious even to me that when he took them he seemed more peaceful and unruffled, and that was the mix that helped calm the seas at home. My father drank occasionally, my mother never, and the only drugs she ever consumed came from the doctor's hand. Their problems seemed to be more internal than external, and when tempered with red capsules and the pills from his brown bottle, their moods were better, which made a huge impression on me.

At sixteen, with learner's permit in hand, we raced down to the secretary of state's office for my license. Paperwork complete and photograph taken, I was finally legal. As promised, my parents gave me my first car. It was my mother's 1965 Ford Fairlane 500 convertible. I was high from the excitement and proud as a peacock.

My two-door dream gave me new freedom and I could finally escape from the ties that bound me at home. I was all the clichés a new driver could be. This was the beginning of an adventurous life and that car—damn, I got a kick out of driving it, pumping gas in it, washing it, watching the man check my oil, and the list went on and on.

My friends and I drove all over the city of Detroit, ice skated at Belle Isle, trolled for boys, hunted for parties, and hung out at the park. I was introduced to marijuana by fifteen and I enjoyed my distorted sensitivity of it, the anesthetized forgetfulness of it, and the "I don't give a damn" attitude of it. I just plain liked it. I learned to drive while rolling it, lighting it, toking it, passing it, roach clipping it, and choking while smoking it. Very quickly I became proficient with every detail surrounding it. I taste it even today; I smell it on my fingers.

In the beginning, I considered every possible hiding place for my stash so I would never be found out and made to feel its loss. The convertible top of my brand new car offered the perfect solution. I hid my loot between the canvas top and the side rails, perfectly out of sight but ready at a moment's notice. In an instant, my car became my introduction to personal and pleasurable experiences like nothing my mother had ever known.

As we laughed and parked and partied, I had not a care in the world. I learned to drive from my father, but who would have thought I could become more skillful, steady, assertive, and cautiously cocky while stoned?

Maybe I was too cocky, because while we were driving around one night, I got a ticket for following a police car too closely.

I was a jerk. I knew exactly what I was doing and I did it on purpose. The cops followed us so much that I'd decided to turn the tables on them, but they stopped me, wrote the ticket, and screwed up my new adventure. Enter my parents, my explanation, a court date, and a black-robed judge. I was dying, and then the judge laughed and dismissed the case, thank God.

Hello? That should have been my wake-up call.

*"Hey, what's going on? I'm not coming over tonight. Yes, I told you I'm going to do this; I'm not kidding. I'll do it tomorrow. I won't chicken out; this is for real. First thing in the morning. It's not harmful. I know for sure it's no big deal. I haven't heard of any overdoses and I've planned on trying them like forever; you know that. You're right, but I just don't want the ones in foil, the street ones. Okay. Sure, I'll pick you up at the usual time. See ya. Goodnight."*

Until now I'd been kind of naïve, but being of sufficient age helped me to understand what the fuss was all about. Initially marijuana was enough for me. This new thing revolved around a subject taught secretly inside but mostly outside the classroom, often by the upperclassmen, the ones who looked like hippies, the straight-looking ones, or the guys who just hung around outside.

Once I put two and two together, it added up to the front hall closet. My father's stash of pills...perfect. I'm sure he never considered his medication of any interest to me, but it was that and more. This was about my head, getting it straight, naw...about fucking it up.

I made my plan. I wanted the tilt and I was ready to administer the mix with no fear. It had been hanging around there for years and it would help; it helped him. Maybe it wouldn't help, but it wouldn't hurt to try. No matter what, I was driven to try it.

*Tomorrow is the day. I'll be safe...it's a medical miracle. Some guys in a lab, a drugstore, buy a free buzz. I don't know what will happen to me once I take it but I don't care; how bad can it be? I don't know what it feels like but I've seen them in action. Very soon I'm gonna find out and what do I have to lose? As long as somebody knows, it'll be safe. My girlfriends know; they'll keep an eye on me. So I'll just see for myself what my father's pills do. This might be the first and last time. Who knows, they might kill me. But it's our family tradition.*

The night left me restless and I was relieved by the rising of the sun. This was the day, and I was ready to put the plan into action. I knew exactly what to do: dress for school, head for the kitchen table, turn right, and open the front closet, Dad's closet. The very same closet we'd passed on that fall day in September, 1953, when they'd brought me home from the hospital. Now, sixteen years later, no longer would I pass it without stopping.

Driven to do it or purely for entertainment, who the hell knows and who the hell cares? Go left, now in front of me, waiting, ahh...the treasure chest. There was no way to avoid the pounding of my heart; my eagerness to receive my "therapy" was at full tilt. I was at the fifty-yard line and moving fast. The excitement of the game and the capture of the prize delighted me and no other emotion would dare attempt to engage me. Then it was done, the waiting game was over, and I sat down at the table in my father's chair and took enjoyment in the irony of the act. The whole process was too easy and the closet pills were mine.

I wondered briefly how my father would have responded had he walked into the kitchen just then to see his bottle of forbidden fruit nestled so intimately in my hands. As many times as I scored his meds, I am thankful the answer to that question was left unknown.

*"Oh, you guys; that was too easy. Hey, I drove us here, didn't I? I look what? Get outta here. Ah man, I do feel it more now; it's hitting me now. I do not look stoned; get the hell out of here...Dammit...but I will tell you, I like this; it's cool. I feel like a rubber band. Like I could melt, sort of. This is a very weird feeling and my head is weird. We've gotta go in there now? Oh man, wait with me for the second bell; I'm not ready; I'm getting kinda freaked. This is freaking me out. Shit, I don't want to get busted. Do you think they'll know? Are you sure? My eyes are open; cut it out! I think it'll get better as it wears off; I'm not used to it, that's all...Okay, okay! I'm coming. Okay, not before school, I promise. You guys kill me! Thanks. I'll*

*see you at lunch, I hope. No problem. My knees are wobbly but really I'm okay. I'll be okay; I like it."*

I liked downers; they had an indescribable effect on me. They were so…cool. The taking was always too easy and I got bolder about doing it. I was good at driving and at covering it up, in and out of school, and it was never apparent that I was on anything. If it was apparent, nobody at school cared. Wobbly, droopy-eyed, and slurring much too often, I swallowed them and I swallowed them and when I couldn't find Dad's pills I took hers; they were easy to find and there for the taking.

*Of all the groups and cliques in school, I belong with the hippies. My days of wearing khaki slacks, miniskirts, and penny loafers are gone. In fact, I was one of ten girls suspended in junior high for wearing my miniskirts too short. The assistant principal actually measured us one day! When my mother came to pick me up after receiving the call, she told the principal that the policy of measuring skirts and sending girls home was ridiculous. I was really proud of her that day. She defended me and we thought it was funny all the way home. The hell with them; the next day I wore another skirt slightly longer. I suppose I had a sharp tongue even then and it was as visible as it was audible.*

*But now it's high school, bell bottoms dragging on the ground, shredding from the scraping of the concrete, and cool shirts and blouses and belts and suede vests with long fringe and self-painted saddle oxfords or platform shoes. Necklaces made of beads. I LOVE beads. My hair is different, too. What was once trimmed above my shoulders now hangs in waves just below.*

*My friends are cool and hanging out with them is like living in an "I don't care that much" kind of world. We're not into sports or anything "jock." I have learned to stay away from the stuck-up cheerleaders and I can't even understand the boys who bring briefcases to school. I just found out about the lesbian group. I know some of the girls but I don't want to march for lesbian rights. I don't want to march for anything. I'm into music, seriously into music. I love the Beatles and anything that sounds psychedelic. I have tons of albums and a four-track tape player in my car that they* tell me will be obsolete soon. I will have to change to an eight-track player and start all over again.

My favorite artists are Jimi Hendrix, Cream, Alice Cooper, Blind Faith, Arlo Guthrie, Janis Joplin, Bob Dylan, and many more. I love all the cool posters but I can't have any in my room and I love black lights but I can't have those either, but as long as my friends have them I really don't care. I'm not home that much anyway.

I'm against abortion, I'm all for peace, and I do not believe in the Vietnam War but I don't attend the protest marches either. My best friend belongs to S.D.S. (Students for a Democratic Society) but I'm not into that either. I don't even know what the hell they do. You might say my friends are liberals; they are way more liberal than I am in many ways, but who cares? We do some crazy damn stuff. Lately we've been spending time with the guys in the band and we go to their practices in the basement of the lead guitar player's house. One foot in the door will give you a contact high and the farther we go down into the basement, the heavier the smell of that sweet happy smoke.

Our friend has black lights and posters and a constant flow of grass and hash and pills. When we sit around on his couches, I can be in a complete state of ease. Hit it or pass it; there's no pressure; nobody cares. We get stoned, we laugh, we come down, and we get something to eat. It just feels so natural. We also hang out at the park, which is no big deal until the police arrive and chase us out for being there after the park closes. They drive around the block in their black-and-white pretending to chase us, talking over the loud speaker, and we run like hell so they can't catch our smoked-grass asses.

By the time I go home I'm fairly straight, but those times when I'm still buzzed and smelling like weed, I load up on cologne and pray that my parents are either fast asleep or in bed watching TV so I can head for my sanctuary with no interruptions. But not every night is party night. On Tuesdays I have dinner with another girlfriend and then we go to her catechism class at the Catholic Church nearby so I'm pretty good after all.

Honestly, if you are looking to find us, we will either be at my girlfriend's house doing whatever or driving around or maybe having ice cream *at the end of the block or custard in Grosse Pointe or we're at the liquor store near Harper and Gratiot buying my favorite bottle of wine and a pack of Cools. No Boones Farm Apple something for me, thanks. Yuck.*

    *The girls are comfortable with me driving because they're all buzzed. They gather up their money and send me in with their order. I go into the store, pick out the bottles, ask for the cigs, and pay for it all with the cash they hand to me, still folded or rolled up in my pocket. Either I am an idiot or everyone else is too chicken to go in there because usually I'm on my own. Long after the party, when my curfew is near, it's my quick drive home to hopefully not face the music.*

There is no doubt that using illicit drugs was very popular in the sixties and early seventies when I was growing up. It was free love America and we were tuned in and turned on and with fists raised high, we were "Right on, Brother." Popular lyrics gave mood to the music and set the pace for a new openness that we had not seen thus far. This was the Vietnam era, and some of our uniformed boys openly smoked weed to help them over there, and once home, it helped them forget the ugliness of war.

Simultaneously throughout the country, protest marches and sexual openness prevailed and the use of marijuana was soon considered just a sign of the times. Once it was accepted, we fell in line. It was unadulterated "Flower Power," controversial, groundbreaking, and peace-loving, and it was for me. There were concerts and mass drug experimentation and free love throughout the U.S. The festival of '69 in Woodstock, New York, was the preeminent concert of musical history. The attendees' poetic indulgence was not quite accepted by middle-class America, but it had its influence on us.

For us, marijuana and alcohol were everywhere. We had become the sex, drugs, and rock and roll generation and my parents thought these activities undignified, immoral, and repulsive. If only they had known about their last born. We were beginning to gamble on our own, with our own experiments, in the comfort of our own homes (not mine), with the safety net of our friends, and we knew who to buy what from, at least most of the time.

Occasionally something was obtained from an outside source and it was due to our naïveté. I was looking for a trip…chasing rabbits, thanks to the Jefferson Airplane, and I knew the medium that would me take me there. If there were other desires and the hallucinogenic cube was not your bag, the guy offered "Weed or hash or uppers to speed up the day, or downers, THC; now how 'bout a little 'H' in that grass?"

Everything was considered but coke. That was the rich man's desire, none of which we knew anything about. I was looking for just the right mixture for my sachet of contentment. "What do I try first; I'll try this; now how about that; man, that was terrible; I wanted to die. Switch over to something else. Bad again, but I'll try it once more just for fun. How about you guys; what's happenin'?"

There were days when I had to talk my girlfriend's younger sister down from her bad trips and dreadful highs and I would wonder, "Why me?" Each time she got fucked up, I would help her. Maybe they thought I had the most experience. Yeah, I did. But I couldn't watch her in this way. I mean, she would lie in bed covered from head to toe and say really bizarre things or sway back and forth in a wild-eyed stare and truly someone had to keep an eye on her.

Once I stepped in, talking her down became my role, and to this day I don't know why she continued to punish herself by ingesting the very chemicals that tore her apart. It was freaky and I was frightened for her. Today she's a fucking practicing psychologist. Hmmm.

In those days I was dangerously uncaring and unafraid and in hindsight I must have been more than wild. Fortunately, I didn't end up going mad. Most of the drugs were merely mood-altering until my first LSD trip, which took me into what I considered a psychedelic realm. I hoped for a powerful road to enlightenment, but I ended up in a hippie experiment with one foot in the door of ecstasy and the other in disturbance.

The spiritual part of this journey was when God spoke to me. He told me something simple and obvious. In a soft powerful voice of authority, my mind heard him counsel, "It's all about love." I was supposed to spread the word somehow and immediately I ran upstairs to alert my girlfriends and they told me to take it easy and calm down.

I tried, but it was impossible. This was surreal. Back in the living room, I sat in a tiny child's rocking chair in front of the TV set, and while I watched the vividness of the colors that emanated from my mind, a lady in an apron came out of the TV and asked me for a pair of scissors. Other than the weirdness of it all, I had the luck of a good trip.

The next time the objective was to dig it in the same way. Amid the colors and God, let's pass on the lady in the apron, I wanted self-awareness and visual beauty, a real heart-racing adventure. Instead, I experienced a frightening spectrum of colorful wavy walls and sounds that were awful and a flight of the imagination, fears, paranoia, and discomfort. Panic filled the brim of my poor lack of judgment. It was too weird; it was too much. I knew and felt everything I never wanted to feel and more. With my heart still racing, voices told me to run, and before I made it out the door, I was rescued.

My friends protected me from myself, but it was hours before I could shake this experiment in mental survival. There was distortion and paranoia and I was out of my mind. Terrified of my own thoughts, I begged for forgiveness and the Lord finally rescued me. At last it was over.

We were high school kids and we knew it all. First kick up the nervous system, then slow it down. I hadn't learned my lesson; it was all too easy to forget when it was over. I was still fired up and there was seemingly no end to our amusement. It was truly by grace that we escaped the impending deadening bite. Simply put, we had too many choices, mind games, stimulants, depressives, and brain rushes.

Wine, oh yeah, we consumed our share. So long to sobriety. It was the well of forgetfulness and nausea and motion sickness, oh God, too many nights of that. But let the truth be known, I was slick. I didn't intentionally try to deceive, but the taste became a remedy. Once the ball started rolling down that mountain, there was no stopping it. As it evolved, picking up leaves and sticks along the way, it began to change in shape and composition. Even though it took on layers of diverse substances, the core was not changed.

I was to recreate or be destroyed. My parents offered me much freedom and I came and went at will without a single parental question. I was into the culture and the exploration; I had opportunity, money, and safe havens. In my head, anything and everything was better than what was. No monkey

## Life Is Like a Line

in the middle, and for the first time in my life I had more than one friend who cared for me like no sister or brother ever had.

*I can't believe I stayed home for this. God, they are at each other again, another night at the fights, and after all these years they can still make me feel this way. I should have stayed out. I hate this shit; they love to bicker… ahh, man, I sure would like a cig or a joint at this point. Who would even notice? It would be the smoke that would get them. A downer, that's what I'd like. Dammit, I fought with her this afternoon and now he's catching hell tonight. This afternoon she bitched and I fought back.*

*"Where did you get this? You found it in my drawer? Those are my notes written only for me and I can't believe you went through my desk. Besides, why are you going through my things? I don't care if you think my friends are disgusting. It doesn't mean anything and this is my room. I know this is your house and I live under your rules but you don't get to read my personal mail. I don't read yours; I don't tell Dad about you and my brother."*

*What a bitch, going through my fucking room. Tonight it starts all over again. I stayed home because I just didn't feel like running around and I thought they would be happy to see me but no, it's bullshit night at the fights. And I won't do this crappy homework either; fuck them. Man, do I want something…a cigarette, joint, wine, I could just choke that woman. Ahh, God. Sometimes I feel sorry for him and now I do again.*

*He walks in the door and wham, but then again she has been sitting home all day going through my drawers (thank God not my car); it's time to pick on someone else. After all, he is five hours past the bell. Shit, I'm doing it again, taking sides, dreading, monkey in the middle, just hoping for a peaceful night but they won't last long; she's gotta be tired out.*

*No matter how much I hear them or how old I get, I am still bothered by the tension and angry voices. It will be over soon; it won't last forever; just get past this hour and the next one will be better. Get past this hour and the next one will be better; get past this hour and the next one will be better.*

*Convince yourself, you jackass. Dammit if life didn't seem simpler when I was younger. There were fewer years with them so I'd heard less of this and I hadn't stored as much as I have now.*

The child in me, now past sixteen and slowly maturing, was every day exposed to them for the good and the bad. But in the bad, the misery kept burrowing deeper into my soul. There was no sharing with the perpetrators of my discomfort. They were not emotionally available to me; they had considerations of their own. I always said I was an only child. Once it became obvious to me that my brother was living a life somewhere near a closet and couldn't come out, all of our relationships became strained, except of course the one he had with my mother.

I had been babysitting my sister's kids for years now, but she still viewed me as a child. Her adult world simply didn't offer a sibling relationship with me other than the contractual one, babysitting. Once out of the nest, she never looked back at me, not ever, not the way I needed her.

Neither of my siblings wished the memories of the turmoil at home. They were aware of my plight but never considered my constant struggle. What occurred in our household might have been commonplace, but as mental abuse punctures the spirit, it bleeds the joy out of life.

In the beginning, I found a temporary release in the liquids, pills, and papers at my disposal. In my deepest hour, I prayed they would release my inner self from its captivity. In all that surrounded me in my youth, there was no substance great enough, ingested enough, mind-altering enough, to relinquish the ache. I endured a lifetime of their collective battles, without eradication from within…me.

> *Just when I thought we were doing book work today, he decides to have a lecture. Why do I care about his lectures anyway? I just want to get out of this seat and leave right now. Pack up and go. Why is the clock moving so slowly? I'll get a bathroom pass and not come back…No, I better not; that will get me in trouble, but I have to go and go right now. I don't know why I feel this and I don't know what the hell this is, but it is just awful. If he catches me drawing he'll have a fit. I should be taking notes, but I can't take notes, not now, not today. There is something inside me that makes me feel awful and I can't really explain it except that I would like to get a buzz right now.*

## Life Is Like a Line

*All I think about is the awfulness of how I feel and it follows me every-where. It feels like there is something following me, hanging over me that I just can't shake. Oh God, this class is going so slowly. I gotta go now.*

*Okay, relax, you're freaking out with only twenty minutes left. Maybe this is about them and last night and listening and listening to them again...I feel bad and there are times when I just can't stop thinking about this stuff and I am afraid of the way I feel, but it's the way I feel and there's nothing I can do about it.*

*Oh man, nineteen minutes, okay, only nineteen minutes more of this jackass, and then three flights up to my locker and one block to my car. I feel like I have permission to escape life, the whole scene. I've put my time in; I have permission because it sucks really; for me all of it sucks.*

*Oh man, this is crazy. I know what this is. I am just panicking. One half of my head says, "That's wrong, really wrong, even wrong to think it," and the other half says, "Go ahead; everything is fucked up anyway. You'll feel better, in a better place."*

*Fifteen minutes and I feel like someone is sitting on me. They're holding me down and I can't move and I feel like I'll go crazy if they don't get off. That's me right now; I hope I'm not having a heart attack. I cannot explain any of this; none of this is making sense anymore. These feelings aren't necessarily new but I thought I'd outgrown them. I had the same sense the night before my sixteenth birthday and today I feel it again and it feels the same.*

*This is freaking me out. Maybe I should do it. Oh God, nine minutes of this. I can't stop having this feeling today and it is just awful and I'll be fine as soon as I get some fresh air. I'll just lay my head on my desk. No, that's bad, too noticeable. I'm not going to do it; suicide is something someone else does.*

*Dammit, my heart is pounding. Oh man, I gotta get out of here. I need to end all the bullshit and the misery; that's what I need to do. It's not as if I haven't thought about it once or twice but I don't go around planning my own funeral; it just appears in my head. It's just there, the thought of it, the feeling, my thoughts are just rambling today and besides, it's not death really; it's just like disappearing, being gone, evaporation, being unseen, which I have been for years anyway.*

*Oh well, I'll never do it anyway. That's just a head full of bullshit.*
*That's disgusting; I hate pain anyway. Grass, that'll do it.*
*Ah, the bell. So long, jackass; I'm outta here.*

In high school I was unbelievably stirred up. I was becoming more and more captivated with the world of drugs; my interest was narrow but my ingestion was great. Memories bring to me the aroma of smoke deep inside my mind. I taste the powder and feel the sensations. It is my dark desire. I feel the substances like a quiver against a bow. I am lost in the memory of its power. I am lost in all the memories.

Within my own obsession I have come to know compulsive thoughts. My thoughts are sporadic. I have not lost myself to the substances of the past though I yearn for them. Today I am taken by the sensitivity of the small child who sits behind the wheel of the car running in the garage. And now she stands in front of her house, struggles to see it. Her back faces it but something prevents her from turning around. This happens to her over and over again; she is glued to the walk; she can never turn around. No one is there to see her or to help her find her way.

Fear wakes me; it is only a dream.

*"Hi. Ya, I visited my father's little helpers today and my mother's yes-terday. So what? I wasn't going to; it's been a long damn time but I just felt like it. I really needed to; they were crazy and they were making me crazy."*

*"No, I don't want to hit that…Where'd you get it? Man, it's early. I haven't even had breakfast; I'll have the munchies."*

*"Okay, I'll hit it one time, then get away from me."*

*"Can I borrow a cigarette? What, no menthol? Okay, I'll have one of yours. Cool. Yeah, any cooler and we would be dangerous."*

*"Oh man, we're going to be late, for God's sake. I'm gonna walk out of Spanish so I'll meet you in the lunchroom."*

*"I don't really care; I hate that teacher and I hate that class."*

In those days, I never realized I had such extremes. The risks taken were so unwise. I would walk out of classes, I skipped classes, even skipped days; second hour it was down the stairs and out the door. I drank at night, smoked when I could, and couldn't care less about the ramifications of doing so. I grew to be cocky. I was brazen. I didn't think about it; I just did it, and I had plenty of energy but many restless nights.

First thing in the morning I would race out of the house to escape the button-pushing fest of my mother's. After my groundswell of irritability, my sarcasm would begin and then I would hate myself and the world and decide to alter my senses.

When we smoked pot, I felt like I was on top of the world, divine. I would walk in the door stoned, I would walk out the door stoned, and half the time I didn't know what I was thinking. When I took my "meds," I felt them in every inch of me, from my head to my toes. Even through the fear, I was fascinated. There were times when my mind was captured in some sort of awfulness and the experience would remind me that what I was doing was risky, but once gone it was easy to forget and start over. In my group, we were in this together, some more than others, but all in all a good fit.

That school year brought overdoses and pregnancies but not for me. Somehow I made the honor roll and I kept wondering if they hadn't mixed my grades up with someone else's. We hung out with one of our substitute teachers, a virtual bearded hippie stranger who was a fox. We would go to his house and hang out and listen to records. I have no idea what he was thinking, but we had a great time partying with him. I am certain I have a guardian angel in my life who kept me safe, if for no other reason than I am here today.

> Things are happening in school that I don't really care about. Everything seems to be changing, but maybe it's just me. My parents have just joined the country club and they golf and eat there several times a week. I meet them there but I am barely interested in meeting anybody. They have been getting along very well and I am happy to be around them but I am not home very much to enjoy their company. The country club is good for them; it's a bonding thing. I join them for lunch and dinner and my sister and her family come too. They have their own lockers and a charge account that I gladly use for a meal but I don't feel like I fit in there; it's like guns, gangsters, cigars, and cards and everybody's son is a wanna-be gangster.

*Dad is still trying to convince me to go away to school, but I just can't bring myself to go; I can't even think about it right now. I can't tell him that I'm really freaked out about it, but dammit, I'm freaked out about it.*

*I'm just afraid to go away. I'm comfortable at home for now, I have a steady boyfriend or two, and I'm busy doing so many other things. Concerts, parties, whatever. Life is pretty good; I still get a buzz and we drink some wine but things are okay. No, life is great, really great. Oh, by the way, I am taking golf lessons and I find golf to be frustrating and fun.*

*Recently I got a job in a department store and I am the only one of my girlfriends who works; how weird. I suppose I took the job because I was bored. I guess they are partying without me. Oh no they're not; I am the risk-taker and the party line starts behind me.*

*Anyway, I am the newest employee in the personnel department and I am having fun. I like working; it's an after-school and weekend thing and I get a paycheck every week, which is cool. My parents don't ask for any rent money like some parents do, so I get to keep the entire amount. Back at home, I think they appreciate me cutting the grass or trimming the bushes so that may be my trade for my living expenses.*

*My boss has asked me to help out in the cash office and although I hate math, using the cash registers is pretty cool. While in the personnel office, I'm adding up the time cards and figuring out the gross income so my boss can do the tax part. Sometimes I screw up because I get distracted, but she catches my mistakes in time. Usually I say hi to the other employees and strut around like I own the place.*

*Working in the personnel office is important. Before I got here, I didn't know a damn thing about working but I'm getting the hang of it pretty quickly. They know they can rely on me and I am capable of learning everything in this department. Just recently I was asked by the security guard to help him frisk the women they catch shoplifting. My answer was "No, thank you." I saw the bullet they took out of the cleavage of a very large, very aggravated woman and that was enough for me. All I could do was wonder where the gun was, but I wasn't about to ask, or look for it for that matter.*

## Life Is Like a Line

*The department store is only a mile from our house and I drive my car to work. Sometimes when it's raining I drive little old ladies home, which makes me feel good. Usually they live in the neighborhood so the drive is short. I am dependable and trustworthy in the cash office and friendly to the customers so they like me pretty well. So far I have not missed a day of work and I do what they ask me to do, so I should be there a long time or at least until I graduate.*

CHAPTER 6

# On Being Full-Grown

W e really had a blow-out the weeks before and after graduation. Everyone was drunk and you could smell the sweet scent of smoke first thing in the morning every morning. The guys with the hot cars were spinning their tires and smoking up the streets pretty bad. We weren't smoking up the tires, but smoking was part of the equation. It was the seventies and we were having a ball. I'm sure the teachers were glad to see us go; I know for sure the Spanish teacher couldn't wait for my backside to hit the door. She wanted me from the start and I gave her all I had for two long years. Her smug smile and ratted, over-processed hair will never leave my memory bank. Adios, bitch.

We hit all the parties and hung around with our pals and were messed up most of the time. But I did get a diploma, ended up on the honor roll (I still don't know how), and had a mixed bag of emotions at the close of the journey.

## Life Is Like a Line

*It's strange to be separated from my friends. Some have gone to college and some chose employment over college. I work in a nearby hospital as a ward clerk and enjoy it most of the time. There are some real characters who work there, but sometimes my life feels dull and mundane.*

*I've recently been in trouble with the head nurse on my usual floor. I keep getting something on my shoes from the chair and she wants me to polish them perfectly every day. I want to take her nurses cap and \*\*\* but then I would have to quit or go to jail.*

*Tonight we had a snowball fight in the hospital parking lot with the fresh powdery snow and that was crazy; you can't make snowballs with fresh powdery snow and it's still snowing. There's a guy who digs me but he's married. He's very cute and very nice but he has a wife and that's enough for me to just be friends. I work the three-to-eleven shift and all my friends work days, so after work I usually just go home.*

*Last night I got stuck in the freight elevator for a few hours. I was pretty freaked out about it but laughed once I returned to the floor. I didn't want them to think I was too concerned. When I returned to the floor they told me someone else had been trapped the day before. I'm using the stairs from now on.*

*Life is kind of a drag. I have been calling in sick quite a bit; it's easy to do since I still live at home. But something feels so strange; perhaps I am bored. I am not a grown-up, yet I am not a child. I am in limbo. I often wonder what being an adult feels like. I wonder if you ever feel your age, ever. Recently I began having dreams that I never graduated from high school. Sometimes I don't feel like I'm moving forward, and if I am, it's just not fast enough.*

I was looking for something new, and it didn't take me long to find it.

*High school graduation is several years past and I have recently chosen a more hopeful path to increase my happiness. College is just not an option for me. I'm still not interested. I know nothing about college; it's just too much to think about, too much to learn before I get there. I am the third offspring to disappoint my father. My brother had a short stint at Eastern and my sister opted for marriage and a family and that is where I am headed.*

*Upon invitation and without hesitation, I recently accepted a marriage proposal from my high school boyfriend. We have been dating since eleventh grade. He was the boyfriend of my best girlfriend but she wanted to be "just friends" so I guess he was convenient. Actually, he was my first non-puppy love so it seems like the right thing to do.*

*I'm hoping our marriage will work. He hasn't changed much since high school, retaining the old habits and the way of life we once knew. But we have made plans and although we have broken up several times, this time is for sure. He is more than anxious to leave his parents; he despises his father and just tolerates his mother. So I'm his way out and he's mine.*

Always fearing that some homicidal act would finally take place, I worried about the life I was leaving behind, but I needed to believe that everything would be all right. Marriage felt like a quick way out of the unhealthy environment of home, away from the life I'd always known.

Our marriage was rocky even before it began. First he got cold feet and wanted out and when he changed his mind again, the wedding was planned. We started out with June and moved it up to February so he could get his grant for school. The ups and downs of our union would last for seven unstable years before it ended, and I wouldn't let it go down without a fight.

*After our wedding, we had arguments because our points of view were different. There is so much room for improvement on both sides. You might say we're both immature; still I am hopeful. My moody temperament clashes often with his; he is cold and detached. Living together has proven that we're extreme opposites. When we dated there were things I didn't see, but living with someone is a real eye-opener. He was my high school first; maybe I felt compelled. I admit I am demanding and expect certain things and I'm just not sure he understands me. Sometimes I remind myself of my mother. I am fast and loose with the tongue and hot with the temper. There must be something to that but my reasons are that sometimes he pushes me to the point of absolute exasperation, but fortunately during the other times we are fine, really fine.*

## Life Is Like a Line

Maybe we became the worst of enemies right from the start but I didn't realize it; somehow there was enough to sustain us, at least for a time. We both worked and every once in a while we smoked some grass or had a few drinks. I bought a little dog he cared little about, and for entertainment we played cards with his family or with our friends. We also bowled with his sister and brother-in-law on a mixed league on Saturday nights. That was fun.

*I just wish he were more affectionate and more verbal; maybe his quiet demeanor is a guy thing. Some of our arguments are quite upsetting. When he's angry, he won't speak with me for days at a time and I hate that. My anger lingers; I am tense around him. I can't stand it when someone gives me the silent treatment. It's a death sentence.*

*I'm not thinking of killing myself these days, but his silence is killing enough for me, and too often when he regresses I want to wring his neck. I quit my old bad habits and have started anew, no grass, no cigarettes. Since I didn't drink much anyway, relatively speaking, I quit that too. Well, I suppose a cigarette during cards or bowling is no big deal, but I am so over the rest of it.*

*I am yearning for his affection. I am so lonely and I'm going to tell him when he comes home. I know he hates it when I show my anger or irritation or get demanding, but I just can't help it. It seems as if it helps to stir the pot; at least I get a response from him. You would think from his behavior that he doesn't really care and maybe he doesn't. I don't know, but I would like to find out. Today there is no small brown bottle or red pill of affection for me. I'm running out of fuel and feeling empty.*

*Our unreliable marriage has been filled with periods of desolation; still I hope that it will survive. I don't want to be single and I can't go home. I'm pretty sure that having a family will be the answer; love and affection are built into children. This will be our answer; I really hope so.*

But he rebuffed any thoughts of fatherhood until, one day, something changed. Perhaps in some small way for some short time he was trying to save the marriage, too. We stopped any remaining unhealthy habits and began to count the days to the ninth month. With three months to go, he became fearful and moved back to the home of his parents. A terrible time for retreat and contemplation; how can you un-ring the bell?

Alarm and worry filled him, but no more than me. His role was so necessary, and life was dreadful alone as I waited for him and wondered and worried all through the night. Activities filled the days, but the nights were restless with the burden of relentless thought. I had a gnawing feeling and a grinding of my teeth and overwhelming panic. But when my upset stomach returned, I realized that the unwanted thoughts and feelings were the result of obsessive-compulsiveness. In that pattern of behavior, I would think and think and think negative tormenting thoughts and worry constantly.

My baby, oh God, my unborn baby and me. There was nothing that mimicked that aloneness. He seldom visited during those dreadful months and was unresponsive to my pleading. He reminded me that I revived negative feelings in him and that I could not force his hand. Depression set in and my anxiety, sleeplessness, and compulsions remained. With a racing heart, my panic would devour me and then a few hours of sleep brought relief before the panic and aloneness returned again. With no money for food, I relied on my parents but I was emotionally wandering. You could speak to me but I heard nothing but my own fear. To concentrate, impossible. For three months I experienced agony and sporadic composure, but my parents helped as they could.

They did their utmost for my comfort, which I so appreciated. I remember when we had bees nesting in the bedroom walls and in the Rose of Sharon tree out front, my father came over to spray them. It made them furious and as they began their assault on him, he fell off the ladder and ran like hell. We laughed over lunch. Then he removed the cat from our attic and then he fixed a leaky plumbing problem. He could repair everything except me.

As the days dribbled by, I continued to slowly…melt…down. Still unsure of any reconciliation, I fell deeper into my depression and felt unworthy to bring into the world our wonderful child. Finally, at the coercion of my father, my husband reluctantly returned.

*We were blessed by the birth of our daughter. My twenty-four hours of push and breathe were insignificant compared to the sound of her voice. I have no idea how to care for an infant and was almost panic-stricken when we arrived at home with my parents to greet us at the front door. We're managing to figure it out, him and me. Afraid still of just about everything, my depression has started to subside. He and I share a guitar and I strum on its six strings and sing from the book. It relaxes me and our little girl seems to enjoy it. The kid in me struggles with lessons at a very young age; it is bittersweet.*

Our relationship continued to be strained at times due to his inability to participate fully in our family; he felt the demands of fatherhood were still worth dodging. His life was filled with nights of bowling and baseball games and school; he did these things while I stayed home with our growing baby girl. Keeping his job meant that we would move to another part of the state. Reluctantly we left our families behind and I was virtually on my own. Thus, the moment he walked in the door, my anger and words of jealousy and mistrust filled the room.

Thank God my little girl didn't really understand the conflict. The take-as-needed Valium prescribed by my family doctor slowed me down too much and so I abandoned them and chose to live life with him in a state of straight.

*"I'm driving down to my mom's. I really don't feel that well. I'll be gone a few days. Why don't you just think about it [you asshole]? I'll call you when I get there [asshole]. Tell Daddy 'Bye bye,' babe."*

Our marriage had been on a rocky path with plenty of peaks and valleys, but I couldn't believe he wanted a divorce right now. I was pregnant again and I didn't feel well and he was telling me this now? I had cramps and I didn't know why; I just needed them to go away. They were scaring me and my fear was that it would take us three hours to get home, but at least I had my little girl with me.

*"No one will separate me from my little girl, not ever. Oh bullshit; he was never home anyway. He won't miss me. What am I supposed to do? I'm trapped. Damn it, it's almost three. Okay, I'll talk to you later. Yes, I promise I'll call you when I get there. Thanks. You're a good friend."*

"Hi, Dad. I'm so thankful to be home; at least we made it. Traffic was bad. When I got into the city it was really bad, bumper to bumper. Just the overnight bag. Oh yeah, there's toys too in the back. I'll get them after I get my little girl. Honey, go see Grandpa. No construction, either. It was clear until we came into the city. Hi, Mom. What, Dad?

"Yeah, a trucker helped us out; my car was overheating. A wonderful man pulled over when he saw us driving on the shoulder and he looked under the hood. He took his water bottle and walked to the ditch and got some water and poured it into my car. First I was afraid of stopping but then I wanted to give him a big hug. I couldn't stop thanking him but it was three long hours, long long hours. Will you check out the car in the morning? No, thank you, I'm not hungry; I just don't feel good right now. I have these cramps and a kind of pressure. Are you hungry, babe? Stay with Grandpa; I'll be right back.

"Oh God, Mom, would you please come in here, NOW? Oh God, should I go to the hospital? I'll call the doctor myself but I've got to lie down right now. I need to just lie here in the bathroom; I am going to be sick. I'm not supposed to be bleeding. Don't look, Mom, you'll be upset. Oh my God, Mom, I see something, oh God."

My little girl is almost three and she is a blessing to me. She is so smart and beautiful and her smile, ahh…I love her. I really hope she doesn't understand what just happened to us. She has seen me so angry and so sad and at other times I'm mad as hell. I just can't believe this is happening. Today I am sad; I just feel miserable. No one should be looking at their unborn child like that. It just passes through you as a piece of tissue. Once it was life and then it's lifeless and I'm holding it in the palm of my hand for all the wrong reasons. God, why have you done this?

"Yeah, but we have to drive home. I have a ton of packing to do; we'll be there until the house sells. Three hours back. I'd rather stay here but something's going on with my brother and my parents and I don't want to be in the middle of that. Although they've been fantastic, I can only take their bickering for so long. It's time to go. No; I'll be okay. Don't I always say that? My saving grace is my little girl. Hey, thanks for calling; I'll let you know when we move back. You're a good friend. Bye."

## Life Is Like a Line

Promising to be better and to spend more time at home was good enough for me, so I let him come back once again. I trusted him fully and fatherhood visited one more time and we managed to live as a family. We also moved back downstate; home at last.

*This time having another baby was his idea. We have been getting along quite well. We bought a house on the east side, close to everything and just three blocks from my parents. We are beginning to have some fun. There has been great joy knowing that another blessed child will soon be ours and we wait anxiously for her arrival. Right on time, she came one night after bowling, faster than her sister and in the middle of the night. The whole process took about three hours. As my mom raced down the street to babysit, he grabbed my bag and we barely made it to St. John's before we heard her cry.*

*And then I saw her and her skin and her eyes and her fingers and her toes and all of her hair and she was perfect. I was reminded of the miracle that never made it lying in my hand on the bathroom floor not long ago. I was sick with the thought but I fought it away. I looked at her and all of my emotions began to flow. It was obvious that our lives were so perfectly changed. Blessed with our two beautiful daughters, we have so much to live for, so much to be thankful for, and a love to last forever.*

Or so I had hoped. Before I knew it, our marriage took a turn. Like fruit fallen from a tree, once it started to decay, it rotted all the way through. Only a fool would be hopeful.

*"Just what is your problem tonight? I waited for you for dinner. I know you're really busy but I need your help. I know you have things to do. Do you know you've been acting funny lately? We're supposed to go out this weekend; I got a sitter. What do you mean you don't want to? I already made plans. You're going where? Why are you such an asshole? God, I hate you. I really hate you. You're never home, you don't care, and what about the girls? You are the loser my father said you were. You are one goddamn loser. And besides, no matter what you try, you suck in the sack. Hate me, but don't even try fucking with those two girls. You are a sorry piece of shit."*

*Oh, man, I could swear at that asshole all day. He is such a weak, spineless snake. His personality is so opposite of mine. I just can't stand him. I'm sure he hates me, too. He acts like it. He's an empty crazy weak stone-cold asshole and I hope he dies in his sleep.*

*Me, I might be just as crazy as him, but I will never be empty. As long as I have my daughters, my life will be full.*

There were times when I tried to keep our marriage together. We were going to church with the girls and I was trying not to pick on him. In too many ways I recognized family traits. Sometimes I just couldn't shut up. Our individual personalities and temperaments were like two opposing forces pulling and pushing in a distressed tension. Not even our daughters could keep him home, and the more I put pressure on him to be involved with us, the more he began to pull away.

It was evident that his interests were the opposite of mine. He liked to sit in front of the TV; I liked to do anything but that. We were like night and day, but I was afraid to be a single parent. Every moment we were together, I was conflicted. I hated the bastard and most likely pushed him away. Fireworks. The differences between us caused fireworks.

*Seven years married but he wasn't that rusty after all. It didn't take that bastard too long to find his next victim. In a damn bowling alley and the slut with freckles is half his age, of course. Once he fell for someone else he turned his back on us and moved back in with his parents. It's sad to see how many times those people have taken him in. He's like their puppy and they clean up the shit he leaves behind. With a suitcase in hand and in my opinion not much dignity, he moved to Mummy's. Oh, and don't forget the cigarettes in his pocket and his damn bowling ball.*

Immediately, I felt a sense of hysteria. My life was unraveling and his new life was beginning, sex, beer, and she was literally just a teenager.

It began to sink in that I had no plan, and I considered my former thoughts and decided, "Be careful what you wish for." I called and I begged and I pleaded and I insulted and I begged some more. He would not budge; he was so over me and so into someone else. And the children, he was over them too, until his mother began prodding him. I kept thinking that someone bad like him was better than someone unknown. Or even worse, better than nothing.

*We were separated for the year and I received an annulment from the Catholic Church. Then the divorce decree was handed down and he married within a month. Bastard. I know this has to be a blessing in disguise. Even though life is more difficult raising children on my own, I know that everything, particularly the atmosphere of our household, is better for them. There's no echo of my disillusioned cynical self and the mêlée that offended me, that never allowed me to be free. In reality, he has no interest in fatherhood, thanks to his new playmate.*

*I'm adapting to the dual role of parenting. Thankfully each decision is mine alone with any chance of parental tangles eliminated. With a deep love and devotion for my daughters, it's clear that my nurturing abilities were not affected by the lack of fostering in my own upbringing. My girls give me so much more than I have ever known before.*

The dissolution of my marriage was painful and often paralyzing. In the beginning, my days and nights ran together. Long walks in warmer weather gave way to Sunday afternoons in the cold spent at the mall fixated on the families that surrounded us. I was able to cover up my daze of depression and my daughters seemed to enjoy the distraction of others. My father became the man in my daughters' lives. He helped us regain our strength and our sense of humor and, by his illumination, my feelings of self-worth.

There were days when my moods reflected a woman deeply despondent and I overflowed with anxiety. When alone, these moods would have their way with me. I had problems with simple tasks in social situations. Often, taking the girls to the movie theater would make me anxious as the walls closed in around me, and any effort to breathe in the stagnant air would choke my sinking mind.

Even with an urge to flee, I could not. I cried a river of tears for me, for the girls, and for the unknown, never expecting that life would actually improve. In my head, for the moment, anything that improved was a miracle.

The girls loved to eat in restaurants and finally I saw the haunting fourth chair for what it was: empty. It took over a year before I was able to enjoy these typical activities without emotional surrender. Emotional surrender, life in a robe locked away in a house. As my mental well-being improved, my ache began to subside.

One afternoon an anonymous woman bought our dinner after telling the waitress that I was doing a good job with the girls. God bless that woman, God bless her, God thank you for my guardian angel that day. I began to feel better about our divorce, but the separation from their father became difficult for the girls.

Even though some of their issues needed the benefit of professional advice, we managed to make it through to the other side. There were times when I experienced symptoms of depression and there were days when the girls were sad and lashed out. It was through diligence that I learned that each of us was going through this process at our own level of understanding, at our own pace, in our own time. I made every attempt to amplify their happiness; I could not prevent the slivers of unhappiness. Those were inescapable.

Once I started feeling better, I made some decisions that would affect my life dramatically. I underwent two cosmetic surgeries; the first was rhinoplasty to correct my deviated nasal septum and reconfigure my round Greek nose. It would take three surgeries to get it right, sort of.

The second was breast augmentation mamoplasty to enhance what was lost to childbirth.

As my frame changed, so did my feelings of self-confidence. I was cocky with my new look and the formation of new features. Changes such as these, especially the breast implants, were dramatic. Never could I have known the extent of the adjustment. Just under the skin, I now felt the sensation of carrying around two grapefruits, gel-filled sacks of the eighties. I had never before known this infinite breast heaviness and horrific fear of rupture and I lived with this obsessive fear for almost twenty years. Now, saline-based and three surgeries later, I'm taking them to the grave! But in the beginning this was my renewal, my metamorphosis, my jump-start to second chances.

## Life Is Like a Line

*"I didn't want to tell you, but I met a man. I know it's soon but I met him at the dry cleaners. No, I'm not kidding you. We made eye contact and there was an attraction and I gave him my number...he came over. Yes, right then. He was an absolute gentleman. We talked and one thing led to another. He was the first since the jackass. Yeah, now I know what I've been missing. Honest to God, I was that comfortable. Amazing sex."*

*"No, they weren't home; are you crazy? He will never meet them. About eight months ago...it's occasional gratification with a smattering of conversation. We take turns at each other's houses and he knows when it's time to go. Believe me, all I want to see is his dry-cleaned trench coat walking out the door. What could be better than that? Don't worry; it's one step at a time. It's purely physical, trust me. A relationship? Uuuuugh, hell no."*

*"I know, I'll be careful. No, I know that. He's not forever, but he'll do for right now."*

That relationship, shallow as it was, brought back the woman in me, the woman who had been lying in wait, the woman I had never before known. I was shy at first; he was my teacher and what he'd learned elsewhere, he brought to me. This first man in my life of singleness prepared me for the list that would follow. With each man I found sincerity and gentleness, kindness and consideration, and an extraordinary culmination of their years of intimacy.

But it was time to get serious, so my ever-inspiring father persuaded me and we successfully obtained our real estate licenses. His placed in escrow; I became a member of a real estate team and interacted with great enthusiasm. Those days were filled with excitement and I was happier than I had been in a long time. I was making sales and listing homes and was very busy juggling the schedules but it came easy. Each day was incredible, with every day like the one before or better. The enormity of my freedom was mind-blowing. Though I tried to shy away from the lunchtime bars, my friendships, momentary partners, and paychecks stood strong.

Soon we had listed and sold our home and prepared for our move to the suburbs. We eased into a two-story, two-bedroom, one-and-a half-bath townhouse. The girls were now nine and five and we were putting the past behind us. I hired a professional moving service, left the keys on the kitchen counter, and walked out the door with no regrets. We never really settled down in the new digs, but we settled in. We met the neighbors and quickly adapted, I enrolled the girls in the elementary school nearby, and our new life began as we hit the ground running.

> *Apartment living has turned out to be the best. Minimal obligation, maximum benefit. We see my parents often; they baby-sit for the girls on a regular basis and usually spend the night. My dating is minimal. I still see Mr. Dry Cleaners but it's getting weird. Sometimes I wonder what in the hell I am doing with him, but he satisfies and he is temporary. He is a booster shot for the years that I've missed.*

My education continued with a refresher school, another confidence builder I suppose. I was named "Miss Congeniality" at graduation; imagine that. But for the first time, I was truly happy to the core. Employment came quickly, thanks to a teacher who befriended me. I was introduced to a notable Birmingham resident who owned an employment agency and had just the right connections. I was excited and office bound. With soaring interest rates the handwriting was on the wall; place the license in escrow and roll with the dice.

My introduction to the three-piece world of sophistication and high stakes was ready, set, go. My persistence was relentless and the girls visited their father every other weekend and learned what a great life they had with me. Their absence was incredibly painful and I was filled with lonely days and long nights. Married seven years and now divorced, I was too naive to realize that I had to reinvent my life and that the surgeon's alterations were not enough to fill me.

Slowly I began meeting and making friends and began to experience a true social adventure. I was becoming self-assured, self-reliant, bold, and playful. After a few years, the saying, "I learned how to party" once again was mine. The attractiveness of single-parent groups, dance bars, and men, especially the men, was magnetic. Still fearless, I found the combination of spirits and the challenge of seduction intoxicating and I was never shy of the casual liaison.

## Life Is Like a Line

Cocktails...dancing...after-the-bar breakfasts...amour. Sometimes in that order, sometimes not. When the night was blah, it was breakfast with the girls, my sister included, and often the restaurant was more stimulating than the dance club. I enjoyed Monday through Thursday with the girls at home but once plans were made for the weekend, the days moved too slowly as I waited for the rush.

During those times of fleeting relationships, I had no interest in commitment, even though there were those who asked for my permanence. My focus was on my daughters and on the fun and nothing more. I was playing the man's role, love 'em and leave 'em. If my friends enjoyed the potions and if my mood was right, I'd be there with them. On any perfect day I was super-mom, super-charged. Still full of myself, I was flirtatious and distracted by my games of seduction. This was my life until I got caught.

*I've been dating him for at least eight months now and my calendar has been filled with one adventure after another. I met him in a bar the night of the Detroit Tigers' opening day. There was a strong attraction and after our mutual glance it was lust at first sight. Thanks to my sister-in-law's abandonment, he made his way to me and I could barely be contained by the intensity of him and at the night's end, too many cocktails and his closeness rendered a spark and then a surge. I was hooked.*

*Since then he has become the pinnacle of my nights and of my days. I love him for his spirit; he is the life of the party and has a very positive outlook. For those who know him, he's like the warm sun on a wintry day. He's a man who lives by spontaneity, which is a departure from my own "always a planner" mentality, so he is good for me. As a rule, the girls do not meet my men but he is different and at some point we have become like a family.*

There would only be the slightest exaggeration if I said that our relationship was pure ecstasy. As time went by, I grew more comfortable with our risky behavior, sexual adventures, and flirtatious endeavors. Never knowing if this was my buried personality or a reinvented me, I was there for the taking, thinking of marriage with shyness extinct. Every desire, every urge, every occasion was extreme, and while extremes can be very titillating, they can eventually devour.

> *Never did I expect this. I have been too removed from this lifestyle for too long to get reacquainted with it now. Once I saw it, everything changed. It was a twenty, it was rolled up tight, and it was under his nose. The powder was lined up sweetly in a row and with my entrance he had the look of a deer in the headlights. I knew I was in trouble. My successfully avoided next frontier was coming to get me and I never saw it coming.*
>
> *The poison—cocaine. My life has been a combination of coolness and control up until now and I have been that way for so long I almost don't recognize myself, but I am infuriated with him. I am so fucking pissed off. God…FUCK I am so pissed. Calmly I tried to discuss it with him and he didn't bat an eyelash. First rage and then calm and then rage again. This was his "thing" and I was shocked. How could I have missed it?*
>
> *I used to think I was slick but I was just a child. This is a mature adult, a self-employed successful man fucking around with my heart. Ah…God. It's his warmth; he's got me. As he flashed me his pure white smile, he assured me that it was "no problem" and the subject was closed. It was an unspoken ultimatum and I was backed into a corner. Not a very pleasant place to be. He had no reason to hide it now; he did it out in the open. As I headed for the door, I could see him line one up.*

In his corvette, on the boat, even on the motorcycle, he had it down pat. My exposure to it was becoming greater and greater. When offered I refused, but then I took up his challenge: to agree or negate his best argument that it was harmless. But the taste in my mind and soul knew that it was not. After too many nights and days spent with that twenty-dollar bill under my nose, too much had changed. With my mood irritated and my desire dissolved, I became afraid. Though I missed him deeply, we were finished.

Our relationship ended and it was over, but over with the other I was not. Obviously stricken, there were days when I couldn't resist lining one up in the ladies room at work, in the bar with the girls, and in my bedroom alone.

## Life Is Like a Line

*I've had numerous salary increases over the years and recently I received a promotion into a position I have absolutely no experience with. Eventually I'll be moving from an administrative assistant position to become sales manager in one of my boss's hotels. In reality, my boss has been chasing me around my desk for years (in his mind) and I speculate about his reaction if I ever stop running. There is no secret to his thoughts; they are written on his face, centered in his eyes. He is gentle and soft to me but can be enraged in the office, and when he doesn't make me feel shy he has me thinking. Whether this promotion is a cleansing or favoritism I don't care; I was getting bored anyway.*

*We have a hotel department now which is located in the Birmingham office and the new hotel manager is Ron JackAss and he really is. He looks at me in an unusual way and I'm sure he is wondering about me and how I landed this prestigious designation, but the truth is I don't have a clue myself. With their budget on the line, they decided to send me to Houston for a hotel show.*

*What a laugh, and getting there almost landed me in prison. As infrequently as I travel, I wasn't prepared for my own stupidity. Mix the airport with security then conveyor belt, purse, makeup bag, and tiny little brown bottle containing my worst still-active bad habit, powdery white and waiting inside. The scenario begins in my head, my body is feeling the fear, and the letters "p a n i c" must be written across my face. I'm starting to sweat. My thoughts are sick. They are disturbingly sick. They are about the loss of my children and lawyers and courts and wounded parents and a life forever changed over one little bottle of a bad habit.*

*I am a fucking idiot! What have I done? I am screwed! "Run to the purse, dammit, then run like hell!" It was a very long desperate twenty seconds or so and then it was over, no long looks or second looks and no looking back. I headed straight for the ladies' room, tossed it in the can, and ran to the gate.*

My dangerously bad habit was not shared with the dregs of humanity but with the educated, the well-respected. The consumers were highly regarded in their fields; they were my lovers and friends and bosses, and they were men of means and influence. It was not the bum on the street who snorted cocaine but the chief of pharmacy at the hospital and the well-known physician and the plumbing contractor and the real estate mogul.

What began as a determination of harmfulness became a willing game of seduction that made me feel tremendous, poles apart from anything I had ever felt or experienced before. Still, many days I was angry and irritable and hypersensitive. Nonetheless, this was my newest distraction, my amusement. My girl pals didn't buy it and my sister thought I was crazy, but it beat the four-dollar drinks and kept my hands free to talk.

In time, it took more to arouse less and I knew that the blazing fire in me had to be extinguished or I would be burned.

*My life is good, the girls are great, and my parents are fine, although my father had a small stroke in the parking lot of our apartment building. It left no obvious damage but it scared the hell out of me and my nervous system was reminded of what panic is. There are no tiny white powder bottles lingering in my closet anymore, though there are times when I do feel the power struggle. I pray for the strength to resist. I still smoke a cigarette or two when I drink but basically I have quit.*

*No dreary sadness for me, not for a long time, but sometimes I miss him terribly and I fantasize about him and I wonder about him. But life goes on—if we're lucky. I've learned how to shelter myself fairly well. No crazy random poor judgment. I have a new mood. It's not frenzy or extreme. I wouldn't call it calmness either. I would just say that I'm no longer dangling on the edge.*

*I have been selectively dating. In between the crazy ones have been some really nice guys. The man I was seeing most recently is in the medical profession. Frankly, he delivers babies; he's a wild and crazy guy just about my height and is a blast to be with but he has that bad habit and I can't be near it anymore. I am sure he has a drinking problem too, which doesn't help matters. We don't click really but I was into seduction when we met. He has a girlfriend and was recently divorced. After we went our separate ways I called him for a few lines but he told me he was out, thank God. He was my lifesaver and he was out of my league.*

## Life Is Like a Line

Once I returned to absolute oneness, I reviewed my past, studying the worthiness of it, and while I faced my own disappointments, I became less proud of my behaviors. My mind was driven and it kept me occupied. Always with things to achieve, explore, busy always, going here, doing for someone, cleaning the house, weeding, planting, always cleaning, I was busy. My mind made no connection with the words "Stop, look, and listen" or better yet "Stop, drop, and roll."

I hadn't realized I was still on fire, but once the flames went out, I was settled. My daughters and I blended together for a purpose, our lives unique, and there was plenty of life to live. History had shown that my brazen approach to life was reckless. Without any forewarning, I had been heading in the direction of self-destruction. It was only God who could have saved me so many times.

I liked my neighbors; there was a young couple with two little kids who lived on my right and an elderly lady on my left. I visited them both and occasionally hung out with the couple. They often played cards on Saturday nights and when I was alone I would join them for cocktails and cards. Sometimes the sweet smell of grass poured out of their living room via her husband and I got the hell out of there to save my soul. Ultimately her favorite uncle would escort me home and, until the wee hours of the night, we would attempt to forget our loneliness.

Then, without reason, the wife started resenting me and I didn't know why until that day. It was a childless weekend and I was in for the night; then suddenly I heard a knock on my door. It was my neighbor and he looked buzzed and he was smiling from ear to ear and he had that glimmer in his eye. Without hesitation I invited him in and we sat at my kitchen table drinking glasses of pop and making small talk but he appeared to be nervous. We talked about his wife and the kids and about my work and his and then his eagerness spilled out.

I was blindsided. I trusted our friendship perhaps too much and felt confident with him and when he asked me, *"Do you want to smoke a rock of cocaine with me?"* I couldn't believe my ears. Was he crazy? Me smoke a rock of coke? Was that possible? I'd cleaned up my act; no more driving idiotic desires.

Then he exposed the wrinkled tin foil that was in his pocket and opened it for my view. It looked innocent enough but I felt confused at what was happening. There were rocks of cocaine in my damned kitchen? A rock of cocaine? Smoke cocaine? How weird, I thought. How do you smoke it?

I had never heard of a rock of coke or a dirty glass pipe. Poor naïve, tempted, trusting little me. I learned later that it was crack, yeah crack, no fucking kidding crack. *"Just one hit; really it's great. You'll like it,"* he told me.

Hmmm, his wife was at work and the kids were gone and he was sitting in my kitchen at night and his breath was getting very close to mine and my heart was beating a little faster and there was this tingle I shouldn't have felt and I was in trouble.

We never spoke again and soon after that they moved away. Though he and I were never intimate, it was never more obvious than that night that he wanted more of me and I feared I might have begun looking more his way in due time.

I suppose she knew of his interest. It was no secret that he and I were friendly, but after that incident the whole relationship turned south. This situation helped me create a new mantra: I must be strong, I must be strong, I must be strong, and I must be wary of anyone who might attempt to sway me to their deadly deeds.

*My new neighbor is a single mom with two daughters and we hang out just for fun. She's a former hairdresser turned lounge hostess. She is sharp and we laugh easily together. There is no subject off limits and no man who is safe and sound around us. The girls won't be home until Sunday night so we have decided to color my almost-gray hair. We're going to get drunk, too. I just feel like it.*

*In hand I have a bottle of Dom Perignon and my dye. She made a good partner in crime and we consumed the entire bottle of my best champagne. Everything was fine until I couldn't stand up to see the new color of my hair and my neighbor would rather I didn't anyway. I asked her, "Am I hallucinating or is my hair fucking blue?" and we freaked more than we laughed and she worked with the shampoo and anything else she could pour on top to soften the blow.*

## Life Is Like a Line

*But there was no denying it; it was the ocean with shades of deep dark navy blue. With nothing else to do, I dragged myself home and crawled up the stairs and made my way to bed, hoping to die.*

*The next day my stylist performed the magic and I was better for it. I moved with less motion sickness, though I could still smell the champagne in my mind. Overall, that weekend cost me a fortune but it was fun in a hungover-sick-queasy-ruined-my-hair-turned-it-blue-had-to-have-it-fixed kind of way. So I swore off fun, waiting for him.*

*I really believe that being single hasn't been all that bad for me. Since my sister's divorce, we have spent quality time together having fun. My mind has been set on trolling for men, though our motto is, "It's better to be miserable alone than be miserable with someone else." We live and die by that creed.*

*Nonetheless, I am still optimistic that someday I will meet the man of my dreams. I pray for him, but I feel as if my prayers go unheard. Maybe I'm not praying hard enough or maybe there are more lessons for me to learn, but if that's the case, I feel like I've learned all the lessons, every last one since 1953.*

*Now I realize that this earthly enjoyment and heartbreak is necessary and temporary and in general this has been a hell of a ride, even with all its peaks and valleys, and in all honesty I'm ready for him.*

*"Despite the fact that I work a full-time job, I am a mother and I am a daughter and I am a sister and I am a friend and I have learned how to juggle schedules and I am hoping dear Lord that you will recognize my efforts and that you will send him to me. If he could be loving to the girls and a kind and honest man and hopefully dear Lord he will have the kind of personality that can tolerate my parents, not that they are bad but as you know they are quite a handful and they are really involved in our lives and we are involved in theirs and if you would send him our way I would surely appreciate it and I would be the best person dear Lord and you won't be disappointed, I promise…I know you are listening. Thank you, Amen."*

That prayer was my salvation. I wanted Him to hear me. I needed Him to hear me. I have always believed, sometimes doubted, then believed, then wondered, and in the end prayed and believed…deeply.

*There is no reason to look for him here but I am always looking. No laws against fantasy yet. I am fifty miles from home. No man of mine will live on this side of town unless he's wealthy enough to move my whole family here. No, my life is on the east side, the east side of Woodward Avenue. I need someone over there. This is my employment site and nothing more; my job is at a construction site that will someday be a hotel and it is filled with testosterone and hardhats. My office is in a remote location in the building and I am ensconced in a room with a telephone and a typewriter and a radio. In a building full of men and sweat and testosterone, I am sure I will not meet him, not this way, not this far from home, and I really don't care anyway.*

Wrong. I was very wrong. I also cared very much, and that was exactly how we met that summer of 1986, a forever-ago moment on a warm day in August. He was wearing a hardhat, troubleshooting problems in the building where I worked.

*Yesterday, clean-shaven with a mustache and delicious with the smell of aftershave, the smell a single woman longs for, in his pressed cotton shirt and ironed jeans and loafers, he caught my eye and now he knocks on my partially opened door. He is standing right in front of me. He's cute.*

*"Ah, you do electrical work and you need a key for what? Do you have a business card? For how long? What room? You can't keep the key, you know; I need it back before the end of the day. No problem. I'll be here waiting for you."*

*Hmmm, he better bring that key back before four-thirty. "Hello, are you kidding me? I need that back today. In the mail? What do you mean your shop is one hundred miles away? I need that key. Honest to God. Lunch? You want to meet me for lunch and give me the key back then? I'm about to be fired and you want to have lunch? Okay, Thursday; I'm busy on the weekend."*

*"He's here now; I've gotta go…We're going to the river. No, it's a red Corvette, not a red Chevy. Oh, he said a red Chevy. Yeah, this one's gonna be a handful. Trickery right off the bat. He better have that fucking key. I'll call you later, sister. Bye."*

## Life Is Like a Line

I had to laugh. My sister and I were palling around quite a bit and having a blast. She often thought of me as being a prude. Jokingly she would bait me into profanities and finally I would agree, the phrase "Fuck you" would suit me just fine, and we would laugh.

He was polite and gentle and interesting and I felt so much better once I had possession of the key. We sat along the river's edge and enjoyed a quiet lunch and the day was quite perfect. I felt the excitement of a first date and the calm of time. Once returned to my apartment, I really didn't expect to see him this way again. But his persistent character persuaded me to give him another look. We had lunch, and then on my way home I tossed his business card out the window. He knew where to find me and I was a challenging perfectionist. My sister thought I was crazy. We both liked the chase and eventually we had another lunch and then weekend dinners when the girls were not at home. He lived on the east side of town and I was at ease with him.

There was mutual attraction. Admittedly he liked me more, but I had that hopeful feeling and one thing led to another. All my friends liked him and my family liked him but through my insecurity I would waver. More lessons for me, Lord. He had been divorced only three months when I met him and I believed he was still bitter over the breakup. His sense of humor was over the top, too much kidding, too much sarcasm, too much for no one but me.

I was rounding my sixth year alone with the girls and I was set in my ways. For the most part I had become rigid, aloof, obsessive, and uninterested in raising another child, especially if a man was attached, and he had two teenage sons. The worst part was that he had an ex-wife as well. She was a pest. Just like all divorcees, she wanted back what she'd given away. She was obsessive and caused havoc every time the telephone rang.

I didn't care about our dating, relationship, sex, or companionship and I proved it by breaking up with him every time I was in the mood. Our breakups were caused by my unwillingness to follow my instincts and something greater than I knew.

*Despite my anxiety, I realize that he is a decent Christian man, a successful businessman, a loving father, and that he has lots of friends and employees who respect him. He IS my prayed-for guy. I don't know what he sees in me, but he's been in hot pursuit since the day we met and it's very flattering.*

*I've found my moods to be fluctuating quite a bit. Anything between "happy as a clam" and "mad as hell." It's tiresome. Depending upon the situation, I am either great or irritated about something and lately he has been rubbing me the wrong way. He also has an ex-wife who is very intrusive. During my irritation spells, I feel like I'm thinking like my mother, God help me and him. On the days that I am easily provoked, unreceptive, confused, resistant, don't mess up my hair, everything better be perfect, make sure you're on time, and don't be a smart ass, I must be impossible. I feel ugly.*

*Soon he will know me as a perfectionist to a fault, and I hope he can live with my expectations. The bottom line is that the nucleus of me does not resist him. He has perhaps penetrated the core of me. I tried to run, but it was in circles. Quietly he has connected with the soul of me because my surface has been a mess.*

I suppose I hadn't realized my life had drifted so far. Without warning, the years had taken me from cool to cold. I feared him because of what he represented and what he offered, which should have been wonderful to me. Any woman with half a brain would have been drawn to this man. I feared change and love and disappointment and pain and disappointment and a host of other emotions. And I feared me.

My feelings were strong and I was hard but his good nature was beginning to change me. Engaged and then wed, there was an "ahh" to my life that I had never felt before. And then a "Thank you, Lord" for my answered prayer. Our simple ceremony brought close to us our relatives and friends and there was wonderful glorious peace.

My parents and sister and her new husband were there but my brother was not. I just could not bring myself to invite him. The years had brought us so much disharmony and unpredictability that I preferred to disappoint my mother rather than have him there. And I'm sorry for that; I really am sorry.

Once married, I learned quickly that the blending of families can be difficult. There were demanding exes and somebody else's agenda, which was never made clear. We had to attend to the children and think of the business.

Ron had two separate occupations, as an electrical contractor and as innkeeper, and at the time of our marriage, we bought out two sets of partners in the inn. This set us back $125,000 but it allowed us to operate the Murphy Inn on our own. The one hundred-year-old inn, once a warming stop for traders who came to town, had seven renovated hotel rooms each with a private bath. Our restaurant complete with full bar served meals at breakfast, lunch, and dinner seven days a week.

We owned and operated the inn for seven years, and in the beginning I wondered where the money would come from for even the slightest of needs. It was all too worrisome. Much of the staff resented me. They made my presence hell. They didn't want change and they had no idea what I might represent. I began revamping the menus and managing and hiring the staff and dealing with the salesmen. Their idea of selling was sampling their booze first thing in the morning, usually before nine o'clock. I saw the fish man and the produce guy and all the others while Ron worked the trade. I knew nothing of this enormity, then came more of the exes and the bank and my parents moved closer. In the summer I was never farther from the girls.

While I started to panic, my new husband reminded me of his promise; we would make it. He was not afraid of work and we were his inspiration, imagine.

I still worried. Everything was new, especially his promises.

> *I don't know this man. I am married to a stranger; what the hell am I doing here? When life was so simple I chose this…chose someone I don't know…or know little about. What am I doing HERE? I should take the girls and go now before it gets too late, but how will I explain? I can't do that. How can I uproot the girls again? They are so happy. I am kidding myself. I can't go. How can I abandon ship? How can I leave him? What am I doing? Oh God, what should I do?*

We made it through the turmoil of the business and the marital aspects of life that related to our exes and the children began to harmonize quite well. His sons were fourteen and fifteen and my girls thirteen and nine. Then as now, my upbeat husband was my knight in shining armor and he put me first always. Living with him was a pleasant adventure and I was continuously drawn to his entrepreneurial spirit, his unassuming nature, and his kindhearted approach to life.

His positive attitude and optimism have often been in conflict with my own outlook, but in many ways his character is similar to my father's in that they both have that PMA—that positive mental attitude. He forgives, and he overlooks my shortcomings. Over the years I have given him hell, but he never judges me and he takes my abuse. He must be a glutton for punishment.

*I should call this period "a time for turmoil," seeing as its effects are causing me to swallow antacids again, one bottle after another of a pleasant mint paste scientifically formed to eradicate the pain that so offends me. Offends me, hell; I am dying another death as the gripping pain invades me.*

*Overrun with my acidic turbulence, it moves through my stomach and forces itself into my chest and then my throat and the disturbance of my system returns. INDIGESTION, always with me. I find that getting the spoon to my lips is no problem; it's submitting to the smell and then the texture that makes it hard to swallow and the antacids aren't working at optimal performance. As the pain grows, paralysis and panic join in. It feels like a heart attack. I am grateful to God when there is relief.*

*I am my chiropractor's worst nightmare because of my neck. It is so stiff I can hardly move it. In fact, I can hear a cracking sound whenever I move it, the sound of bones disintegrating, pleasant encouraging sounds of my body's resistance to its own existence.*

*By the time I get to him, I'm a mess. I'm a head-pounding, shoulders-curling, can't-move-my-neck, feeling, looking, acting-ugly mess. He tells me my neck pain is caused by tension and he gives me a lecture about stress and exercise and he also says my problems are mostly physiological, whatever the hell that means.*

*He should have explained himself. Maybe he doesn't want to be my shrink; maybe he thinks I know. But he could have advised rather than just collected my money and set up another appointment.*

## Life Is Like a Line

*Okay, I admit it—I have stress and I don't handle it well; I never have. I don't do yoga or meditation or alcohol or drugs or smoke anymore. I handle things; I bury things. I know what "physiologically" means; I've heard of therapy and I catch his drift. Here's my answer: throw away his business card and double my over-the-counter analgesic.*

*How do you dispel stress anyway? It invades me, I stiffen up, I can't move my neck, I get indigestion, I feel my throat tighten, and my head starts to throb. I am irritated and cynical. I don't like feeling it and I don't like when I show it and I probably don't like what leads me to it, but I can't help it and I can't stop it.*

*I suppose the stress has caught up with me. I thought I was coping but all along I have been getting more easily agitated. I have been terribly difficult to be with but everyone still finds me when they have a problem, so I can't be all that bad. I don't resent the kids, of course; I love it when they ask for help. It's the problems of everyone else. Honestly, I enjoy the unraveling aspects of troubleshooting; I am the letter-writing muck and mire aficionado. My direct responses from CEOs of Fortune 500 companies prove that the art of letter-writing is still effective, and oddly enough it helps relieve my tension. It must be the getting it down on paper and out of my system that is so liberating. It is this non-emotional troubleshooting that I prefer, but my life is abundant with the other.*

*My life has revolved around my parents and my interest in them has layers of involvement. They are a source of constant concern through no fault of their own. It is their physical health that concerns me so and often I am on the edge. My dad just had a serious operation and putting up with my mother and her whims is not for the weak. Both my father and mother have taken turns being ill and the juggling of their needs has been crazy. In order to spend more time with them, I have to work by the light of the moon so I can be available when my mother calls. Often her calls relate to the trivial and her expected drop and run mentality has become so tiring.*

*The problem is my parents' schedule doesn't allow me to take care of my own household. I have overgrown grass, I need to clean, and I haven't made a home-cooked meal in ages. Not only that but I have a business meeting at eight in the morning and I can't move my neck because, ahh let's see, the damn neck is physiological or there's an elephant sitting on my shoulders.*

All of the business and the harmonizing and the matrimony and the children and my family...it was potent stuff. After a few years of pretty good times, it seemed as if we were finally over the hump and into the rhythm of life. That is until peri-menopause stepped in. Sleep problems were already my enemy; now I was adding hot flashes and more mood swings and a plethora of other symptoms, all thanks to my deteriorating hormones. Though I didn't know it then, today I believe I was living in a state of excitability and apprehension possibly controlled by a mood disorder; I had all the symptoms.

Once our business began to run itself, I started looking for other ventures. It was amazing how many business owners didn't know one another, so I started talking with a select group of entrepreneurs and we organized the town business association. Our first meeting, held in an elementary school, brought one hundred citizens, some curious and others ready to join. I felt blessed to be part of this community and I knew that camaraderie among the players would provide the cooperative spirit that is necessary for small businesses.

With the enthusiasm of an army, we worked diligently on the first business association and I, as founder, became the first president. I was passionate and my fervor spilled over; I couldn't wait to bring the circus to town. We organized a "Fun Run" and political debates and mixers. I was running every day with a different type of stress but it affected me just the same.

I could hide my moodiness from the rest of the planet most of the time, but once at home it was difficult to keep the lid on. We were in the midst of renovating our home and it was a mess; we were living in construction dust with no appliances. We even had to climb up a ladder to the second floor and then crawl through a window to find our temporary bedroom.

There were days when I awoke to a moody ugliness that consumed me until it left. My physiology kept the good feelings down, my mind always fighting my body, fighting my mind, and on some days I tripled the acetaminophen and ibuprofen stored in the cabinet, but in truth it was never enough. In no way did I realize how much of an effect my growing level of stress would have on me, or how much I internalized it. I was high energy with the potential for heightened irritation. Not a good combination.

# CHAPTER 7

# Along the Water's Edge

*My parents are doing well and we are blessed to visit them often. It's easy to do given their new surroundings. I was able to find a home nearby in a beautiful location right on the river and without hesitation they made the purchase and moved. I'm delighted they're closer to us; everything will be easier. The house is a simple one-story ranch and will be easy for them to manage in their retirement years, though regrettably my mother says "It needs quite a lot of work."*

*She has begun tearing out and replacing, which will probably cost more than a fortune but it will keep her occupied for years. My father is delighted to be here because he is very attached to the girls and has a reputation for "just dropping by" with goodies and laughs. He brought tears to my eyes when he told me he has missed them since we married, and I assured him that our marriage changes nothing and his fear of losing them is unnecessary. He will always be their "Grampie" and they are as attached to him as he to them.*

## Life Is Like a Line

*Overall, the water plan was a smart move. They have a beautiful loca-tion in a better neighborhood and they have more of us. They concur that this is the last move for them and I'm relieved.*

But as soon as the sun came up over the horizon, my father went back to work. Too much retirement and too much time. An opportunity to sell equipment for the automotive industry came chasing after him and he couldn't resist. Mentally, physically, he needed this. He was too young to sit in a rocker and watch the freighters pass by. He wouldn't last six months, and even though he said they would have to carry him out of the house, he didn't want to speed up the process.

Financially they were comfortable, but the word "no" has never rolled off his lips so he was back at it. Leaving love notes on the counter, he was off and running once again. Between the lines of their turmoil still lived a flame and a memory.

*I seem to be caught in the middle again because I've dropped by during a skirmish. Why do I just drop over? The debate today is about my father's increased work week, from eight to nine and some days ten hours a day away from her, and he tends to dismiss any discussion of cutting back. I know he'll never cut back and that he expects me to carry his weight with my mother. I swear, if this is his way of escaping from my mother, he is doing a bang-up job.*

*Stop this. Stop dwelling on this; stop going over this in your head. Nothing is going to change. This is his continual rejection, and her stress today is mine. I know she is fine on her own, but she is caught between a rock and a hard place. She desires companionship with an entirely different but exactly the same man, but her resentment runs too deep.*

*At what point does her life begin? She drives a car so she can get out of the house. She can go to the store or the movies, but she goes alone and why should she? What is my father thinking, feeling? I'll never know.*

*I should just give up. What the hell am I doing? Stop it. Here I go again; turn it off. When I think of all the years spent living the way she has, I am sad. Why do I mull over this every time I'm here? It's difficult to be with your loved ones when they are in constant misery and all you can do is stand beside them in a perpetual state of powerlessness in a situation fated to fail.*

*Stop this, goddamn it. Stop thinking about them. This has been a life-style for them that I see as hopeless but I have to try; I have to do something. There's nothing I can do but it eats at me. How do I make this stop?*

*God, there are no boundaries to my thinking. Whether I'm asleep or awake, I'm always working out the angles, always thinking. I'm pathetic; my limitless feelings drive my own behavior and determine what is left of me. I wonder how many more years I will be filled with conflicting feelings of them, drained by their situation, feel this distress.*

*We have a Japanese exchange student living with us and having her here has been quite enjoyable. Brought in by our Rotary Club, she needed a place to call home so we "adopted" her and she has settled in very nicely. We've taught her how to speak English and when I bring her to my Rotary meetings she's a hit. All the family celebrations and holidays are spent at our house, so she's had an opportunity to meet my family and has taken a liking to my father. Usually a shy young lady, when my father visits she has a perpetual smile that gives her away. She calls him "Grrrrammmpa." These past few weeks have been quiet on the southern front and I am fully enjoying the, shhhh, listen to it...the silence.*

*They're leaving for Florida this week and as official "snowbirds" they won't be returning to the nest until spring. Until then I have custody of their special checkbook; I pay all the bills and oversee the house. Even when they're not home they keep me busy, but it's bicker-free.*

*I understand that my brother will be visiting my parents in the spring though no one tells me directly; I heard it through the grapevine. I think the schedule goes something like Michigan one year and Florida the next and so on. Lucky us; we are blessed to entertain him this year. Of course, the "we are blessed to entertain" certainly doesn't include me as we are still estranged and that's just fine with me.*

Time moved so damn fast I could hardly believe it. It was impossible not to see the changes we were going through, in my mirror, in the girls, and in my parents. Because of that and my father's recent heart surgery, I had begun thinking about the future and mentally preparing for the unknown.

## Life Is Like a Line

I had begun to notice some differences in my father's state of mind and it was upsetting. I didn't know if he had this problem during the day while working, but when home he had begun having periods of dramatically fluctuating moods and his behavior was much more aggressive than usual. I worried for him, terribly.

I didn't really know why my mother didn't speak up when she noticed problems like these. Maybe it was the fear of admitting a problem and then losing him to it. I could analyze it for a few hundred years, but I'll leave that to the professionals. When he closed himself off from the rest of the world, it offended my mother and she reacted as she always had, but this was expected. Not a new behavior, just an old habit that was never broken.

His cardiologist was an incompetent oaf and prescribed some medications that I believed may be of harm, but neither my mother nor my father would allow me to speak to him about it. Of all the eight or ten medications that were prescribed, the one I worried about most was Halcion, a sleeping pill. I believed it was either counteracting with another medication or he was having a reaction from it. Either way, I feared it might lead to trouble. His noticeably glassy eyes and temperamental flare-ups appeared without reason and sounded the alarm.

He was occasionally losing his way when driving home and became agitated easily. With possible side effects of amnesia, agitation, disturbing thoughts, and insomnia, it was quite possible this medication was the culprit. Honest to God, all I thought about was one of them murdering the other. I worried about them; I worried about another catastrophe, and often I felt doomed at the prospect of yet another disaster.

*I'm over for a visit and they are in their rooms watching TV. Fortunately I've missed the skirmish, but I haven't missed the sulking. It looks like they don't really need me but it's too late to turn around and run. I'm not taking sides today; I swear to God I'm not going to get in the middle of their insults and denigrations today.*

*I'm in my mother's room. She seems fine. She has her ginger ale and snacks but her anger sounds like retaliation for her loneliness.*

*"Yes, Mom, I know he is every expletive ever created. How about if we do something this week? We can go shopping and have lunch or something. Does that sound good?"*

*I always go to my mother's room before I see my dad. If I don't, she will resent me for going to my father first, and that's another burden to carry.*

With the sound of the pre-dawn Monday morning bell, my father, now restored, was off and running, back to the enjoyment of his weekday reality, while my mother was left to carry on with the responsibilities of household supervision until his return. She has learned to spend money in his absence. I believe it is her way of filling the void of him and of herself.

I was safe in my own home. My morning bell rang after sunrise, and in my bathrobe I bathed in the heat that filled our sunroom, longing for something more numbing than the coffee in my cup. I had thoughts I couldn't escape. I thought about my attachment to my parents; I thought about how they warmed my soul when they were near. I thought about how I felt torn when I was with them and how I was mended when I was not, and with all that behind me, I thought of them some more.

It was still true even in adulthood that I was their marital sounding board. That was my load. I need not ingest it; subconsciously it engulfed me. They tore me up when they ticked off their harsh offenses toward each other and when I experienced the bitter taste of their devotion.

"Your mother is a very sick woman," he told me. "She is emotionally ill. You don't know how she is, Cindy. She is sick."

God, not this again. I was fucked every time he took me back there. I was this goddamn little girl hearing him and grown woman despising him. There was no objection to his words; I was consciously concealing my fury. The rage that lived down under began pushing itself up, farther and farther, nearing the point of exit, and I conversely pushed it down, down, suppressing it only with my fear of lashing out with my strong Greek temper. It would solve nothing. When they stepped on each other, sooner or later they stepped on the eye witness.

His mouth kept moving and he was defending his side of the dispute but I couldn't hear him any more. I didn't really plan my departure, but suddenly it was 1963 and I was back in Detroit. My father and I were sitting at the kitchen table; he was reading the paper and having coffee. I was reading the comics, drinking a glass of chocolate milk, and waiting for my mother to come downstairs.

I admired my dad; I looked up to him. Sometimes he read articles to me and we discussed them. He was very smart. He was the man in my life, my hero, my dad. It was a wonderful Sunday morning when my father injured me. It was a sunny and warm summer day until he showed me the coldness in his heart. I helped myself to a glass of water. "I'll be right back, Dad." I was heading for the bathroom when he interrupted.

"Why don't you go upstairs and check on your mother to make sure she's still breathing?"

Oh God, help me. Words as fresh as yesterday sadden me still, especially on my worst days. The responsiveness of my body was immediate. He shattered my security, the little girl was troubled, and the woman she grew up to be never stopped checking on her mother.

I hated him for that. I loved him always, but I hated him simultaneously. But it was so long ago. Events of long ago do not necessarily equate forgetfulness. I soon forgave my father for his callousness but I had no loss of memory. Without understanding why, I became aware of his aloofness and his detachment. He hurt me that day and not my mother. She never knew. I could never break her heart.

> *Feelings are mostly crap. The lousy ones are the ones you remember the most and they cut you into pieces with no shame. You pack them away; keep adding to the heap, one after another. The body is vast, the mind endless, and if that is where the excess of life resides, there is no limit to what you will naturally accumulate. Feelings are the emotional upheaval of the human being. They encompass the commotion, disruption, turmoil, interference, and distraction. They are tweaked by your outlook, approach, manner, and mindset. Finally I get this feelings thing.*
>
> *I once lived by thinking alone; I never knew how to decide with my gut. Now I feel my feelings and I would rather think with them alone. Feeling them sucks. As I write this, I want to throw up, just throw up, and do you know why? It's the feelings; they are mostly crap. And that's God's truth.*

Accelerate time. What seemed like an eternity lasted only a few minutes, but right then I knew my visit was over. I glossed over what he said and set aside what I remembered and I kissed him goodbye. I did the same with my mother. I felt guilty for leaving so soon, but I couldn't stay a minute longer. I couldn't put my finger on why I felt bad; I just felt bad.

*"Run Cindy, run. See Cindy speed for her escape."*

Memories are buried treasures in my mind. Recollections of emotions or feelings reduce me to ashes. The mind-body connection is phenomenal. My mind connection is the emotional disturbance, the happy, the sad, the arousing, the disturbing, the exciting, the mentally affecting.

My body connection is the mind in charge of my body. This causes emotions that result in indigestion, tight shoulders, stiff neck, headache, nausea, panic attacks, hyperventilation, and dry heaves.

Mind-body connections, the emotions, the feelings, are all stored in the cabinet called me.

CHAPTER 8

# Fire Power

Depression takes on many faces, and none were immediately distinguishable in my father. His coverup was natural. He had practice, but his ways were "just Dad" to me. His spark and energy and playful manner were welcoming and addicting, but they were not a constant. My eyes tell the tale, but not my father's. Masterful, this melancholia wasn't apparent, so if he was down in the dumps or fighting the start of a depression, he struggled to pull himself out of it.

In my father's opinion, admitting to depression would show a personal weakness and there would be none of that for him. Even so, he continually searched for answers in the volumes that lined their bookshelves. My father believed in the power of a positive mental attitude and it was not unusual for him to give counsel on the subject. Norman Vincent Peale was quoted as saying, "Change your thoughts and you change your world" and "Your enthusiasm will be infectious, stimulating, and attractive to others. They will love you for it. They will go for you and with you."

Without a doubt, my father was a student of this positive outlook. He aspired to live this philosophy every day, but for reasons that weren't always clear, on certain beleaguered days he could not. Most days he was vibrant, enthusiastic, and encouraging, sharing stimulating conversations and teaching as he went along. Unfortunately, every high point has its down side. The time spent at home didn't require the salesman persona; there he behaved as he was, naturally. It wasn't always Mr. Happy.

My mother compared his salesman shtick to his slightly dimmer manner at home and felt disappointed. The source of her agitation would last the length of their marriage, and on behalf of my father it was defensible. My mother never worked, so she never fully understood the dog and pony show, the five-day grind, the "keep smiling" attitude of his generation.

On the more bleak days, even my father's famous positive mental attitude couldn't change his mood or the yin and yang of their collective personalities. As they alternated moodiness, they blamed each other for their disappointments. In the night, they blamed each other for their disappointments. And me, I was their child, their ally, their go-between, their interpreter, and I never fully absorbed the concept of PMA. How does attitude overcome inherent behavior?

Standing within the circle of their squabble was like standing in front of a freshly disturbed beehive. There was no room for positive mental attitude. Any sane person would have run like hell. Make no mistake; I was close to them my entire life by choice. It was what I had always known. In the worst of times I have fought my instincts to separate myself from them and I have loved them through it all.

> *Maybe I'm addicted to the turmoil…What an extreme fucking thought. I don't know if he takes his pills anymore, but I wish I had one…bottle. I haven't seen them around in years.*
>
> *Usually I feel well but I have had a female malady that brings me to the table, literally. With some sort of cause-and-effect mentality, I am now facing my second gynecological surgery. It looks like a complete hysterectomy, this time to put an end to my symptoms. I am told that many women*

have diseases and conditions that require this type of surgery and it is an option for the condition of endometriosis, fibroid tumors, pelvic pain and pressure, heavy bleeding, and pre-cancerous conditions.

They say it can enhance sexuality (they should have told me that before), but I'm not putting any credence in that yet. I realize my moods have been up and down and up and down and I am not easy to live with. The problem is that when these moods occur, I'm driven by an ugly, short-tempered me and I'm not really in charge. Why would any sane person want to fly off the handle for no reason, be untouchable, alienate everyone around them, embarrass their children, and generally be a major pain in the ass?

That's a good description of me. I know it and I don't like it, but it's who I am and what I continue to be, for now. And honestly, if I were that bad, my family would tell me, right?

No, I don't think so. They're either too kind to say anything or they're afraid for their lives. My wrath…not worth the gamble. Either way, it seems as if they wouldn't notice if I lived the rest of my life standing on my head with a chicken up my ass.

If I told them my behavior was perfectly normal, they would agree. Overall, I'm counting on this surgery to be my cure-all. The human body, fantastic. Tear out something from your abdomen and stop being a bitch. What a miracle.

If for some reason I decide against the surgery and at the last minute continue to live this way, there will be no end to the discomfort and the pressure and the pain and the moods and the emotional upheavals and the worry and the hot flashes and the sexless sweaty nights of misery I have. Oh, that's attractive. Based on a few of those day-to-day discomforts, I'm going to tell them yes, yes, YES.

Well, the surgery is over and my Greek gynecologist reports success with no sign of cancer or any irregularities other than that fibroid tumor the size of an orange nestled deep inside me. I thank them. One obgyn and two up-and-coming physicians got the job done without slicing me open and soon I will have it all behind me, lock, stock, and barrel. Ron came every day and the girls called and our friends surprised me on my worst day and the time went by.

## Life Is Like a Line

*Even the motion sickness from the recovery area to my room didn't seem too bad once the anesthesia wore off. Uggh. The nurses, the "hospital cuisine," all of it okay but I have known for quite some time that my father and I would have a medical conflict and now here we go. Just two days ago my father was admitted to another hospital for open heart surgery and on the day of my discharge, he undergoes it.*

*I was denied discharge based on what they knew and then I had to promise. My doctor has asked me to go directly home and to not pass go and I have assured him that I will but of course I will not. He's a great doctor and I respect his opinion medically, but this is about my heart and my father and how a daughter views life and death and mystery.*

*My father got bumped not once but twice today by emergency room patients and now a late evening time slot gives way to an early morning recovery. He is prepped and ready to go. With wheels under my feet, my husband is rolling me through the hospital corridor to the surgical waiting room. It is nearly seven o'clock in the evening; I have missed the kiss for luck. My mother and my sister are anticipating and they look up.*

*"Whoa, what a look, ladies. What, you didn't expect me?" This time it's my turn to ask the volunteer for surgical information. I thought that being in a wheelchair would help us obtain more information or that at least I would have the sympathy factor for leverage but I was wrong. The volunteer was less than amused with my sense of humor.*

*He's been in surgery for quite some time. Silently, I am feeling ill. Light-headed and nauseated. I give it no credence in hopes that this too shall pass. I can fight my weakness by staying in this chair for as long as I can and I'm in the right place if I pass out. The good news just arrived; he is in recovery. I watch the clock; Ron watches me. We get the word; we take turns seeing him.*

*Looking into his eyes, I can barely stand to see him this way. It is upsetting me and I am soaking wet with sweat from worry. He recognizes us. It is good. Now I can go. I am not anxious anymore, though I have been in and out of panic mode. I am really lightheaded and they tell me I'm as white as a ghost. "No jokes, you guys. Ron thinks I look pale enough. I'll be here tomorrow. Bye. Love you."*

*I have been back to work for over three weeks and it's so good to have my life back, life without the female discomfort that dominated me for years. During my recovery, they counseled me on this thing called surgical menopause and the negative effects it can have on my body and my mind (probably too late for that) and that's just great.*

*I expel discomfort and replace it with insanity.*

CHAPTER 9

# *"C" Is for Change*

$\mathbf{M}$y father strove to educate himself and others at every opportunity. He was a professor at heart and he talked about his heritage and the background of the people who are the essence of who we were and are. We are of strong Greek stock: hard workers, generals in the war, members of a special group. We are the givers and the doers of life. This spirit is our foundation; it is my father's proud legacy.

We are also members of the "Type A" club, of course. My father always believed he was born an extrovert with this particular personality. After all, he was a naturally high-spirited workaholic, friendly, cheerful, driven, outgoing, and rather excitable as well. Every member of our family is a Type A and no one would dare say we aren't cheerful or driven or outgoing. The truth is, our family has accepted my father's conclusion as a feature of our personalities and has never questioned it because it makes sense.

## Life Is Like a Line

My family and friends would probably describe me as energized with a sparkle in my eye, a creative and entertaining sort, willing and able to do anything, with known periods of excess as I go beyond even my own usual comfort level.

Unfortunately, this behavior pattern is also typically marked by tenseness, impatience, and aggressiveness, often resulting in stress-related symptoms such as insomnia and indigestion and possibly increasing the risk of heart disease. Perhaps this explains our impatience and tenseness with each other and the loud exchanges between my parents.

The Type A personality was first described as an important risk factor in coronary disease in the 1950s by cardiologist Meyer Friedman and his coworkers. Friedman characterized Type A behavior as time urgency (or hurry sickness) and an easily aroused irritability or anger or free-floating hostility.

> *Type A, you are the incontestably perfect explanation for my intermittent negative temperament. Whether this temperament is of consequence or circumstance, it is positively mine, and by the luck of the draw it is shared.*

I suppose my father's explanation of our character is more socially appealing, but I know firsthand that our Type A temperament embodies qualities and behaviors that can be detached and even hostile. I am certain my father was enamored with the appeal and excitement, but that temperament also has the potential to bruise with abruptness, to blemish relationships, and to destroy lives.

Even though Type A individuals complete tasks in record time, their trademark impatience and tenseness can be destructive to others. Whether this Type A trait is an aspect of our ancestral temperament due essentially to the complexion of our genetic makeup or is a learned behavior, it can be detrimental. It has been an unfavorable dynamic in my personality and has set the mood and pace of my manner, but it has kept me distracted as well.

> *With the leaves changing color and coolness in the air, the year 2000 will soon be just a memory. We are still self-employed and our construction company keeps my husband on his toes. It's wonderful that he enjoys what*

*he does because he works very hard and never really gets a break. I try to hold down the fort and it is much easier to do with our office in our home, but I have guilt because I am pulled away quite often.*

*Owning a construction company has afforded us the opportunity to move into some of our newly built homes. Our first home, a renovation, was a much loved abode and although I have never have been too attached to any one home I have had my favorites. With each we have significant memories, some memorable and others not. The children have grown and we are so very proud of each one of them and look forward to our home being filled with grandchildren. We have one daughter with us still and it appears as if she is on the cusp of a lifelong relationship. The greater family circle is unchanged, but my father has been rather ill again, which alarms me. His heart surgeries seem to come more often and they have been more challenging. His participation in state-of-the-art trials at a major heart center seem to have been beneficial to him overall, but with each surgery a little more is taken from him. Mentally he seems sharp; each time they implant a device in him to keep his heart ticking, they manage to leave the essence of him behind.*

Nothing has really changed in my family's relationships...we could be described as people who have descended from common ancestors who lack a harmonious spirit and shared affection. With that, I am being very kind.

The depth of real love and affection came to me through the birth of my two daughters and my marriage to my husband and the melding of our families. I never knew such a connection existed in that way until then, and now I proclaim that my memories are not just black and white glossies anymore; they are recollections intensely painted on the canvas of my mind.

*I have started working on my diet and exercise, and I am looking and feeling pretty damn good. My neck and indigestion problems seem to be in control, physiological components and all. If I were to adopt my father's philosophy of "mind over matter," life would be a bowl of cherries, so I am trying to have a more positive outlook, trying to live the positive life. I believe that as long as I am crisis-free, I should be able to pull it off.*

## Life Is Like a Line

*I am slimmer than ever, down from a size ten to a two, and I love being so thin. I look in the mirror and I am almost gaunt. That is so excellent. My husband and my family tell me I look fantastic but my sister says I'm anorexic, of course. I'm probably a little of both and slightly paranoid that I might gain some of the weight back and I have heard that there is a "high" in weight control, especially when you can get down to here from there and if that is true I feel higher than a kite.*

*I don't know if it's healthy, but starvation has been my method of late. Through this process I have taken diet pills and slim drinks and I eat less food. I'm really into this diet thing and I find it to be a challenge to my psyche; it's a conflict of me against me. I'm not as irritable as I was in the beginning but I am noticing that lately I have a loose tongue when I talk with my husband. Along with the harshness I have toward him, I am driving like a maniac, fast, switching lanes, and without much patience.*

*I have no explanation for this; I just call it my wild spell and this too shall pass unless I drive myself to the funeral home. My thought for today: forget the radio channel called Lite; this wild side of me digs the rock.*

*Everyone tells me I look frail so I have hired a personal trainer to help me build some muscle but what I really want to do is bulk up. Truly, I like the delicate look. Oh well, they tell me women have a tough time without the use of steroids to get bigger so I suppose I'll go for the concept of muscle for health; how boring. I have plenty of energy and feel enthusiastic about my training program, so I'll get up and go for the movement of my life.*

*Ron has always had this "work like a dog" mentality and when we first met he was shuffling the responsibilities of two distinctly different businesses, working from dawn until dusk. I, on the other hand, worked your standard nine-to-five job and at the end of the day returned to my life as a relaxed homebody. But the early days were filled with the responsibilities of children, our personal life, and our business and very quickly I learned that in order to be with him, I had to work alongside him. Ever since our honeymoon, I have learned about dawn to dusk and only going home for a few hours to see the girls. In our restaurant, working late meant chopping onions, making nachos, washing dishes, waiting tables, and playing office clerk, housekeeper, hostess, innkeeper, troubleshooter, and boss.*

Now, in our construction company, I know all about dirt and mud and rain and how frigid it is working in the elements. I'm damn good at cleaning the site and back-blading with our skidster and I have thoroughly enjoyed being behind the wheel of our backhoe maneuvering over the terrain to take a scoop out of the earth at will.

Today, I really think I can do most anything if shown how, thanks to my husband who has helped me evolve by exposing me to all these occupations and trades. It may sound crazy, but I'm sure I could do brain surgery if someone would just show me how.

Lately I find myself counting things automatically, naturally. I don't remember when or where it began but I think I have done it for a long, long time. Four, five, six, seven: random things, everything. The holes in the ceiling tiles, light bulbs in fixtures, the black squares on a black and white floor. I am walking up the stairs, counting my stride, walking down steps, five, six, seven, four, three, two; anything that moves, everything that is stationary, is counted. It is subliminal but it is no big deal. It is controlling; it controls me; it nevers stops. I have told others but no one seems to be alarmed. I am on an escalator, twenty-six, twenty-five, twenty-four, twenty-three, twenty-two, how many ribs in each stair, five, four, three, two, one. I am on level ground. I am on to something else. My keys, I unzip my purse and look for them; I zip up my purse, unzip my purse, zip and unzip and look for the keys. I get sidetracked by this disturbance. I see my keys; I know they are in there…Dammit, I check again; I touch them; they are there. Today I cannot shop; I cannot shop today. Dammit, I am going home.

My husband tells me he is lucky; his woman is never boring since she is ever-changing. My man, I could have foolishly walked out on him so many years ago, but through it all I love him, I am attached to him. We have a great life together; he is my strength and he loves me through it all.

# CHAPTER 10

# Infinite Thoughts

In my youth, I felt life to be a rather helpless existence, but the aid of a helper caused a simple turn of a mental switch and I was changed.

The "off" switch threw me back into the darkness; it brought on my sadness, which came to me without any conscious indicators. I suppose this "off" position was driven by weighty occurrences that directed me. I always loved my parents, but I was affected by the storms of their relationship.

Even now when there is a load upon me, every breath I expel is a sigh of hopelessness transformed from a physical purpose to a distinguishable reverberation of my soul.

> *Working out helps me to sleep better, but once the daylight hits,*
> *I find myself facing days of fighting the fight of infinite thoughts. To*
> *deter my wandering contemplation of doom, I make every attempt*

*to occupy my mind with good thoughts, digging deeper every day as the situation evolves.*

*I have been so worried about the health of my father. The truth is, I have idolized him my whole life and as I look at him now, the slightest signal he sends is too much. Perhaps my loss would be a comfort to him, but as he finds the light, mine dims. It is unfortunate that my mother is so angry with my sister and vice versa. We should be a team, a fighting fucking team, faking harmony if we must, all for our father's tranquility.*

While the thought of my father's passing terrorizes me, I realize I can serve him by helping him through his struggle and by assisting my mother to stand strong. In the big picture, I am still only a spectator. Dad doesn't seem to want to be saved anymore and we have to respect his wishes. He seems to have lost the positive mental attitude that has been his lifelong trademark. We all share the same emotion—sadness. I do my best with what I have and the rest is in someone else's hands.

*Okay, the recent encounter with Dad's cardiologist in the hospital was heart-wrenching bullshit. He didn't want to be questioned, but he's been wrong before. I don't need that jackass jumping down my throat; it's tight enough as it is. And damn it, if he had been speaking any louder, the bastard would have been yelling at me. I kept on talking and he didn't get the upper hand and he couldn't get a word in edgewise, the bastard.*

*The truth is he didn't have any answers anyway, so I really don't know why I bothered taking him to task except that once I started, I was on a roll and I put him in his place. I fought to look unshaken but I was a ball of nerves inside. He was getting to me and then he almost had me but it ended just in time. His ranting and raving affected me more than I thought.*

*My legs and hands are still trembling, but I'm glad it's over. God, I hate it when my heart is pounding. I hate that bastard doctor. I hate it when my throat feels tight. I should have stopped them from going to him years ago; he's always been a lousy doctor. In my head I kept hearing, "He always bounced back, but he always bounced back."*

I felt that day for many days to come. My physical symptoms roared like a lion, first the throat, then the chest, and then my chest and back. My pulsating head gave no pause, so I popped the pills (ibuprofen) and I drank the mint and I begged and pleaded for relief and I promised myself I'd relax.

Even when my father was physically better and was back to work more than full-time, he was different. He seemed grouchy and moody and he didn't want to eat once he came home, although he ate out often, especially at the lunch hour. There would be peace in the house if they stayed in their neutral corners, but too often they were agitating.

On that Saturday my mother was a pistol and my father was acting anti-social and had no desire to visit so I went to a graduation party without them. I had literally just arrived and was forty minutes from home when my cell phone rang. It was my eldest daughter.

*"Hello. Why are you scared? You want me to come home? I just got here; what's wrong? Grandma was sitting on a chair and you were talking. She passed out and you can't wake her? Where's Grandpa? He won't come out? Okay, shit...sorry, call the ambulance and I'll be there soon."*

*I seem to always be racing and now it's directly to the hospital. So far the ER physician has sent her for a chest x-ray and an ultrasound shows a mass in the left upper quadrant of her lung. With the ER physician vacillating between this and that, they have finally determined it is pneumonia but since it's so severe, she is being admitted for further tests and treatment. I am nervous about trusting their judgment because, in my opinion, this hospital is good for scrapes and cuts and nothing more.*

*My mother has been given antibiotics and will probably stay in the hospital for a few days under the care of her personal physician. Lately I've been running back and forth between parents, from hospital to river house to home, and it is exhausting. For the past so many years they have relied upon me to assist them in scheduling and transporting them to their medical appointments and I have done so at the risk of becoming completely engulfed in the flames of their relationship.*

*After so many years, I have come to hate the receptionists and their phony smiles, never looking up when they speak and never missing a beat when they say, "Complete and sign all the sheets on the clipboard...and without your insurance cards and your driver's license you'll have to reschedule..."*

## Life Is Like a Line

*Eye contact, bitch; does the head move? And gimme that fucking clipboard so I can smash it on your desk.*

*To date, much of the medical profession has brought to us questionable diagnoses, an overspent cast of disinterested players, and physicians whose revolving door is dizzying. And because so much of my time is spent troubleshooting for my parents, I find my heat, my short temper, my headaches, and my indigestion. But soon our pace will slow down just a bit and my parents will return to their good health. I know they are frustrated and I am the same. I want to live my life again. I want to be romantic with my husband. I want to spend my days at home, not in a medical institution. I want to stop worrying.*

They sent my mother home with antibiotics and a follow-up appointment with our internist. I remember it was in the morning. I was in the office going through the mail when the telephone rang.

*"Oh man, it's just been a few months, Mom. First Dad and now you? What do you mean an ultrasound? You had that already. For what? They told us it was pneumonia. They don't know what the hell is going on. Sure, that's no problem; that will be fine; don't worry. Is Dad working tomorrow? Maybe he wants to go. No problem; it'll be fine. I'll be with you. I'll pick you up at eight. Love you."*

*We already have our remedy for the pneumonia. They've given us an antibiotic or two; that's supposed to be the damn cure.*

*The second ultrasound proves it; it's something more; it is much more. My mother is placed in the hospital and the doctor gives us the news: the radiologist says it looks like lung cancer. It's as if we've been struck by lightening. She is there three more days.*

*Every night in our home I lie in bed watching the ceiling fan and listening to the sounds of nature on the other side of the glass. The frogs are the loudest tonight and they celebrate their existence noisily. They live among their thousands of relatives and friends who are hatching with them, celebrating their lives until they are frozen with the season, frozen before knowing what hit them.*

*I understand their plight, frozen in this crisis of her season, and with every thought of her illness I feel the coldness as it pushes over me. Illness as I know it has always been my father's and I've become accustomed to the routine of it; I know the business of it inside and out.*

*I do not know my mother's dilemma but it feels strange and it is beginning to take her away from us. I can only imagine what she's thinking and feeling and fearing. Although I want to pretend this isn't happening, I have to stay in the reality and not in my hopefulness.*

*Giving my father the news is difficult. My hands tremble and my voice reflects my fear and with every word I speak he looks away. Meanwhile, I search for words, nice pleasant words, some comforting group of words, and the proper intonation to ease him through it. Dreadfully, not one word softens the blow. How does a daughter tell her father that the beast called cancer is in her mother?*

I found him to be detached; he told me they were wrong and that I should take care of her.

I thought, "What? What in the hell is going on here?" and I began explaining the pecking order. He was on top; this was his responsibility, not mine; this was his wife, not mine; this was his problem first and then ours.

He told me she was my responsibility and I told him that was bullshit. I said that just before my injured self wanted to wring his neck. I wanted to tell him how I felt, I mean all of it, beginning with my childhood going all the way up, starting at the basement with each year being a floor, forty-six of them right up to this very moment, but I could not.

Something was happening with him that I couldn't put my finger on. I was scared and alone and as supportive as my mother would allow. My father continued to be disinterested and he was bringing out the memories I fought so hard to ignore. But I kept my disappointment in him to myself. We exchanged kisses, goodwill, and goodbyes and my frustration followed me home.

While I raced down their driveway and rolled past the stop sign as usual, dear God, I made my escape. Never fast enough, I was like a race car driver weaving in and out of traffic, crossing the center line to break away from the pack, racing to the finish line with no effort to avoid or fulfill death's wish. I was a bandit stealing my heart from them and taking it back home.

Even in my short drive home, the silence was my respite and it gave me another chance for peace. But my thoughts did not vanish and I remembered again what I wished not to know and the more I became involved in my thoughts, the worse I felt. I was no calmer than when I was with them; I was achy with each reminder of the day and I was everything and nothing once again.

> *Honest to God, my soul is ill. I am not a good wife. I will leave him. I have so many feelings and thoughts. I don't know what I want. I have no desire; I feel no warmth. I am shit and all I see are the flies.*
>
> *Forgive me; I am a miserable person. Dear God, I am a fucking miserable person.*
>
> *It's been a day since I told my father. My mother and I spoke for a long time today but my father still has no interest in her condition and he isn't about to visit. He has his whatever-the-hell-they-are reasons for his disinterest. I have no fucking clue what they are, but it's hurtful. It makes me remember, and I hate to remember.*
>
> *Since my father is disinterested at this point and my mother needs decision-making help, I'm her best hope. She has relieved my father of his function as her patient advocate and has elected me to step in for her. Doing this is nothing different than what I have done for years and I am pleased to help her. She's asked me not to tell him or anyone else for that matter, so I will respect her wishes. However, I am concerned that he will be upset when he finds out and retaliate against her, which would not be surprising given this newest string of events.*
>
> *It's been a long day and hospital hours spent as a visitor can drain the life out of you. Eight o'clock in the evening means that visiting hours are over and I've just been reminded by nurse Hatchet, whose stare equates to "Get the hell out of here," so I'm off to check on my other parent. Since he wishes not to see her, I will bring the information to him. His refusal of her, his unwillingness to believe in her, his rejection of her, is disgraceful.*
>
> *Given his heart condition and high blood pressure and the bottles of prescriptions he takes, including Halcion and Valium and the random vitamins*

*and herbs, I feel his mood may be prompted by a serious medication problem. Some of these may be contributing to his mental and physical downfall. I've begged him to reconsider taking them all, but I have lost the argument.*

*It's funny how my age doesn't preclude me from fighting right along with them and against them when need be. When I am their adult, I troubleshoot and reason and convince as I must, but when I am their child caught up in their conflict, my heart can no longer deal with the emotions that rise to the surface.*

*When I am caught between them, through no fault of my own, the suffocation begins and my life feels the pull of the gravity below. My father, receptive always to my visit, never asks about her and my stay is short and sweet. Tonight I am suffering. I need my husband, I need to feel warmth, I need my home, I need my little dog. I need my ceiling fan and my front porch and the street light across the street.*

*While I kiss my father and depart from his gloominess and make my way to the door, I have opinions of him and I am paranoid at the potential of my thoughts. He is mentally fixed upon nothingness and I cannot help him tonight. I will give my mother his messages and add a few in for good measure.*

*I am losing the battle in Physiology 101. My body is tense…yup, neck stiff…yup, it hurts like a bitch…how about that familiar headache I know so well…yup, fucking yup.*

*Bury the feelings; drive it home hard. No traffic, speeding like a pile of pills, no threat of smashing up the Suburban, a scream in the car that nobody hears. God, please take me…home.*

I wasn't able to sleep for worrying about her condition, and night after night I was fixated on my parents. The potential of this illness frightened me and the depth of this ill made me more than uncomfortable. I realized my need to know would not be fulfilled until its time. My father pulled away so much that all I could be was irritated with him and I was saddened as I had been so many times before. I loved my father and never expected him to act this way, but there were more realities in their relationship than I knew. I didn't want to feel this way every day, every day. I didn't want to think about this every day, every day.

## Life Is Like a Line

*Why do I feel with each day that he'll come around? Why am I so damned optimistic about him when in essence I am going against my pessimistic self? My pessimistic self is perfectly right about him. The schedule has kept her hospitalized over the weekend but thankfully she is having a stress test early Monday morning and then we'll know.*

I thought I would make it in time to see her go down for her test, but I missed her by a few minutes. This was the test we'd been waiting for. Near the end, the technician began to slow down the pace. That's when he spoke, the reprehensible cardiologist barely able to speak English. As I was soon to learn, it was my mother, the technician, and him in the room.

She was there for the taking, and he decided to give her the news. Despite my explicit instructions that she not be told yet, this three-piece-suited self-proclaimed big-shot took it upon himself to tell my mother that she did indeed have lung cancer.

She nearly dropped to the floor. Until now, we'd had no confirmation of the diagnosis and we hadn't wanted to frighten her.

Why did he do this? Because he had an opportunity to be his pompous callous self. If telling her like this was his way of feeling powerful, I'd hate to see him in bed. If frightening a weak, helpless, eighty-plus little old lady for absolutely no reason made his day, then he was about to get the ethical shit kicked out of him. No words could describe my brand of upset and no pacing could relieve my anxiety.

Once more another medical genius was caught fucking with all that was sensible, all that was honorable, and all that was mine. There was no stopping me once I went into confrontation mode. I was engulfed with rage. He would soon be returning to the floor for some charting and as my heart pounded, my body trembled and my shoulders rose to the ceiling. My palms were so sweaty that wiping them didn't help.

I waited for him. My battle cry was "Don't fuck with us." The nurses knew I wanted him and I paced up and down the hall from her room to the desk, from her room to the desk, until I heard his accent. I felt weak and strong and anxious; the tightness in my throat reminded me of how I had felt so many times before. I could feel the rage inside me but it was purposely controlled.

I began reviewing the series of events in my mind. Chanting them over and over again in my head, I practiced my speech, searching for better words.

They came for me, I was led to a consultation room, and he sat down first and offered me a chair. I stood near him instead, almost over him. I stayed in his space; I was in his fucking comfort zone. I wanted a piece of him and this was the first step.

As I began, my voice didn't quiver and my words were perfect and he knew he was wrong. I could see the look on his face as he began to search for words. I heard him hesitate just long enough to reprimand him again and under his accent he could say no more. He never got the chance.

The nurse stood behind him as witness, I suppose, but she was cheering for me. Her body language and facial expressions were all mine. This was just more of the same. Excessive self- importance. Welcome to America, you pompous son of a bitch.

With each hospital admission, some major jackass had fallen down from the ceiling and landed on our family, but I swore no more bullshit from any more fly-by-night, two-bit, over-the-ocean morons.

Fourteen days later, I took my mother home. When it was time to leave, I jumped in my car and nailed it all the way, face forward, radio blasting, same feelings, the need for speed. I needed to go faster; I needed the speed. I was going fast, fast enough to get home before I had to open my eyes.

I thought many times about my grand escape. Taking myself away from the jaw-clenching, teeth-grinding stomachaches, the pounding heart, frozen neck, shoulders on the rise, headaches, irritability, sarcasm, withdrawing, anxiety, panic attacks, and physicians falling from the ceiling, but I could never leave them.

> *I have come to believe that my sinking self on earth is a slow under-mining of my soul, a torturous lifetime of dread, and any part of it can be deadly on every level.*

As for my mother, our prayers were answered. My plummeting self would rise to the line once more.

## Life Is Like a Line

*I am panic-stricken as my sister comes into the fold. The specialist she recommends performs a battery of tests and it is written, our mother's mass is completely gone.*

*I believe the good Lord healed her and that is why she was cleared of any malignancy. She has pneumonia after all and it's not as bad as originally thought.*

*We are told to keep a close eye on her health. We accept this as a miracle, thank God, and watch her like a hawk.*

Not long after, my father, with his sixth sense, began to "put his things in order" and it wasn't clear at the time why. My parents decided to clean up loose ends, so they adjusted their wills and made unfriendly family choices and decisions. Though my father was the business mind and my mother micromanaged the house, in this instance she made the business choice; it would in due course be about her and she was strong and adamant.

As we drove to see their lawyer, we spoke about everything but the business at hand. After an overview of the formalities, my mother's medical advocate was chosen and she confirmed again that it would be me. Then questions and answers about the administrator were next and I left the room. The duties were discussed and my mother was asked whom she wanted to help her should my father be gone. She was quite determined that the lone conservator of the estate, the child who would continue to care for her as she had done her whole life, would be me.

My mother felt I "had always been there; no one else has bothered." My sister and I had been co-advocates at my suggestion. The original trust and wills written in 1992 were to be changed and now she would be legally prevented from playing any part in caring for our mother.

The attorney warned me that, "These changes will be monumental to your sibling relationships." Additionally, he said, "This will be the most difficult thing you will ever do; they will declare war."

I glossed over his words. I had done everything in good conscience. My parents picked who they wanted on their own, they sat with the lawyer alone, and they signed alone and I did not interfere. I am not ashamed of advocating for my sister the first time and I am not ashamed of doing nothing for her the second time. I knew I could handle the responsibility alone. I knew the work, I knew the parties like no one else, and my mother was adamant like never before.

With my principles intact, the will was finished, but the attorney was on the mark when he told me about the subsequent war over the wills. My sister believes I have manipulated our parents and I have been called every dirty word in the English language. Though I don't wish conflict with any member of my family, it is an uncomfortable reality with her. The blending of our history and our chemical makeup provides a breeding ground for our sibling rivalry, with no real desire for a solution. Nonetheless, the darkness of her mistrust makes me sad, and as it continues to come to fruition, the wrath is incessant.

Lunch at my father's favorite Italian restaurant after the attorney's office brought memories of the past with him both well and ill and I remembered what had been said and what they had signed and how I had been warned and how I didn't fight for my siblings. I became mindful, too, that this was a significant admission of my father's condition. As before, my physiological process began to kick in. The more my mind focused on him, the more my body fought a losing battle.

> *We're having a small Christmas celebration at my parents' house and surprisingly my sister will be joining us. My father is weak and it is agonizing to look into his eyes. There are so many memories in those eyes, so much to remember.*
>
> *My mother has decorated sparsely and music is playing in the background. This is a painful holiday for our family as the sureness of Dad's death is becoming more and more evident. As the gifts are being opened, I watch them and all I see is him and I must withdraw.*
>
> *Despite being surrounded by the love of my family, nothing can erase his image and the panic I feel. Subconsciously I am me, I hear my voice, I see my hands, I do the work, I go through the motions. Privately my husband consoles me, but I have no real warmth or enthusiasm and I am unable to respond to him and in the course of this I have lost the line between pretense and me.*
>
> *Having our daughters home for the holiday is pure and comfortable and a necessary distraction to my life. They have that contagious spirit, they*

*are full of life, and they are not afraid. I remember the holidays when they were small; God, those were good times. I used to think, "Enjoy this Cindy, because someday they will leave you," and although I hoped they would never leave, I didn't pray.*

*When they were young, I held on to them as they to me. They were my lifeline and I kept from drowning. And though they have left me, they are still my lifeline and they are all that they were and more. I close my eyes and moments in time stand still.*

An apple dissected cannot sustain the removal of too many slices before its purpose is fulfilled, its core is excessively exposed, and it no longer can offer what it formerly was. For the apple, the removal of each bittersweet slice is a stress, and as each piece is removed, the structure breaks down little by little.

In an abstract way, the same has been true for me. Each major stress I have faced has slowly dissected me. Each bittersweet slice out of my life has been a stress upon my core and has broken down my structure little by little.

My parents are my major segments of life, and it was becoming clear that they were beginning to break down. Consequently, so was I.

With the imminent loss of my father, the marital engagements of both our daughters, my mother's tender condition, the separation of my sister, and the construction of our new home, I was overwhelmed with too many changes. All was passing from one state to another; some were beginning a new journey and some would soon be leaving.

It was too much life, too many alterations, too much sadness, too much happiness. I was confused at how I should feel; there was just too much life. I was fighting it and I was broken with the loss.

*My energy for the season has weakened since my father's decline and visibly he has weakened too. He has told me many times that, "There is a time for every season," and I know exactly what he means. All I can do when he speaks this way is cover my ears and turn off my mind.*

*I just don't want to hear about time and seasons; it has never been my subject of choice and I am sick with the truth of it. It is obvious to all that my father is gravely ill and has deteriorated quite a bit. With my visiting every day, I am finding it more difficult to watch him and I have no tolerance for the sight of his suffering. I go there with a sick feeling. It's in my head, then throughout my body. Nothing hurts but I am very ill. While I visit, I adjust his oxygen and then help with the inhalers, medications, and visiting nurses who are twenty-four hours on call.*

*I think my mother needs help but she refuses the "intrusion." The physician-ordered bed has arrived and she hates it, hates the idea that he needs side rails. Not all but some of my buttons have been pushed and I have just arrived. Soon she will be very close to a detonation, it will be me, and it will take place right here in this living room.*

*I will again try to maintain order in my head while I search for calmness in my heart. I suppose I'm like her in some ways and, God forbid, not in others. I hear her sarcasm and see her aggression and watch her moods control her as they seem to turn on a dime from an accommodating person to an uncooperative one. These are the behaviors I fight and fear my own mirror sees.*

My mother had a way about her, a rather offensive way, and after all these years she still couldn't recognize her troubling behavior. Spending time with my parents under these conditions one day after another seemed impossible and it was shocking that each day was worse than the one before. My visits made me tense; I was heartbroken and helpless. Between my father's illness that crippled me and my mother's hostility and panic, life with them was maddening. I felt an anger that never left me and a rage that must remain within me and never come out.

*I am compelled by my personality and lifetime involvement to stop her condescending attitude toward my father. Her easiness at criticism can only bring him lower mentally so I shall reprimand her and face her firing squad. "Mom, don't kick him while he's down. He's ill; he can't help himself; can't you see that?"*

*That is just a taste of what I want to say but I dare not question or criticize her motives any further today. That would incite a riot. "Sure. Okay, Mom. Do you want me to put more water in the oxygen machine? I'll just put the tube along the wall so you don't trip and fall; will that be good? I know you don't want the tubes showing down the hall but he needs his (fucking) oxygen. Okay, I'll cover it up with your throw rugs.*

*I know she must be trying to kill me; she must. She's going to kill me and all I can do is think my thoughts; otherwise I will be killed in battle.*

*"Geez, won't you insult me more? You mustn't be finished, that's not quite enough. I fucking beg you, please break me down. Can't I be that daughter you love to hate? Oh yeah, I already am. Shit, you can do better than that. Come on, sorry, that's right, it's all about you and you're freaking out, but don't you think I'm lost in this too?"*

This was why I always got into trouble. I just couldn't keep my mouth shut. I riled her up and set myself up at the same time. I questioned her about the oxygen and her retort incited both of us into a near rage. I stormed away before I broke everything in the fucking house. Then I started thinking and my head was saying all kinds of things that couldn't be verbalized. I wanted to warn her, if she really wanted to go head to head with me, I'd win. My sarcasm could beat her ten to one but it wouldn't be kind. So I shut my mouth and shut it some more.

Truthfully, I'm great at cutting sarcasm, insults, criticizing, and the like. If you don't believe me, ask my husband.

*My father's illness and these horrific days of watching him deteriorate have begun to wear me down and I am feeling drained and sensitive. I suppose it's time for me to leave them because I feel explosive and I have concealed my upset and put it where everything else goes. I cannot cry; I can only think. I wish I could cry but there are no tears available for me. Seems all I do when I'm away from them is worry. In the shower I worry, driving in the car I worry, I pet my little dog and worry.*

*I'm a different person. My thoughts are fixed on them and I am unfocused on everything else. For those who know me, this is my life until I return to them, and once with them I am fixed on them in person until I leave them again.*

*I am in a complete state of parental absorption. In a world of conscious oblivion, I am living the life of two minds. I am their caregiver and I am their child; I am their counselor and still I am the student. I am the water to rinse away life's dirt and I am the sponge that absorbs it. Immobile, I am often the punching bag that grows weaker as I ingest this same sight day after day after day. As my throat carries the terror of my father's death, I fear that normalcy will be gone forever and I'll not only be weak in the knees but also weak in the mind.*

I was helpless, angry, terrified, and worn out. I was preparing for my escape. My mother had been a bitch that day but I chalked it up to stress. I gave my kisses and words of encouragement to both and I was out the door, messed up and running. Driving home fast, passing in the no-passing zone, I hoped to run the amber light but it was a solid red. I didn't care about the death-defying danger. My heart pounded and today I felt more of the same, more and more of the same, just like every other day.

Finally home, none too soon, my tires screeched in the driveway near my haven but I couldn't erase what I saw there and what was said and what I heard and even the smells lingered. For the moment I was a little girl again, frightened, feeling too much, and angry.

*Once I arrive home I try not to blow up at anyone but I am alone. Hopefully nothing annoys me, and as I slip into the house undetected I face one fewer hurdle. When I feel this way, usually the first one to irritate me wins and loses. If I can come down to calm before my husband comes home, he will have beaten the rap. He is a good man and doesn't deserve the highs and lows of my alternating moods that just keep getting worse. He is the innocent bystander; he is exposed to my fluctuating levels of intensity, unaware of their cause or direction.*

*Because my behavior has become more hostile and upsetting, he has tried to steady his defenses for his own protection. While he is uneasy with my ugliness, he is mostly concerned about my condition through it all. It is safe to say that ugliness is not a feature I aspire to have, but it has me.*

*I don't want to be this way…I am caught within their upsetting turmoil. Through this process I am more intense, my thoughts are more vivid, and my desires are more powerful. Because of this process, I walk in the dark. I am terrified in this life. I am simply terrified.*

## Life Is Like a Line

*My father is dying. The stress and sadness bring out the ugliness of my unpredictability. My underlying frame of mind is anger. I am angry and it is an upsetting, fearful state. I am worse when I am subjected to the stress of my new familial reality. I am worse when I am forced to swim upstream. I am worse when I aspire to do my very best and it is never good enough.*

*On this day, I want to get drunk; this is when I just want to be drunk drunk drunk drunk. On this day, I feel confused when I want to be enlightened. I don't know what I want or where I'm going; nothing satisfies me and I am restless. This is the day I want to lie down and die and count my visitors while floating from above. This is the day life is too boring; today I can't concentrate, I can't read; on this day I will put some bubbles in a bath and try TV.*

*My husband is on one couch and I sit with my little dog on the other and while I pet her, I am comforted in a way that I will never be comforted again. These are the days when my imagination considers prohibited substances. I am relieved if only for a moment and I have peace and I forget. I have no idea why I have these desires; perhaps they are historically based.*

*Drugs, death, thoughts in my head, dangerous sporadic gnawing haunting desires that I have not entertained so severely for decades. Stop, please stop, but they, like my parents, never listen. This is my plea from one sector to another but my thoughts defy me. They are all too weird; they are not my conscious idea; they are ideas spontaneously uninvited.*

*There are days when I don't really give a damn; days when it's all too much, days when it's all too dark, days when it's all too sad, days when it's all too slow. Perhaps it is because life's timing is not my own. I know I need rest. I hope tonight will bring me rest; I pray tonight will bring them rest. I didn't want to leave them. God, my poor mom, ahh, my poor mom.*

*When I wake up in the morning it is the same until I go back to them. There is heaviness in the air and I'm not prepared very well for today. The oxygen machine is running at full throttle and I stop the nurse on her way out to get the report. "Same, Cindy; everything is the same." Her expression kills me. I find my mother and realize her capacity for stress must be getting close to full. I dare not look at her today.*

My guilt took over while driving to see them today. I know for certain that while I tossed and turned in my bed, my mother barely made it to hers. She reports a bad night and now I feel like shit for being so judgmental the day before. I am her scapegoat and she is mine. God, I hate guilt. I hate to judge others and be so critical. I hate that shit. I hate flaring tempers and rage. While I'm here I'd better rectify my failings as I search for my coping skills and put them into play.

I easily slip into anxiousness and I am filled with sorrow when I'm here. God, this hurts; it's so painful. I hope Dad isn't suffering mentally through this; I wonder if the mind shuts down. I hope so. I'm going to ask him if he's all right later. It is true that most of the day is spent in turmoil, while I am giving support, assistance, making Jell-O, washing bathroom walls, doing what needs to be done. My mother is cleaning and vacuuming and performing every task that is physically possible. I am so fucking helpless here, helpless to what matters. I am prepared to leave now so I'll pray like I do, for another tomorrow, even though I have no idea what tomorrow will bring.

I have given my kisses and words of encouragement and hate like hell to leave and offered to stay again tonight to no avail. Once in my car it is the same routine; I drive down their long driveway and crank up the radio but there is no radio loud enough to drown out my body's sensations and my mind's automatic thoughts.

I drive home winded, fast, and it's worse than before. Another day spent with them and I am filled with this sticky gloom that has attached itself to every living part of me. My fear of loss is rising inside me. Perhaps this is panic; yes, that's what it is, panic. I feel this way and then I have this overall unwell feeling that I can't put my finger on. I just feel sick and I can't eat and I feel so ugly. I'm so fucking ugly. When I am home I am ugly. When at the grocery store…

"Don't drive in front of me! I warn you, I will hunt you down and give you hell!" My disposition is critical; I am angry and easily agitated. I am so critical. I want to throw things, smash things, smash everything in my path, and walk away from the mess. Smash and walk away…

## Life Is Like a Line

*I have a new enterprise idea. I am full of fantastic inventions but this one is right up my alley. A small store, nothing too fancy, walls lined with a metal of some sort. Now add hundreds of dishes to the mix, white thin dishes, all of this in exchange for dollars, and the idea is that you can smash dishes one at a time, on any wall, anyway you like.*

*With this activity you get a full face mask, gloves, and a body vest similar to the one the dental technicians lay on you when they take a molar x-ray. Smash and run, oh God. In reality I can see my behavior and I can hear what I'm thinking and it doesn't seem healthy but I just don't know what to do with it. I am sure this too will pass. This is a crisis of major magnitude. Ah, back to my thoughts.*

*They are coming to me too often and without conscious effort. They are inconceivable thoughts, constant and invasive, and they feel right at the time. They concern something I have the option of doing. Actually, everyone has this option but some are more aware of it than others.*

*Some think about it and some don't; this is a decision for three, for me, myself, and I.*

*I analyze these thoughts. I pick them apart. I dissect them. Each thought has a different scenario ready, waiting, unknowing and knowing all of me. My thoughts are chilling, graphic details of my seemingly worthwhile demise.*

*This has always been my deadly secret. I have thought about it more times than I will ever remember, but no one will ever hear me speak of it or the possibility of its success. This is my fucking daily assault, my unkind desire. And to date this has been my most successful failure because I have not given it a worthwhile try.*

*I can never express fully the reasons for my thoughts and it would be harsh to blame this on my parents' fragile condition. Nevertheless, my heart is heavy and my state of mind feels delicate and our loss is close. It feels like it's all too much and I fear that I too may fall and I wish I would. Negative thoughts fill me; my mind is relentless; I am consumed with panic.*

*These feelings are unusual for me because I have never been shy of a fight, but I am ever so aware that illness, death, is a fight I can't win. Often I am kidding myself. "You'll go when I tell you it's time" is a joke*

*about the powerlessness over death, but I am an asshole and if my driving*
*is any reflection of my mood, get the hell out of my way; I'm on the brink*
*of a catastrophe.*

*I tried "lovemaking" today; it was senseless. I was cold and detached*
*still, cold and detached still.*

Of all the years we were together, this was the most difficult time and the most intense time and the most precious time. It was evident that my father was withering away and nothing I could do prepared me for this conclusion.

My mind was filled with impossible tasks and my duties seemed endless and more difficult to accomplish. Many of the decisions brought discomfort to him, which brought heartache to me. Each turning point was a temporary victory until he took a turn for the worse. Every day I mentally dressed for battle. I couldn't please my mother, like that was a shocker, and my father needed hospitalization.

There were problems with the hospital. My mother hated hospitals. She didn't like this, there were problems with that, the floor was dirty, he didn't have fresh water, the nurse wasn't nice to her, the roommate was noisy, too many visitors, blah blah blah.

The water in his lungs needed to be aspirated and it was gruesome and painful and we felt each draw of the syringe. Confrontations, daily questions. Who was doing what when, each new procedure, all the hospitals seemed the same, no lunch for my mother, grounds for my immediate verbal scolding.

It is no secret that my mother cannot handle these types of situations and panic is her first line of defense, especially on the medical playing field. As the attention was directed to her, we watched him grow weaker and weaker and he wanted no more tries and no more cures. With the possibility of his departure, I felt blank and engulfed with worry.

More decisions to be made and I questioned and fought and carried his sword and did what my mother couldn't do. The drive-through or pizza took precedence over home-cooked meals, alternating with days of starvation. I buried the emotion and any physical signs that might show I was in so much pain.

## Life Is Like a Line

I had apprehensive feelings and mental strain but I really didn't realize to what degree at the time. My adrenaline kept me ready for what was necessary. I found myself pacing and I was bold and I felt fearless but confrontational; I had the testosterone way of thinking: get the job done.

But I had problems at home due to my stress and my behavior. I was cold and detached. *"Hold me in your arms against your chest but I cannot hold you back."* Don't ask me to hold you back and don't feel bad when I can't.

I don't think I have ever been tougher on my husband and he didn't deserve my wrath. I just didn't know how to swap my battle gear for a silk bra and panties. I am truly the nicest hard ass you ever met, but I needed to be tough. The demand on my body was great; I popped stomach pills, something for my headache, and the mighty minty liquid to soften the daily blow. I was really screwed up and I knew it.

> *Back the next day and he is right where I left him and she is still cleaning, same as the day before, so I sit with him, reassure him, entertain him, and he strains to tell me things, details about things I must know, and with my funny side I try to lighten his load.*
>
> *He is too ill now to talk about his customers or politics or the automotive industry or any of the subjects that gave him joy but he looks at me, he watches me, he loves me, and my heart is breaking and I force myself to have control of my conduct.*
>
> *I am here as they need me and I am here as I need them. This is not pleasant, this is sickening, this is really unbelievable. Watching a loved one die is just terribly wrong.*
>
> *One step forward and fall to your knees. Today I am beaten up, aggravated, and feel unjustly wronged. I am living the lawyer's truth and it weighs on me and I want to scream at the top of my lungs. Things have changed. We were at bad; now we're at worse. I feel strange and it's not just physiological and I'm worried that I am so worried. I am grinding-my-goddamned-teeth worried and I barely sleep and I have anxiety.*
>
> *I know anxiety; I've lived with it and I am filled with it. My father is a skeleton and I am certain that the end is near. He is suffering so. My nonparticipatory sibling lives in New Jersey and is devoid of any appreciation of*

*the situation and the mere presence of my sister has created such an uncomfortable environment that it is difficult to be in the house together.*

*My mother is someone who is speeding naturally on her own adrenaline and I wonder how much is left. Panic-stricken, obsessive-compulsive, underfed, sleep-deprived, filled with terror, and coping with the help of her pills.*

*His body does not bear a resemblance to our father. There is no "Type A" left. He has lost his muscle mass. His legs cannot hold up his frail body, but he will still attempt to ease your pain and give you comfort. The shell that surrounds him has been altered and his soul is prepared to be undressed.*

*My husband and I stop over for a visit. It is Sunday after church and we want to surprise them, make them breakfast, bring fresh faces, new stories, a few giggles to forget about his health. We ring the bell but they do not answer so I use my key. Once inside, I yell to them, looking for a response, but there is silence and then commotion.*

*Running to the back of the house, we find them. He is in the bathroom, face up on the floor, and she is standing over him. He is unable to move; he is just looking up. She tells us he wouldn't use his walker and he fell.*

*My mother, bless her heart, panic-stricken, unable to help him up from the floor, was too upset to leave him to call us for help. When my dad saw my husband, tears welled up in his eyes and I began to fall apart. "Fall apart" meant that I wanted to scream at the top of my lungs and throw up soon after and then smash everything in sight and smash some more.*

*So many questions come to mind…How will we live without him? He is the girls' "Grampie" and my confidant. My Saturday dad, he listens to my mumbling; he's the family glue, our positive mental attitude man. This man is a man of strength, of kindness to his children and grandchildren. He would have been married almost sixty years and now he is lying on this floor, this goddamn bathroom floor.*

*All I want to do is throw up. My insides are shaking and I'm thinking bad thoughts, really bad thoughts. No one should know this but my husband sees; he is looking into my eyes and this time he knows. I have to handle this; I can keep my head up and be strong. I'm the one in charge and I'm the one in fucking charge. I want to scream out, "I don't want to be strong, Dad," not this time, please not this time.*

*I want to fall apart but I don't know how. Does that make sense?*

*My husband carries him to his bed and we visit for a while and then we leave them to rest. I just can't turn off my thoughts so we go home so I can pretend. Pretend that none of this is happening.*

# CHAPTER 11

# *That Sixth Sense*

I didn't know how to respond to the feeling. In fact, I rolled my eyes most of the time when someone described it, but it's an occurrence that happens to some in our family. My father and I talked about it; I suppose you might call it intuition or premonition. It was well known that my father and his mother had hunches, that they were tuned into unspoken feelings. As kids we were always shocked when Dad instinctively knew certain things.

There have been occasions when I have gotten the message or felt that tug called forewarning. My father's mother was a devout Greek Orthodox Christian and she liked to read tea leaves. She also had a special awareness of the moon and earthly cycles. She believed in the mysteries of the universe, she had a sense of the tides, and she was ahead of her time. She was not a witch or a seductress nor did she believe in witchcraft; she was just my grandma: drop a fork and if it

## Life Is Like a Line

points to the door, you're going to have company. This was a grandmother who lived with other family members so consequently we seldom saw her.

I'm not sure how many generations of my family have learned to follow their instincts, but I haven't learned to rely on them yet. Although there have been many times when I have felt that nudge, the unrevealed coaxing has not been scientific enough. And I am often compelled to ask, is it knowledge or nothingness, wakefulness or unconsciousness?

*Given a split second to make my assessment between premonition or imagination, I am torn but must decide. Is this some heavenly pull for deeper awareness? I am happy today, full of enthusiasm, but I have this foreboding voice in my head right now, at this exact precise moment.*

*Is this my intuitive sixth sense here to provide me insight or show me ESP? Instinct or inspiration? I am aware of a particular urge and I must make choices. With this process happening quickly, I must choose. I understand the thought completely and I am alert and all my senses are involved, but I am unsure, unsure of how to respond to the feeling.*

*I question the reliability of the source. Is it intuition or imagination or my mind playing tricks on me or paranoia? My body is involved and it is happening too fast. In a nanosecond, my silent voice is directing me. It's all in my mind. Overwhelmed with thought, I am thinking. I have always had this unseen connection. Do I listen? Do I follow? Do I go the way of my second sight or do I rebuff the impulse?*

*This time, I rebuff; I do not submit to the feeling. I give no credence to this impulse, initially certain that my hunch is my imagination and nothing more.*

*Now in doubt, I am worried and unsure and in fear. Thankfully the pull subsides and my inner voice is hushed, the thought replaced by other thoughts, but deeply I wonder: premonition or imagination? It is in hindsight that the question and the answer become clear. In retrospect, I am sick in the knowing.*

*There is no expressway traffic this morning so I am certain it will be smooth sailing all the way. God…it's such a beautiful day, sunny and mild; it's a perfect spring day. I am great today; the world is heaven today. Right after class I will go grocery shopping for Mom and then I am free. I'll talk* with Dad, do what needs to be done, fix something or whatever, and head for home.

Oh, stop; STOP! What am I thinking? "Good thoughts instead of bad." That's what Dad would say so stop thinking these thoughts. Okay, turn it off, death thoughts are not healthy. Why don't I listen to myself? Why do I revert to these depressing thoughts? Why do they take me over? Why am I panicking?

I can't stop thinking about death, him, I hear it over the radio, loud and louder still. He seems so close to the end; he just can't fake it anymore. Honest to God, he must have cancer. I told them he has cancer. You can almost read it in his face and he won't let me help him because his ember is burning out.

Geez, better thoughts, you jackass. Okay, I wonder how Mom is today; she looks like she could go to pieces any minute. If it is her intention to care for him alone until the end, she is going to kill herself. She has some resentment already because of all the work. She is exhausted and showing it. If her goal is to care for him twenty-four hours a day, alone, always on the ready, day in and day out without a break, this martyrdom will do her in.

At least I can walk away, at least I can go home, I can have some distance, I can take a break, I can scream into a pillow and eat myself into fucking oblivion. Ice cream…gotta buy ice cream. She can never walk away. Seeing him this way is bad.

My father, forty-eight years of loving him, relying on him, being so like him, knowing him, we hung out and had great times, and he was there for the girls when we needed him. Now he's leaving us behind. It's unfair and will be hell. I am concerned and worried and nervous and restless and scared and I don't know what will happen to Mom.

Today I must drive my car right into the river, yep, drive my car into the fucking river, drive my car into the fucking river, fucking fucking river. Then who will be there for them and duh, I'm afraid of drowning. Shit, that will be my punishment, fucking drowning. Naw, I'm in the garage, radio loud, my running car, and my little dog.

Why do I think this crap all the time, God? I know he is at the end. Dear God, he is at the fucking end.

## Life Is Like a Line

*I don't mean to jump down her throat but she has such bitterness with him; she uses that tone, that same I'm-still-a-kid-listening-to-them tone, and she is so easily annoyed. I've got to stop dwelling on this. I will pray more, pray for the whole family, pray for my siblings who are estranged, pray for forgiveness, pray for strength.*

*I also have to stop swearing. I can thank my sister for that. Oh, the fun we had, drinking, dancing, men, and swearing. God, that was fun. But now our relationship is history and she hates me and the lack of affection we feel for each other is disgraceful. What the hell am I thinking? No more thinking about loss, ahh, father, sister, brother. God, what a mess.*

*Just five miles from the usual exit; that means only twenty minutes further to the college. Oh geez, what now? What the hell is this? I think I should exit at our exit. I have this strong desire to take our exit and go home. Why do I feel like this? I'm not supposed to go home but I'm unsure now; maybe I should. Maybe this is a premonition or mental telepathy or something but it feels like panic. My feelings make me panic. No, something is drawing me home. If this is being one with the universe, I don't know what to do.*

*Shit, should I go towards home? It's a force, a very strong force; I feel apprehension that I should go home, get off the exit NOW.*

*Fuck, I went straight. Well, I'm not getting off. I am acting crazy. This is stupid. I'm thinking like a crazy person. Every time I think I have a premonition, it isn't anything. Okay, I passed the exit and the world didn't end. Oh shit, maybe I should have gotten off. I didn't listen this time. I have a sinking feeling and if this is my inner voice and if that was for real then I am screwed. Now I am worrying big time. Just keep going and stop this; nothing is happening.*

*I'm finally at school for this damn class but some idiot locked the door from the inside and I really don't feel like waiting. But then they hear me knocking and at the same time my cell phone starts ringing. What the hell is going on? I look at the number and my heart drops. It's difficult to catch my breath.*

*"Hi, Mom. What? What do you mean? You have to call 911? What about Dad? Calm down for a minute; I can't understand you. Calm down.*

*Call 911 now. You have to hang up; do you understand? I know. I under-stand; it's not your fault. I will call Ron; he will get there quickly. Don't worry, but you have to hang up RIGHT NOW and call 911. Okay, I'll call too; we'll both call. Do you understand what you need to do, Mom? Are you listening, Mom? Hang up and we'll both call. I'm on my way."*

*"911, yes, oh my God, I have an emergency, I need an ambulance. Someone just called in? Thank God. That was my mother; she did it. Oh God, thank you. Okay, thanks, please hurry."*

*My father called me last night...He told me if he never sees me again that he loves me very much. I told him that nothing would happen and that I would bring him Chinese for lunch the next day. Goddamnit, I fucked up. I fucking fucked up. God!*

There was no room for panic; I was beginning to go into troubleshooter mode, my usual self, but I could feel my panic grow in spite of rationale and all of my fear that the worst was yet to come. Unlike the doom that drags upon me, the panic kept me edgy, which weirdly enough seemed like the better alternative. I had to have the appearance of positivism. I had to be calm, but I heard it in her words, I heard the tone of her voice, her fear, her terror; she made a guilty plea for his life. My heart was pounding, pounding in my chest, edging up my throat and gagging me.

Pharmaceuticals kept him alive and then they stuck in his throat; what terrible irony. My guilt surrounded me. I should have gone home; why didn't I listen?

*Damn it, I should have listened to that fucking voice. The exit, the fucking exit. The goddamn fucking exit. I am such an asshole. I am freaking out, just fucking freaking out. Where did I park? Five minutes ago and I can't remember where I parked the damn car. My cell phone, here it is. "Ron, something bad has happened. It's my dad; you've got to get over there fast."*

*I can't get there fast enough and I want to run every traffic light, pass in every zone, and beat the mostly parallel train. Thank God traffic is light. My heart is pounding and I am ill, I have the dry heaves, I am having an anxiety attack. I am stressed from my head to the very smallest cell in my body and I have this tight feeling in my throat. Now I want to throw up; it is my trademark.*

*Why does my throat get so tight? What am I thinking? Stop it, stop thinking; this is full-blown panic; I am just panicking. Calm down, just be calm. What is happening now; what happened? What will I find when I get there? Please, dear God, help him. This can't be happening. I should have been there; why the fuck wasn't I there? Maybe I could have done something if I had listened to that fucking inner voice.*

*Dear God, please don't take him, please help him, let me see him, please. Dear God, please. Now I'm pushing the speed limit and each moment is getting more dangerous. Why are there so many old people out in the morning? GET OUT OF MY WAY. Okay, look for cops; I don't need to get stopped.*

*As I move from lane to lane my distance is becoming shorter and shorter and I am afraid...I am here.*

*Oh God, no place to park and they are beginning to disperse their emergency vehicles and the ambulance is moving. It must be going across the street to the hospital and my husband is here as he promised and he's waving me in. Thank God for my wonderful wonderful husband, my rock through it all, my very kind rock. I'm running to him and I can see the worry on his face. He is trying to be affectionate and he is trying to explain and I don't want affection; I want information. Please don't hug me now; I need to be free; please just tell me. As he gives me what I ask for, I struggle to grasp it all.*

*The truth is that my dad recognized him and my husband spoke with him but after that moment we never heard another word from his lips. The alarm inside my body began to go off louder and louder and louder. My father was still alive, alive, he recognized my husband; dear God, he was alive and once the medics prepped him for the trip to the hospital they went quickly; fortunately the hospital is nearby so no time was lost.*

*"Tell me again, please. And they started to do their thing...what? They hooked him up; they laid him down on the living room floor and put him on the...I didn't hear you. He was still alive, right? I didn't get it; he was alive, right?"*

*I'm panicky and feel flushed and I can't concentrate. "Please tell me
again. I'm sorry; please tell me again." My mind is filled with doom; my
thoughts too loud to hear him.*

I had tried to prepare myself for this day. I had envisioned it for as long
as I could remember. Even as a child I imagined how it would go and I
outlined a scenario, thinking it would go my way. But it was not at all like
I had imagined. Everything seemed so far away, in another dimension and
out of my control.

*I go home to get my mother and she is waiting for me inside the house
and she is all alone. She tells me she is to blame and I can tell that she is
mildly hysterical and in shock. She has been the lion of late and her cub is
in danger and she continues to pace in worry even after I arrive. As we make
our way to the hospital, she needs reassurance from me and I try with all I
have to comfort her and manage to drive down my own uncertainty.*

*I am anxious and I don't deny it and I am apprehensive and probably
I am irritable too. There is grave concern today and when I feel my blood
rushing in this way I know I am somewhere I don't want to be, but my mind
is razor-sharp and my senses are kicked up a few pegs and I have horrid,
unthinkable thoughts.*

*We are born and we die and today I fear that I have come to the end of
a life, the life of my father. And so here we sit in the bullpen of survivors just
outside the doors to my misery in the waiting room where all the smells and
sobs drift through the air, and while we wait we share our pain without even
an introduction. I am getting anxious and I'm going to ask; wait here.*

*They call his name. Oh God, be careful what you wish for. We three
get up, my mother, my husband, and I, and head for the swinging doors
that will take us to him. I have dreaded facing this day; oh God, please
help him. We are here and my mother goes in first and I am like a child,
worried, worried sick.*

*Courage. All I can do is look at him and my eyes never leave his face.
He does not have any intravenous fortification; there are no heart moni-
tors or blood pressure cuffs. Only a face mask filled with oxygen. For the
moment, as I stare, I feel detached from him and my body feels weak and*

## Life Is Like a Line

*ill all over. While I avert my tears, I yearn for collapse for it will take me out of my misery.*

*I keep watching him and two nurses stand almost in the corner and watch us; they don't leave the room. I long to rewind the day and erase this awful conclusion but this is not within my power and he is nearing his destiny on the road to paradise. It is so evident by the way his solemn features are exposed and by his breaths and body of lifelessness. We are allowed into his room and will watch his spirit leave us for the other and my mother is hovering over him, nervous, waiting, begging, sobbing, and she makes no room for me. While she begs for his life, I consume the scene as it consumes me.*

*Yet I understand her; they shared all of life's emotions, bitterly, sweetly, in nearly sixty years' time till death do us part. They struggled through it. They had the stick-to-it-ness we lack today. Even though she wanted to and he wanted to, they never walked away. So we are here, and with a soft entrance the ER doctor introduces himself and tells us they are evaluating my father and he will give us our options very soon. It is even clearer that the result will be extremely soon; he has the look and the sounds and I know the time is near and I am stunned at the sight.*

*I keep looking at him and looking away and looking again. There are still the nurses who never leave the room and they watch and chart and it is rather unnerving.*

*Dad, this is Cindy; I am here with you now. There is no need to suffer anymore. You can let go now, Dad. You are a wonderful father...Dad, I will miss you so. I love you.*

I never got close enough to speak to him; sympathetically, I gave her the floor. It was not in the cards for me. I shed no tears, but I have felt the crush and I have wept inside a million times and it has changed me. It was the way it was and it was done. I recognize that I will never have a chance like that, ever again, to speak with my father. I will never forget the lesson: seize the day, say it when you can, tell them with the utmost of urgency, never wait.

I believe I will obsess over it forever, obsess over those last breaths together, forever.

*My husband is a wonderful man. He is with us, he is my anchor, but he cannot stop me from drifting into abandonment. He looks at me with loving eyes and I get his message but I can't respond to him. I am cold and detached; I have no room for loving eyes today. Please don't make my heart reply. Oh…God, this is an agony I have never known, deep and piercing and everlasting. I cannot catch my breath or slow it down. I am breathing fast.*

*"Really, I'm fine, really." I look at him and look away, look and look away, and my mother is begging my father to stay. The nurses offer me a chair; I just can't sit but thank you very much for the offer. I am pacing. Ill myself, all that I am is a physical dizziness. The nurses are very kind; I am hot and sweaty and I want to make it stop.*

*Out of the shadows my mother remembers her prodigal son and there is not a moment to waste. But I am here; look at me. Do you see me as your child? I will always be here for you, but I cannot respect this request. Please don't ask me to leave!*

*She doesn't see me for who I am but for who I am to her. My father and I are pals; please don't make me go.*

*Oh God, here comes the doctor.*

*"Mrs.…This is the time when you have to make some decisions…"*

*I stand closer to her while he speaks.*

*"Your husband has had a massive…*

*I watch his lips move and with each word it gets worse. Each word seems distorted. I am not in my body. I am not interested in his display of kindness. I want the details. What happened with the pills?*

*"The reason he couldn't swallow his pills was…"*

*There it is. I finally have the information; now what in the hell do I do with it? The doctor is trying to let us down gently. Codes and living wills and end-of-life decisions are not exactly what I'm looking for but it's all we get.*

*I sign all the papers and concur with my mother and he is set free. No life support per their agreement; he would never be the same anyway. My mother speaks. Now that it's done, it's time for me to be her messenger. I am dismissed.*

## Life Is Like a Line

*"Go home, get the telephone book, tell your brother about Dad, and tell him I'll call him later."*

*Fuck, why do I have to do this now? I shouldn't be forced to do this right now. I don't want to go; she can't make me go. I'm not leaving this ER. I'm going, damn it, I have to; it's the right thing to do. I have to go for her and for him.*

*I am so conflicted. Oh God, it is out of respect purely because it's not rational. I have to call him, her prodigal son. I'm going back to the place where death began today, to that miserable disturbing house.*

*"Honey, let me go. You stay here." My husband is so predictable, but I ask him to stay with my mother. Besides, I need some air so I can catch my breath, maybe throw up, maybe with any luck get obliterated by a fucking truck.*

*Oh God, why am I leaving? What am I doing? I hurry, I look for her yellow telephone book. I am so damned mad at that woman for making me do this. My hands are trembling. God, this is so weird. I push the chairs back into place and turn off the lights.*

I made the call, he started freaking out, and I thought he was putting it on just a little too heavy, but when his secretary called me right back to confirm what I had said, I felt bad because I had mistrusted his emotions. She made me promise to call him back and then I rushed like hell back to the ER. I was so afraid he would leave us before my return.

Back in the hospital, the emergency area was full of injuries and illnesses and even though each room was occupied, I could hear only her, weeping and begging from inside my father's room. There were no other voices to discern, no other sounds to be heard, nothing but her wailing and the sensation of my pounding heart to be observed. Actually, I noticed my throat, my emotionally tight throat.

*Ron, bless his heart, was waiting for my return, and just as he stepped out of the room to look for me I came upon him. Because of his expression I thought for sure I had returned too late but Dad was still alive, rails up, grayer in color, struggling with each breath. The two nurses remain and I haven't asked why. They stay with us always, in this death trap, and they check his vitals, and the ER doctor keeps coming into the room to evaluate, then one more no-turning-back signature and the oxygen is turned down.*

*There is nothing left of my nerves and probably nothing left of my mother's either. It is clear that he is moving slowly to the side where no ill health lives. "Damn…" The word just came out. "Don't you think I should call Sharon?"*

*That was not what my mother wanted to hear. She had no problem injecting an undertone of bitterness at my suggestion, even in front of the nurses, but I didn't give a damn about her personal animosity or my sister's recent harshness to me. I would have preferred not to call her, I'm no fucking hero, but this was a necessary action no matter the tone of our relationship. There is a connection even by virtue of our hostility. Five in our family, and all five share one thing, the propensity for hostility.*

Thankfully the attending nurse could read between the lines and offered me a private room used by families in situations such as ours. I remembered to dial nine first.

*"Sharon," I start to say as my voice begins to break up. She sounds concerned and my voice is now quivering and I am trying like hell to suppress my hysteria. Just hearing her voice makes me feel better but I start speaking fast. "You have to come now right now; Dad is bad, really bad." With that, my hyperventilation begins and I'm seeing those dots and hearing the buzz.*

*Good God, I said it. I called her and admitted the worst is about to happen and that means we are fucked. He is leaving us and we are all fucked. "Mom gave him some pills; maybe he tried to take too many but the doctor doesn't think so. He started to choke…They just told us he had a massive heart attack at the same time." I can't say this; both my voice and my body are trembling. I can barely say another word but this is my job; this is what I've been groomed to do.*

*There is an unfamiliar fear in her voice. She will leave now, but it's going to take over an hour.*

*I don't know if she'll make it. If he'll make it. "Okay, but hurry."*

## Life Is Like a Line

In his name, I did the honorable thing. I made the call to Daddy's little girl, his first-born daughter, the one with the adorable ringlets, and it was behind me.

The next call was to the Catholic Church. Then I quickly walked back down the hall and headed for his room and it was as surreal as any tweaking of consciousness has ever been. Back inside his room, I could plainly see that the man lying in that antiseptic bed was not the man I'd known. This was either the worst dream I'd ever had or a science fiction movie I hated.

With time moving as quietly and gently as his death, the ER physician had come into the room again and was examining him. My mother, at his side, was still begging my father not to leave her. My shaking body was sensitive and I could feel blood rushing through every blood vessel, every vein, every artery, every capillary. I would have heard it moving within me had it not been for the pounding of my heart, which masked everything but my worrying mind.

*They offer me a chair. I must be pale; breathe for God's sake. I feel weak and confused and I return to the foot of his bed. I am pacing and quietly praying. I am on edge and feeling helpless. Helplessness is another tragedy against the soul; it desires deeply what you are unable to do. Helplessness is watching his lack of movement and his slow labored breaths. Helplessness is having no idea what to do except fight the emotions and keep up the front.*

*For in this hour, he is almost gone. I hate myself for not speaking to him as he lies there preparing for his journey. I should speak to him, go there, tell him now how much he is loved one last time, but I have given the floor to my mother to weep and to wail and I am afraid. I am making a fucking mistake and I will take it to my death.*

*Softer and softer life. Seconds closer, I am feeling severe panic, holding onto it so it won't be seen. His color has given way; all has stopped. He is gone. I have been looking at him for a long time, staring, just staring. I am frozen, helpless, paralyzed, emotionless…I am consoling her. Consoling her like the little Cindy I have always been, the little fucking Cindy.*

*The nurses in attendance verify what we already know and my mother, now frantic, is holding him. The priest has come and is praying over his still warm body and I'm watching him and staring at my father in shock. Prayers are quickly said, many prayers, and we thank Father for coming.*

*The curtain is opening and my sister, still breathless, is told. There is nothing on her face but shock as she races to his side. She has little or no interest in me, which doesn't bother me.*

We called the girls and gave them our awful news and walked back into that very sad room. I was dazed. Once there I wanted never to leave. My sister reprimanded my mother because of her constant wailing and it began. Our family storm.

*Oh God…That's our baby daughter in the hall. Ron meets her but she hasn't come in. Arm in arm with her fiancée, she waits but I can't go to her. I am frozen in place. As the drape is opened, she is full of grief and her weakness brings her to the floor, where she leans on a chair until escorted down the hall. But her strength brings her back; she sees him and she weeps at his side. She is but a child, my child and his grandchild, and her heart speaks through her eyes. There is nothing left to be said.*

*The loss of my beloved father leaves me brokenhearted and with so much to do there is no time for my personal lament. Our first responsibility is to meet with the funeral director to discuss the "desires of the family." While I'm sitting and he is speaking of the "departed," I'm thinking, "Who in the hell died?"*

*I can barely listen to his soft voice; I keep wondering if my father is hovering over the table above us. Going through the motions, catching every other word, we parade like soldiers, single file, to the casket room. Oak or pine, brown or blue, pick out the music, bring his suit and tie, how about the cemetery, cremation or not, call the priest.*

*Oh God, when will he stop talking? Funeral director, how can you love this job? You can do me at my time, but this is too tough; for God's sake, when will you be done?*

*I know, I know, we're making important decisions at precisely the wrong time…It is all too soon. Finally we walk in silence up the stairs and select and select until it is finished and with strength and perseverance through my daze I am able to finish this task.*

## Life Is Like a Line

*I am numb, my mother has no idea what is happening, and my sister is in a self-imposed state of estrangement. My brother hasn't arrived yet, and thank God Ron, my strength, is at my side in his caring way. The edginess of the women is palpable. We should have gathered and hugged and forgiven but we are not capable of this. It is much better to hold grudges while time passes us by.*

*It is difficult to see my sister and be so close and not have our old relationship back, but we have had too much anger and too many feelings for too long. We could have patched things up, put aside our differences out of respect for my father, but there is not enough affinity. Once my father left us, so went our link.*

My brother arrived a day before the funeral but I didn't visit him at my mother's. There was no love lost for me, not at this time. When I laid eyes on him as he walked into the funeral home, my mother on his arm, I felt it should have been me walking her in. I could feel my resentment with each step they took. After all I had done for that woman, I had been cast aside. Not a surprise. War baby, number one son…of a bitch.

I tried not to show my irritability but it was difficult; it's a shortcoming of mine. It is a pain to hide feelings felt deeply and to behave in another way. My anger for my brother really didn't surface to this degree until my parents moved to the river house and I began to see them more often and hear of his adventures, which reinforced the fact that my brother was not to be trusted. He had a lifelong agenda and it was clear my mother would never grasp it.

There have been hundreds of days when I have wondered what I did over the years to deserve her wrath and to feel so much pain. I didn't want to be a whiner or a complainer; you know, that "poor me" bullshit again. It's just that too many times and for too many years I was made to feel replaceable, but I overlooked it, thinking it was no big deal.

All my defensive behavior returned with the prodigal son. This reunion of our twenty-year separation received no sibling embrace, no handshake, no indication at all that we were related. I said "Hi" and he forced a smile and that was it.

Yet standing near our father's casket, I could see that he was just a mere image of the brother I'd once known and I was torn over our estrangement. There was so much more we could have been if the circumstances had been different. He was a detriment to our family, and as I looked at him, I wondered what it was that made him so desirable to our mother over my sister and me. I wanted to know, what did I lack? Whenever he was near, all you could see was Mom and her little boy.

> *There's no denying this is my brother, but his lack of hair makes him look different and he's surprisingly unkempt, which makes me wonder about him. Despite my mother's comments to the contrary, he looks unwell. The years have not been generous to him. If the bluish yellow tinge of color under his eyes and his crooked smile are not enough, I can't help but notice the very poor condition of his teeth and the overall funkiness of his appearance. In fact, he came to the funeral home dressed along the lines of shabby chic. His clothes are wrinkled and fit poorly, his shirt is not ironed, and I have this feeling that all is not that well with the earth.*
>
> *Needless to say, the days of him being shuttled to work in high-flying helicopters from New Jersey to New York City have ended. He looks helpless, but I know he isn't harmless.*

I felt a nagging mistrust that I didn't want to confront. As I saw him and reflected back through the looking glass, my feelings of anger and frustration blended with the feeling that, thanks in great part to him, we were cheated out of a family.

We were gathered together now for one purpose and one alone. We would never have been in the same room at the same time otherwise. Suffering in our own way, the tone was heavy with tension and there was no fondness among those who were left to carry on. My brother did not need to say anything to make me mad. In fewer than twenty-four hours, he was beginning to invade and infiltrate.

As if he read my mind, he smiled. He was wearing Dad's favorite necktie and diamond tie tac, raided from Dad's closet in Dad's bedroom located in Dad's home on the river. The tie should have stayed memorialized there. I felt it was insincere of my brother to wear it, given their lifelong estranged relationship. It was my mother's doing. It was a bond of the twisted pair. Mom and her little boy, hurray! Unbeknownst to him, he was walking on the edge of my temper. I was hot while my father lay barely cold.

*It is easy for something like this to alter my mood. In fact, this is the exact fucking thing to set me off. I am getting hot under the collar, no pun intended, and when I'm hot I can barely keep my mouth shut, but I stand in silence studying and thinking and saying nothing, trying not to be furious.*

*He flew in with two days' notice and he doesn't own one fucking tie? That's precisely what I'm thinking, damn right. I am sure this will activate his first tale of, "Oh, all my ties were stolen while I was blah blah blah," or "My roommates' dog ate them even though they were in a sealed box and the dog...blah blah blah." Lies—just open up his mouth and watch the shit fall out.*

*I sure as hell am not going to be drawn in, and I won't even dignify any of his stupid tales anymore. He's remarkably somber and keeps to himself, which is smart of him, except for the visiting with our daughters. Lucky for him he's behaving.*

*The dreamlike funeral days have gathered my aunts and uncles, friends, and Dad's business acquaintances and the room is warm and friendly. Forty-eight hours in a funeral home and my job is to assist my mother. I am troubleshooting; you could cut me and I would not bleed; none of this is really happening. People come and go and I greet them with my usual flair. My mother, emotionally distraught, is oblivious to most of the visitors but I introduce her just the same.*

*Funeral days, oh God, they're horrid and I feel horrid too. In the past two days we have been surrounded by so much love and kindness, one would think that aloneness could not subsist. But I am living this day through someone else's eyes, in someone else's body. My sister stays in the back of the room while my brother sits right up front with us. I am watching myself go through the motions. I hear my voice, but my responses are impulsive so I must be careful.*

*I am compelled to speak for the sake of keeping up the conversation so that no one is embarrassed by the lull. Make everyone feel comfortable; yup,* do this while you feel the sting of a bloodless sword slash across your throat and into your stomach where no mint chalk can penetrate.

I find myself in someone else's body. Either I am delusional or this is a mechanism to keep me from screaming at the top of my lungs. God, I would like to scream right now. I know for sure that wherever my head is, it's much better than being here. I have never lost a loved one before, at least no one that I have been half this close to, so I have never known the abruptness of losing a life in such a way. But Dad was not just a life, he was a way of life.

I think there are two types of funeral families, the haves and the have nots. The haves are those who say "Alleluia, praise God" as they look adoringly at the sleeping beauty boxed and ready for the dirt. But I am a have not and I am weak. I see my father is not asleep but gone, absolutely inert, dead, unresponsive, motionless, not breathing, lacking spirit, vanished, the once-living soul gone from his body, missing and disappeared, worthy of our search, and search we must.

Christianity tells me he is with the Lord and I rejoice and am comforted in knowing that, but I struggle to suppress the other side of my feelings and I am bruised by his passing. My "Alleluia" is anxiety and my "Praise God" is really "Please send him back" and to rejoice is to be silent with aching separation.

I want to scream the same scream out loud that I find inside. Please let me scream. I don't grieve for him because he is in paradise; I grieve for me because he left without me. And on that day he told me he was going to die, I made light of it and told him I would tell him when it was time to go but he went anyway. Silly fucking me; what an asshole. I don't know shit about life or death; the only thing I know is that I'm in a world torn between both.

And now we face it, the funeral, the last chapter, and I am filled with nervousness and sadness and fear and though my new responsibility should be very similar to the old, it is my mother, a handful needing comfort and care, essential if I am to keep my promise.

I know her well and she knows me. Oh God…here it comes. Panic, breathe, just breathe, sit down, oh God, stand up, walk, head for air. Oh, *they're in the doorway; they're blocking my escape. "Ah, how nice of you to come...They came too; thank you for driving all that way." Walk over there and do what you do; what is her husband's name, ugh, shit, I can't remember. "Yes, he suffered so much, yes, thank you."*

*Small talk. This is what I learned from the master. He does look good for a dead person. Oh shit, I hate it when people say that. Do what Dad expects, okay, brain? Shut the fuck up and for the sake of all that is holy, keep up the charade. Miniature conversations, small talk, devised to break the uncomfortable sense of self; what would they do if I screamed right now? They would honest to God drop dead.*

*I hate that word; it's what my father is and what I have aspired to be too many times. Smile, we're almost through it, talk and be natural; stop shaking, knees; what the hell is going on? Answer stupid questions. Whoever said no question is stupid was stupid. Smile, damn it, see the funeral director, check on the food and the pop, be the hostess and don't look pitiful, be amusing and remember their names; that's important. This is Public Speaking 101 on behalf of Dad, and while undercover, try not to throw up on anyone's shoe.*

Each day visitors filled the funeral home and as the melancholy music played and the sweet fragrance of the flowers wafted through the air, I felt more anxious with nowhere to go. My husband and our daughters were a tremendous comfort, but when you are vacant, nothing can touch that place inside. In the old days, I would have gone to my father's closet and reached up on the shelf, excitedly twisted the Miltown bottle open, and washed one down with some O.J.

It was a partnership that knew me well and settled me and for a last resort a Seconal, the prettiest red capsule of pain relief I have ever known. But my father and mother had no little helpers waiting for me now, so without chemical alteration, my mind stepped in and tweaked itself enough to protect me from my extreme thoughts. Somewhere along the line, I shut out this awful reality; the brain can do just that.

*We are into the last day and I am accustomed to this place but after today I don't want to return. It will remind me that he was here, handsome and youthful and free of his pain. The music is soft again and the flowers don't smell as strongly as yesterday and while I go through the motions, I've got that "putting on the face" down to a science. My quivering self has returned to me and I fear that my nervousness may cause me to say something stupid or offensive to the guests. I want this, our last day, to go perfectly.*

*The girls are here with us and my sister just arrived. She made no eye contact with us as she headed for the casket. I don't know if I'm pissed at her or if I forgive her; still I'd like to kick her in the shins for all this senseless bullshit. I am so conflicted about our recent fallout. I will never hurt her but she mistrusts me, which is probably a reflection of her own aspirations. Our separation is wearisome, distressful, and ill-timed for sure.*

*My mother has just arrived, escorted by my brother. She looks out of it again, foggy; I suppose shock might explain it. It is what keeps us dazed and confused. As my sister moves to the back of the room, my mother is taken to the casket and she is crying. My brother, by her side, is standing over our father and it looks as if he is deep in thought, foggy or buzzed. One by one friends and family begin to file in and small talk begins. What a shame; my father wrote the book on small talk. It is such a twist of fate. All his family and friends are gathered in this place to honor him but he would be honoring us one by one, doing what he so loved to do. Today we are left with the soul-free shell of him that only our memories will fill.*

Among our other aunts and uncles, my father's brother came; he is a Greek Orthodox priest and the pastor of his church. He is very well-known out east and in the circles of the church. My father would have been thrilled to see his brother; ten years had separated their embrace.

*Closer still, the service will commence and then lunch and the time is nearing for me and I struggle to see him in that box. The thought of that lid being lowered slowly down…down…click. I see him there; I am a forty-eight-year-old little girl standing on my tippy toes looking up to see him. I'm hanging on to the side to get a look, feeling the smooth wooden rail under my small fingers, seeing the bright white cushion of his new bed. I am not tall enough to see all of him, just his shoulders and the side of him, but if I could just get a lift, if someone would hold me over him, he might see me back.*

## Life Is Like a Line

> *But there is someone to lift me up, dear God, and now I clearly see him. No longer needing a boost, today I stand as a woman married with children accompanied by my husband, our daughters, future sons-in-law, and our son and his wife. In my lifetime, I've looked up at him and down at him but today I just cherish the years with him.*
>
> *My self wishes not to acknowledge this setting and although I've loved him and hated him and have been mad and adored him, my eyes see what my mind will not. There is no box or vase, headstone or hole in the earth that is my reality. And if this is really happening, hopefully he will hear my thoughts and if he can, then hear me say, "Dad, please get out of there before they close the lid."*

My father was my confidant. A confidant who also rescued and taught and listened and was always just a call away. Never before alone, there is a vacancy in me, a portion of me that is empty, a gaping hole where my spirit may spill. And my mind is put on hold.

> *Oh God, why do I have this condition? There is nowhere to run and I want to run, run where, what is this? What is this sense of self or sense of lack of self? I have again the tightness in the throat and my hands are so cold. I shouldn't worry about the cold, not me. I greet them one more day and with respect and adoration for him there is storytelling and reminiscing and many have reflected upon his decades of passion and enthusiasm for life. He was generous and knew no limits; he gave to the homeless and lived exuberantly and had many shared adventures.*

At the appointed time, his brother "Father" performed the service and his wonderful words were stirring, especially when he spoke of my father's journey from here to paradise. The way he said it was so relieving, so joyful, and so absolute. He praised my father, his brother, and a child of God, and he prayed for his heavenly eternity. I am certain that if my father could have heard this, he would have cried.

And then, without me knowing this was coming, our eldest daughter was introduced by her great-uncle. She stepped up to a podium in front of the casket and gave a moving eulogy. My tears flowed like rain. Her words were a wonderful tribute to her number-one man, "Grampie," whom she loved unconditionally. During her speech, I tried desperately to focus on her. We were so proud of her courage and her strength and her flawless recollection of the relationship and adoration she had for him. My firstborn is a college graduate, all grown up. A public speaker, now speaking to and about her grandfather, she boldly proclaimed her devotion for the first real father she had ever known. I was so moved by her proclamation of affection that I forgot my own grief to realize hers.

Soon the service ended and we said our goodbyes to our family and friends and stayed with Dad a bit longer. My mother, still in shock, went first, arm in arm with my brother. Then we all took turns looking at him and saying prayers and saying goodbye. The girls and their beaus sent him off with their love, and then I said what I should have said in the hospital and I prayed and touched his forehead one more time just to feel him. "I couldn't reach his hand; I'm too short," the little girl would have said, but I touched him for her. I reached in and I touched him for the last time.

We went to the prearranged luncheon and afterwards we returned to the funeral home to select plants and flowers to take home. For me, there was only one flower to take home but he was already gone. Left with only an empty space, I started to think and panic and once I let it begin I couldn't stop it and I panicked and obsessed some more. I might have had more sorrow had I not realized I could have no more, and without advance notice I moved into despair. I despaired and I covered it up again, just like forever.

> *And now the reality begins to set in. "Oh God, my father died; what will my mother do?" I worry about her needs and her safety. I wonder how she will respond to living alone once she is over the shock. There is one thing I do know for sure, that when this is all over I want to sleep for days on end. I want to board a plane to destination nowhere, alone, and never come back, and I want to enjoy one of my old habits a hundred thousand times more. Most importantly, if it is possible, I want to be more numb and then hope to God it will dim just enough to remember and forget and get on with my life, get on with my family, and then and only then I'll be me...if any of me is still worthwhile.*

## Life Is Like a Line

*I understand that if grieving is to be upset or mournful or distressed or saddened or depressed or brokenhearted, I have been all of them. And if only one of them is grieving, then I shall no longer breathe despair.*

Some conflict remained after the funeral, but not from my brother. He returned to his life back east and for the moment that provided calm. My sister on the other hand was still angry and strongly disagreed, but I have insisted on fulfilling my father's request for cremation. Not surprisingly, my mother was stationary and confused.

*Time is of the essence and the funeral director has called and I bear in mind what I was told by my father. She was not there, she would not know, she lived someone else's life, so out of respect and honor it was done. It was not a control issue; it was a matter of fulfilling. So I continue with the paperwork and the sorting and making contacts and filing the legals and authorizing and advising and with a bit of luck all that is required will be done.*

*Whether it is with the lawyer or the accountant or the stockbroker or the government or the insurance company, oh God, there has been no end to the necessary authorizations and proof of signatures, inquiries, red tape, and so on and so on. Familiar with my father's portfolio, it is easy to finish that which is required of us and I shall persevere, but I do this in a rather detached and emotionless way while staying on task.*

*My mother, on the other hand, has lots of emotion and her highs and lows often drive her into irrational thought. Some of what she wants to do is unreasonable and mean-spirited and will hurt a family member unnecessarily. I continue to urge her not to do anything during this time, but she is tough and inflexible and so our debate over a beneficiary issue remains. Obviously, my persuasiveness has no effect on her as she has changed an account from three beneficiaries to two and my sense is that she would change all from three to two if given the opportunity.*

*The problem I have now is that when my mother pushes me too hard, I have a tendency to push back, which I have fought not to do but she is doing just that, pushing me. I am angry when I leave, and while I drive home she leaves a message on my answering machine and once again I am ready for a fight. My mother knows very well that changes in her will are not an option but she is insistent and argumentative and although she still has the power and control of her estate, I will block any further action. I am co-administrator; everything requires two signatures. Think, Mother, think. I've been in enough damn trouble already. All I can do is suggest and pray and take my purple pill and scream in a pillow and swear and drive like a maniac.*

*Even though my sister is still as angry as a bee to a swatter, she will never know, believe, or appreciate how I have protected her from our mother and her cantankerous desire to cut her out of the will. They are ganging up on me. My mother comes at me from one way and my sibling from another. My brother doesn't dare make contact with me but he knows how to get what he wants; he goes direct. They are coming from all angles and it's tough not to crack. There is too much resentment swirling about in our family and the hurt is more than simple annoyance; it is destruction. But today, fuck my sister; she should have been my shelter. We should have had allegiance, but she left me alone in the middle of a war, a defenseless little girl fucked from the start.*

*My mother is trying to settle in as a widow though we never use that term. She has become increasingly irritable and seems to incite the same in me. We have gotten into some heated disagreements over subjects not worth arguing about, but it seems as if she wants to interact with me in this way. I try to hold on while she points and pushes and jabs at me. I am the replication of her former easy mark, now dug into the dirt. There are days when, tongue in cheek, I declare that she hasn't driven me to insanity yet and while that is true, the mere keeping my head above water is a challenging enterprise.*

*I don't deny there have been numerous days when I've slammed my foot down on the gas pedal, hoping for a head-on collision, praying for my death, but the law of averages does not console me in that way. I am certain the collision that comes my way is from my mother.*

Her demands began increasing after my father passed away and redecoration was soon on her mind. I knew she and Dad had talked about buying new furniture and carpeting when he was well. I didn't think the timing was great right now, but she didn't appreciate my two cents' worth. Experience

# Life Is Like a Line

has shown me that her snap judgments have done nothing but cause regret and waste dollars so, rather than cut and run, I continued to hang tough and take my punishment.

We continued to debate, and she got so involved in the confrontation that she forgot the issue at hand, but most issues aren't that serious and overall our relationship is on firm ground.

> Time is sweeping us along and my mother's new independence and confidence fit her well. She seems to be willing and able to care for herself and the house and although she seems ready for this new journey, I am still scared to death when I leave her on her own. She is an eighty-two-year-old woman and although she has been taken care of all her life, she is ready to take over. But I have become the parent; I will never stop worrying. I have been reminded that the reality of her new self has only been folded into the old as her behavior and temperament remain harsh and cutting.
>
> Her comments, thoughtless and unappreciative, push me through my own emotions. And when I remember through my childhood eyes, the adult resolve shields and protects my spirit. My newly found self has realized new limits to my staying power. When my self-protection insists on escape, when I need to run but feel trapped, I am overwhelmed with the same fear I have felt a million times before. Without my father my sense is to "Run from here; run as far and as fast as you can go. What are you waiting for? Go!"
>
> This is my anxiety, and once it starts I overflow with a translucent heaviness. Mentally I feel panic, and while it moves within me, it consumes my mind. It is more than just a sense; it is mentally painful, and like a migraine headache it is just as excruciating. No x-ray machine or MRI scanner will ever detect its image, but it exists. It is confusion, it is fight or flight, it is rapid, and it has my full attention until it leaves me.

The truth is, I made a commitment to my father and there is no escape for me. There never has been. My youthful experiments were simply my way of medicating my feelings. Those trying times I didn't medicate myself, I should have, but all my remedies for my anxiety only temporarily softened the blow of life's poison apple; they could never become a permanent solution. For in the human challenge, the perfect escape does not allow a return to this earthly reality. And in the temporary fix, once reality returns to your psyche, you're back to square one, planning your escape all over again.

*Spring in Michigan is such a beautiful experience if the weather cooperates, so today I'm taking advantage of it, pulling weeds, picking up the fall leaves, and mowing the lawn; 'tis the season. I am reminded of being with my family, of being with my father and working in the yard, of picking up the leaves. I have learned to juggle my time now that the landscape makes more demands of me. I still visit my mother almost every day and fit in the other work as time allows.*

*Our office in the basement gives "home work" a whole new meaning. Our basement is such that you walk directly outside to stand on Mother Earth and if it is the sound of nature you long for, the spring frogs are effervescent with birthing verve. There are many nights when sleep resists me and so I work until the wee hours of the morning, perhaps sleeping three hours, and then do it all over again. I don't really like to be in the basement alone but I have my dog, all six pounds of her, and I turn on all the lights along the way.*

*It's quiet downstairs in the office…God, I love that noise. I can breathe down there. There are no telephones ringing that I wish not to answer, no searching for answers that won't be considered, and no temperament that offends me. There is only me and my thoughts and, shhhh, the silence.*

*Recently I bought a puppet just for kicks and I keep her in the office. I have been a puppeteer ever since my sister's children were young, and once they grew up, my puppet character changed. My girl is a full-bodied, wide-mouthed, blue-haired, blue-jeaned, checkered-bloused, tennis-shoed, rudely-sarcastic-swearing smarty pants driven by mild sexual overtones. She measures about three feet tall from head to toe. Her name is Morph II.*

*The original Morph was named by the manufacturer; she is my old puppet. She came from the Detroit Institute of Arts where our pal works. We met on Christmas morning and she was my alter ego for the first year. She's "Morph" because you can change her facial features by removing them from the fabric one eye, one cheek, one eyebrow at a time or two if you have someone to hold her down.*

## Life Is Like a Line

*Everyone thinks Morph II is short for Morphine, which actually is her full name and not a bad way to go. They tell me that someday I'll have to explain her name to the grandchildren and I say okay, whatever; I'll let the fucking puppet do it.*

*In actuality, the character is a twisted me, it is shock therapy, it is comic injustice, and she mirrors my thoughts right down to verbally knocking someone upside the head.*

*Tonight I have no desire for sleep; I just don't want to try and I have plenty to do. Besides, how many times can one watch a ceiling fan spin in a lifetime? Sleeping seems like such a waste of time. I just can't face it tonight; I just can't.*

*Morphine and I are going visiting via the superhighway with a few stops along the way. We have our victims selected, so on with the show. God forbid the e-mail addresses get mixed up.*

*Tonight my little dog watches me from her bed at my feet. Her little brown eyes speak volumes to me and I am in love with her all over again and I know what she's thinking, "Insane asylum," and I tell her, "Whatever, dog, but if I go, you and the puppet go with me, you little shit." And that's our night, me and the barker and the big mouth, and for some reason I can face another day without driving my car into the river.*

*I'm here at their house and all is going well and she offers me tea and some cookies and we talk and on that day she needs to be rescued and I am very sad for her and my sympathetic heart weeps for her. We have a nice visit and I take care of the bills and some correspondence and after several hours it is time to go. I hate to leave her alone but she insists that I go and I get her message loud and clear. In fact, there is nothing more I can do for her and I need to be home. I am exhausted and hungry and feel the pressure of the tasks ahead and I'm trying to help her without being too obvious. She'll have to get used to being alone after nearly sixty years of marriage, but it's tough. I'm here if she needs me; God knows that is all I can humanly do, be here if she needs me.*

*The loss of my father brings so much heartbreak to our broken family and nothing will change because everything is still surreal. "Goodbye, Mom; make sure you lock the door. I'll see you tomorrow. I love you." And I'm off. I wave goodbye and I'm on the highway. The radio is on, it's Jefferson Airplane, and I turn it louder still. The loud radio and racing tires mean I am upset and the speeding puts me in control, the same control I lost back there, only that control was my heart; I lost the rigidity of my heart.*

I had my pedal to the metal and I couldn't wait to be home and "Get the hell out of my way, you jackass!" God, the way people drive. I was tired mentally and physically and starving. God, I could eat a whole pizza and cheese bread and a bowl of chocolate ice cream.

> *I felt that desire again today. It started with the racing heart and with that an instantaneously unwarranted thought. Subconsciously I am fixated, analyzing and mulling it over. I am still analyzing and analyzing still. A few moments feel longer. It comes from my mind's eye and I watch it like a dream sequence played out before me. Consciously, I am not the producer; I am the set director and I perform the feasibility studies.*
>
> *It is a subtle proposition but it engulfs me. All is vivid and natural and quickly I come to a decision at the right time. I am not distressed. Then it is over, over with the same swiftness as it came.*
>
> *The receptive thought of suicide, my sweet escape hatch, engages me, entertains me, but does not control me.*

Life was becoming more normal and the passing of my father was sinking in and my mother was struggling; time had not healed her wounds. We kept going to the cemetery. I wanted her to spend some nights with us, but she declined. His death came in that house and she couldn't leave him. His aura was everywhere. He had existence there; her reality was there. There was no actual speaking, but I tried to anticipate reconciliation with my sister. My senses advised me to wait, and likewise there was no softening of the relationship between my sister and my mother.

> *Then "tick, tick, tick"; it was just a matter of time. No way, nope, no way. I'm caught completely off guard; this can't be fucking happening.*
>
> *There are phone calls and upsetting conversations and depressive moans. I hear the gut-wrenching stories, blah blah blah. Just two months after my father's burial and my mother is becoming more able, LET HER*

## Life Is Like a Line

*BECOME MORE ABLE! It is every day, every day he calls; it's been their routine for almost fifty years, but the direction of their conversations seems to be taking a dreadful turn.*

*My brother has been finding fault with life but now it is much worse. Each phone call is worse. It's about the ruin of his life and his separation from roommates and his bills and his work and it's bad and he cries. Literally, he cries and sobs and sobs and complains some more.*

*It doesn't take long for my mother to panic. This behavior of my brother's frightens the hell out of her and she caters to him and coddles him. It has been a lifelong commitment; it isn't going to end now.*

He was not my father's son. Once sobbing, twice sobbing, okay five times sobbing would have been allowable, but this was nonsense and it happened each and every time he called. I brought her some groceries and met the lawn maintenance man and then she hit me with it. "*My son is coming back home.*"

"Oh my God; are you kidding?"

Her reply: "I don't care what you say. You can't control me. He is coming and you can't do anything about it, Cindy."

Predictably, she made the plan and he agreed; he was coming home to her and she would bring him back to health. He was having a "breakdown." My unspoken retort was, "We're all having a breakdown!"

My stomach churned. God, what anger. She used words I hadn't heard in a long time and her tone reminded me of everything. It reminded me of my father and how he loved me and her tones of angst directed to him and for no apparent reason to me.

I am very sensitive to tone of voice and can get pissed off hearing the wrong tone at the wrong time. So after I pulled the dagger out of my chest, I started to panic and I felt that neck tension and my engine running. What in the hell was going on? While I drove home, upset and confused, I reviewed our conversation.

"Pardon me? He is what? Moving in—here? All of his things? What do you mean by 'all of his things'? Moving van, leaving his pals, and moving here for good; you need money for his trip?

"This is not right. In my town? Coming to my town? What do you mean, this is none of my business? This has everything to do with me and don't forget about my sister; she is involved just like the rest of us and I will not be willed away."

Dad gave me this job forty years ago; it's called "Look after Your Mother" and it means I must protect and defend her at all costs. And when she called to tell me she was in charge now and calling the shots and I was no longer her trusted confidant but her hired assistant and nothing more, I said, "Okay, geez, okay! I'll call you tomorrow." I was crushed and worried. It was acceptable when our parents would slip us a few dollars for doing menial tasks now and then but money was easy for my mother to dole out. It was either her money or her emotion.

As usual, she was ragging on me and pissed at me but that was nothing new…guess it would have happened sooner or later. But her home was far too close to my sanctuary and it brought fear to a life where bouts of happiness once were plentiful.

> *Home is my safety. It is my breathing space, and when my heart is pounding and my throat is tight, when I am overrun by anxiety and when it seems like there's nowhere to run, it is here I run to. It is here where I live with my love and my little dog and our memories.*
>
> *There have been too many days when I have hated him and thought I wanted to divorce him and then end my life with my little dog in tow, but our home; I recognize it is my refuge. It's where we celebrate birthdays and holidays and the good of life. Home is where the phone rings and the kids call. It's the destination of long-distance travel, it's where the blowout parties are, it's where we laugh and joke, and it's where the sexes become engaged on the pool table.*
>
> *It's the roaring fire under blankets drinking glasses of wine and it's two in the tub with the dog rolling her eyes. It's my solitude, and perhaps I have taken it for granted. I am so afraid that living on cloud nine will soon be replaced by living under cloud nine; streaks of lightning will soon be thrust upon me.*
>
> *I am anxious and irritated by the sound of his name. He is my pain-in-the-ass brother, period. My fear is that he is coming to my mother's home for*

*an undetermined amount of time to perhaps deceive her and ruin me. I'm hopeful that she will soon find her pal to be her intruder, but just in case, Dad, if you can hear my voice, please stay close at hand.*

Ron and I moved again, and we found our new home to be bigger than we needed and more beautiful than we could have predicted. There was an indescribable comfort within our walls; it was our refuge and my seclusion. The design appointments of our French Country home were the essence of homes found in custom magazines; this new house was our most prized creation.

Our master suite watched me as I came and went, looking for that space of hopefulness rather than unhappiness. There was no escaping the fact that this was a major abode that I barely had time to clean. I gave it my best shot most of the time, but it was overpowering. The house was five thousand square feet from bedrooms to basement. In addition, our three-car garage seemed to be my mind teaser. The garden potting shed was the size of a one-car garage and sat as the matriarch in our spacious yard.

I was sickened when my father died. Selfishly, I'd wanted him to see this home; this was his kind of place. He saw the plans and the clearing of the land, but by the time he saw the foundation, he was too ill to appreciate it. My dad was generous with his compliments and he loved my husband as his son. He enjoyed all our homes and bragged to his business acquaintances about our work. I know for certain this home would have knocked his socks off.

In the beginning, my father had a difficult time warming up to my husband; he felt the same way I did in many ways about his edgy sense of humor, but soon his fears were eliminated. If his realization had not come through discussions of politics or philosophy or current events, it would have been through the electrical or construction business they both knew so well. Each man was so deliberate in their quest for knowledge that often they shared publications and were never at a loss for words. My father would throw out a subject and my husband would bite; it was cool to watch. For fifteen years, I observed their mutual love and admiration.

There were differences, but I saw a logical likeness, the kind that would cause a woman to leave her family for another man.

CHAPTER 12

# Invasion and a
# History of Ruin

*Our bedroom has an eighteen-foot cathedral ceiling and is
painted the softest Cayman Island blue, so very reminiscent of
the warm water we enjoyed on several of our family vacations.
But on the nights of sleep lost to worry, all I can see is the white
of our ceiling fan and the cold breeze of its spin. It is related to
my misbehaving mind, filled with dark foreboding thoughts of my
brother's return, my mother's lack of cooperation, and me, stuck in
the middle again.*

My mind wouldn't rest on my time; it rested on its own. And
although every room in that house offered us solitude, it was difficult
to break away from the anxiety I felt. There was no doubt that I feared
many things, and my brother's return was significant.

*The telephone rings. I have a sense of who the caller is and I
know I have to face the music, so to speak. The reminiscent ring*

*has interrupted many activities. It wakes me from my sleep, interrupts sex, echoes splashes in my tub, disrupts dinner, and stops the riding lawn mower and the washing of the car. It has too much power. Family, friends, tele-marketers, wrong numbers, so many calls in a lifetime. The land line and the cell phones, some crucial, some crazy, some wanted, some not, some enjoyable, some aggravating. While it's ringing and ringing, I start reviewing the day and try to evaluate what I may or may have not done to activate the bells, and as it rings another time I know that soon a machine will do its dirty work.*

*"Hello, I'm sorry we can't come to the phone right now. If you would leave your name, number, and a…" I don't find evasion an appealing alter-native and I know the caller so I answer, dammit, and get it over with.*

*"Hello. Hi, Mom. Mom, are you okay? Are you upset? I just left you."*

*"I just talked with your brother. Cindy, I want you to…I think I should have…I have to get ready for your brother to come home, so I need you to…"*

*"But Mom, don't you think we should wait before we buy bedroom furniture for him? You do have a sleep sofa; that will be just fine. I realize you can buy what you want, but…we have to use our best judgment. What do you mean, 'Why don't I like my brother?' Do we have to go into that again? He has never done anything to you and he is my family. What are you talking about? I don't like him? Who told you that? He is my brother as well as your family."*

*That woman is crazy. Goddammit, she hung up on me. I can't fucking believe she did that again. This brother thing is going to be the end of me and he hasn't even arrived yet. Why am I so pissed off? Why does she do this to me?*

My husband, his usual patient self, avoided any conversation about them and tried to get me interested in his day, very difficult. I told him I was clenching my teeth night and day. He wasn't really paying attention and that pissed me off and I didn't like his tone but he has always been good about my family bullshit. He knew that every time the phone rang it was usually my mother complaining about something and then my reaction would become a swearing fit.

I realized my father's death was very traumatic for my mother. Not to minimize her feelings, but this was not about her trauma. This was about my brother and her flight of the imagination about their relationship.

The most frequently heard words out of her, other than curse words, have been "I want to buy that" and my father heard them all. The phrase lives on, but now it's my cross to bear and it never ends. I am working for the estate. My mother knows that and the taxes are almost ready and yet she insists, "I don't care what you're doing, Cindy," and then somehow the conversation moves in another direction.

*"Mom, you know how I feel about his coming here. This is going to be bad; Dad wouldn't allow this," and now my mother begins to rebel. "Well, your father's not here."*

*Oh God, she shouldn't have started with that sentence. I could jump over the fucking kitchen counter. She is challenging me and she is bitching me out and is using the power struggle game. She keeps talking and then threatens, "Not if you know what's good for you, blah, blah, blah." Now if you drag that out for ten more minutes or so you're standing in my shoes, partially. And I start to seethe.*

*How about pushing a few more buttons? Okay, that's perfect; here we go. She just doesn't see the potential catastrophe that is coming to town. I get this blood-rushing-through-my-body feeling, a familiar experience, and I am so fucking angry, so horribly angry, that I don't know what to do, and now I'm swearing like a sailor and there's nowhere to turn and I want to smash things and I need that relief. That minty stuff in the refrigerator is quick, down and dirty, and I beg for its remedy and honest to God I am drinking it out of the bottle.*

*My mother is destructive. I know this and I have ingested her verbal abuse and as soon as I calm down I can look the other way and I don't know why I even bother. If only I could get wasted without this fucking liquor allergy kicking in. Dammit, I so need to get wasted.*

There is no doubt that when I promised my father I would care for her, neither of us could have predicted my brother moving here or perhaps he did have a sense of it and just didn't say. I knew that if my mother didn't

Life Is Like a Line

put up her guard and heed my warnings, she would be rummaged through and trashed. Here's what I thought: if this was a plan of God's, I submit to you that he has too much time on his hands.

Oddly enough, my mother and I had pretty much smoothed things over until the news of my brother came. I had worked hard to overlook her nasty outlook on life even though what I needed from her was still difficult for her to give. For all our recent time spent together, I just wanted to know. I needed to be sure, and I have never been sure yet. I wondered, but she didn't say. It was about us looking at each other face to face, mother to child, woman to woman, about wanting her to know my heart. I see me back there; I am there often. My heart is very young, and still I wait for her.

Life should not be filled with the scraps of a parent's affection. It was my brother, he was it, he was always it, and he would have the hours of her affection again very soon. Most of the time I hid my feelings of needing her approval while I devoured her irritability, and then I found myself somewhere I didn't want to be with much to consider. My cherished father had passed away, the family offender was coming in for the take, and my mother was not thinking clearly.

I didn't know what to do first; I had no guidance. Ron listened, but every syllable I spoke, every emotion and sensation, brought forth that tightness again. He offered little of himself for fear of being devoured.

In my stomach, an upset. In my head and shoulders, an ache. I was angry, really really angry, and worried, worried about what would soon take place. My anticipated disaster would occur, but it was the details I lacked. In my mind, I began to have little hope. I was wounded and fucking angry. After she called again, wanting more of me, I struggled for my composure but kept raising my voice. By the time I hung up the phone, I just wanted to lie down in the middle of the road. Just my form lying in absolute darkness; in silence they would follow the dull black pavement right down the middle. I was fragile and frustrated. I no longer knew how to pass for normal, and no one knew that what was left was just a trace of me.

*I understand that he took our father's death very badly, but after living away from our family for over forty years, his return now brings just one word to my mind: suspicion. I am very shocked to hear of his desire to move back. Why for the love of God would he want to move in with his mommy now? He has lived the better part of his life establishing a family with a multitude of others somewhere else and now he abandons that lifestyle for our sleepy bedroom community?*

*Fuck. He is about to penetrate the safe haven I have in this quaint river town and knowing his reputation, this does not sit well with me. My father would not have allowed this had he still been alive. This would not be happening, dammit, and in my father's absence I worry, I fret, I pace, I don't sleep.*

*But my mother's intimate relationship with her boy is undeniable and no amount of clamoring on my part will keep him from his chosen destination. My mother and brother have had more closeness than any other relationship in her life, including the one she shared with my father. She has been quite defensive regarding his return because she knows I do not appreciate his perversity. By that I mean his deceitful nature, not the fact of his homosexuality. I was shocked to learn that his best female friend thought my daughter was his daughter for twenty-five years.*

I didn't go there to greet him but my mother called me to let me know he had arrived. He brought some personal belongings in his little sedan and while they waited for the moving van I dwelled on the fact that I was going to have to become involved. This was a mess and I knew I was going to get screwed, and not in a good way.

I called my mother every day and she was giddy, like a young mother seeing her baby for the first time. I tried like hell to stay away and let them familiarize themselves with each other without my intrusion and so went the days.

*The first few weeks are uneventful, especially since they are feeding each others' needs, which in fact isn't such a bad thing. They are spending time away from the house and by the looks of things this is settling well with my brother, but recently my mother who has no problem with the say-what-you-think strategy is becoming verbally cross with him, which is not a good sign.*

## Life Is Like a Line

*To put it simply, before his arrival she was settling in psychiatrically if you will and now she almost seems to be hostile with the intruder as he is creating havoc in her ideal little world. Funny though, the "ideal little world" she creates revolves almost solely around the very presence of the intruder.*

*But the fact is that her trueness, the very essence of her personality, can no longer be suppressed in the course of this disarray. Perfect son or not, she is beginning to exude a new thickness into the air. She has lived her earthly existence under the notion that all is synonymous with perfection and she knows nothing of disarray; she also knows nothing of her guest.*

*A messy man (such as my brother) to a perfectionist (such as my mother) is like gasoline to a match. And then, with her short fuse, a slow burn until multiple explosions. It has started…toilet seat up, not flushed…underwear on the bathroom floor…dishes in the sink…garbage can dripping Chinese takeout leftovers from last night.*

*Should I, the daughter, scold him? That immaculate house is in disorder. Aha, now you have your son back! Her quick temper, her threats, are laughable. He laughed. Me too; we were in stitches. She is so funny. This isn't believable. Throw him out? Oh, yeah, please.*

*Though my father complied with her rules, my brother will not. With thoughts of perfect sugar plums dancing in her head, he brings a flutter to her air. It is a dance of the fanatic and I, neither the producer nor the director, do not want to be too close. It is true that after almost sixty years of marriage, my father was a well-trained machine. It was forty hours or more on the job, brow-beaten and quiet as a mouse, Navy clean with toilet seat down, mustache and hair just so. He could cook and pick up and wash dishes when necessary. He scheduled maintenance on the cars, often made his own bed, wiped up his bathroom shower and sink, was generous to her, took his clothes to the dry cleaner, and so on and on and on. He was a tough act to follow, for wife and daughter.*

*My brother will never measure up to his standards and my mother does not know this yet, and until she comprehends it she will continue to be ugly and insulting and critical and mostly make my life and his life miserable. She wants me to do her dirty work for her but I cannot fix this, even though*

*I want to kill him and ship him back to whence he came. I am just in the middle of their love-hate relationship. I defend her and she defends him; will I ever win?*

*Each time I am at my mother's house, I am exposed to their newly-shaped relationship. It is terrible to be with them and their relationship is getting worse.*

Something was happening to me and it was unlike my usual self. My mind was firing at speeds that were unrecognizable and I seemed to be argumentative most of the time. Fortunately, we had opportunities for respite and on any given weekend our cottage in northern Michigan awaited us. Although our home on the lake gave me relief from my turmoil, I seemed to have paranoia when we were there. The four-hour drive was grueling as I persisted in criticizing my husband's driving ability, and in my mind's eye I experienced an imaginary crash, the swerving, the roll, the windshield glass shattering all our dreams.

Each day, every moment, I concealed thoughts. With feelings of impending doom, I was obsessive and compulsive, repeating tasks for no apparent reason, and my mind felt chained to feelings I didn't consciously call to mind. I worried so much, so much about everything, and I almost could not contain it anymore. I was going through a phase; I thought I could breathe underwater, breathe without oxygen.

What in the hell was that all about? I didn't know...Honest to God, I didn't know anymore.

On the next visit to my mother's house, I jumped out of the car and walked to the garage, heading for the door. My heart was pounding and I noticed a series of very prominent black scratches and dings along the drywall in Mother's immaculate garage. The dings were right next to where my brother parked his car. He was smashing up the garage, for God's sake. I knocked and went in. "Mom? Hi! Did you see that John hit the inside wall of the garage and made a mess?"

She said, "He has a problem backing out. I'm having the garage painted anyway."

That was all it took to begin the cycle all over again. If it were me and my car...ugh, she'd be mad for days. I'd have to screw the painter to get

# Life Is Like a Line

him there lickety-split. Only three minutes into my visit, they were already tearing me apart. I insisted to myself, "Okay, simmer down. They are not worth it," but it was very difficult. It was both ends against the middle, me the fucking middle man again.

My brother knew what he was doing; it was classic manipulation and my mother loved the attention. That was not the worst of it. He falsified and received government assistance, he got into a fender-bender in town and drove off, he kept hitting the detached garage while backing up, he was dropping and spilling food, he wouldn't get a job, he fell a few times and my mother couldn't get him up, he was on the computer dawn to dusk. It was bill collectors and buddies, all reminders of his life left behind.

I thought of him as nothing more than a jackass, busily destroying my reputation and ruining my life.

*"Mom, did you say anything to him about the garage? You're afraid to? What does that mean? I know he lost his job, but you have a right to be angry. My God, what the hell is going on? Me, being critical?"*

We were in the garden and she told me more. I became furious because of her fear and I marched back into the house for a confrontation. He was sitting at his computer, facing the pornography rather brazenly, and I began to speak. With a quivering voice and angry as hell, I said things that were true but I said them in a very brutal way. He began to defend himself and I gave him the ultimatum: he had two weeks to find other accommodations or I was calling the police.

*The look on his face is quite defiant, and while my threats mean nothing to him, they have to be said. At last I am no longer capable of homicide and I return outside to where my mother is hiding, still pulling the weeds. I give her the rundown, then the blow-by-blow exchange, and as my last sentence ends, she flabbergasts me once again.*

*"I will NEVER throw him out, NEVER, and I don't care what you do. He is my son!"*

*Goddammit, what...the...FUCK! SHIT! Why the hell did she send me in there? I feel my knees begin to shake. My voice is beyond a quiver, my heart is racing, and I think I am likely to explode but I don't know what explode is exactly. I keep it all in, push it down, jam it in. I defended her, threatened him, instantly became enemy number one, who I was likely to become eventually anyway, but for what? For fucking what? She wants her sonny boy more than she cares about his push and shove, his cursing, his catastrophes, his threats.*

*I am going home. They can obviously take care of themselves and she deserves him anyway, that bastard. With only half my sanity left, I am backing up out of her driveway. Crap, I just ran over the neighbor's lawn and I am mentally somewhere I shouldn't be. Nine out of ten times when I leave here I am thinking fast and recklessly. Leaving her road, heading for the highway, I roll the stop sign, pull in front of a delivery truck. Who in the hell cares about a goddamn truck anyway? I'm racing home; God forbid anyone should be in my way. I wait for the closing of the drawbridge in town with music blasting, foot tapping; I can't wait.*

*I speed to our subdivision without incident, then pull into our driveway. At times I forget what a beautiful home we have. How striking the pastel carpet roses are as they edge along the circular driveway and how strong the trees are that go beyond the towering house. Whenever I return to this magnificent sight I am encouraged, but in my unhappiness, in my rage, I do not appreciate, I forget.*

*I am still on fire, and as the garage door begins to close behind me, I'm thinking. Finally I turn off the engine. Fuck 'em; they won't do this to me, this vicious fucking cycle, suicide. Fuck you, fucking suicide.*

*As I unlock the door, I hear her sounds as she rushes my way, my little dog, and as she approaches me she shows me how happy she is to have me home, my little Yorkie, six pounds of woman's only friend.*

*It is so good to be home; there is nowhere I'd rather be, but I am exhausted and full of fury. They have pushed me further and further away from something and towards something else and it feels bad. But now I am home and there is only peace. I don't get it quite yet; I still feel violent and everything is worth destroying but I am in control. I hate control. I hate control. I hate control. I fucking hate control. I hate control. I learned from my father, "Don't let them see you out of control." Goddammit, Dad; I am sure that is bullshit.*

## Life Is Like a Line

*My little dog and I are lying on our bedroom floor watching the ceiling fan spin and she is jumping around licking me and I am where I want to be. As I pet her, she cannot contain her excitement, and as I turn off my mind and regain my calm, she will never know just how necessary she is to my survival. No human has ever consoled me with such little effort and as she puts me at ease, she brings me down from the highs of rage and brings me up from the depths of despair.*

*She has a fix on me and I am treating her in the same way I would hope to be treated if I were her. Perhaps it is the innocence in her big brown eyes that generates my tranquility, but I have a sense that when our eyes meet, she can see into my soul. I know what she is thinking. No matter the reason, it is she who stops me from smashing everything in my goddamn house and screaming at the top of my lungs, for there are days and nights when it takes all my effort not to do so.*

*I thank God for my shelter since my brother has surrounded me with such madness. My shelter is where my heart rate is better, where my shoulders don't touch my ears, where I still have some control, and where I don't need to consume bottles of ibuprofen to make it through the day.*

*What I have now is my little dog and my apology. "I'm sorry, but I can't help but cry today. You help me, you know. You help me pick life when I really want to die. Pick life over death. I love you, my dog. I am so sorry to leave you to be with those idiots. Your attention today has saved me from myself."*

Every day I went back to the Bermuda Triangle and day after day I listened to my mother's tales of woe. She was filled with stories of how he had misbehaved and how frightened she was and at last she was fed up enough to get rid of him. Her version was not the same as mine; hers was to put him up in an apartment, outfit it, and give him money.

That detonated me; the internal violence was unleashed. Anger and rage were beginning to be commonplace; I was visibly angry and invisibly in a rage. I had never known this emotion in such a way before and it became worse as the months went by. With no desire for physical confrontation (not three hundred twenty-five pounds of him), I tried the talking-convincing method but he wasn't buying it. He had his partner lined up and money coming in and he was set.

I'm a Greek woman; I have a sometimes okay, mostly horrible temper and you probably don't want to mess with me when my back is up against the wall. I was going after him in a big way, even if the price was somewhere between a nervous breakdown and homicide. His anger began looking more like open violence and my gripe list was ever-increasing as his infractions became more and more noticeable with each situation he brought into the house. My drive was the usual. Speeding down the highway, get the hell out of my way, heart racing, explosive. I was a ball of yarn beginning to unravel.

*Living in my little town of five thousand people consists of neighborly behavior where shopkeepers know your name, the names of your kids, and even your dog. We are a community bordered by rich pastures of milking cows to the west and sunrises over the forceful attention-grabbing river to the east. Life here is nothing like New Jersey or New York where a million or so people reside. If you are unscrupulous, you can fall between the cracks there but not here. If there is anything to know, people know it.*

*My mother, who to some extent already regrets him being here, worries that his traipsing around by himself could get him into trouble. He is stealing bottles of plum sauce for his take-out meals from our local Chinese restaurant, a place where we dine often and know the owners well. When I saw the bottle, my blood began to boil. Seemingly such a small infraction, I contemplated homicide. Immediately embarrassed by his behavior, I became so pissed I could barely see straight. Confrontation means nothing to him and each visit brings awkward moments.*

*My mother, either intimidated or ignorant, shrugs off his behavior as is convenient, as if it's no big deal. She is protecting him still. This is exactly what I expect from my brother, but it doesn't preclude me from ranting and raving at him. I come from a genealogy of high-strung talent. And while positioning myself with him, I am forced to correct my mother whenever she interferes, reminding her that her comments are not helpful to the situation.*

*As usual, neither one of them cares one damn bit about doing the right thing. Neither cares about honesty or self-respect, and as far as making any permanent correction, I have no power so I offer no consequence. My father was not a perfect man but he aspired to do the right thing, and he kept my brother's ass in line because he knew my mother was putty in his hands.*

## Life Is Like a Line

*I know my brother is my personal time bomb; all I can hear is the "tick, tick, tick" of the countdown to real disaster. There isn't a day or night when the traffic on his cell phone isn't constant. His past is beginning to search for his present and, as predicted, the funds can only last so long without employment.*

*But it's a damn good thing my mother can save him with her dough. She bought him more minutes on his cell phone, paid his car payment, and dished out more money for what random area code calls were coming in. It's becoming a mess, a real fucking mess, and I have little control over him.*

*He is going to barrel his way through my mother for his desires and that's that. He is ill-mannered and she longs for the perfect roommate, even if she has to create him. In their land of make-believe, I only know one thing for sure and that's that I am screwed. He is sending the last of his brokerage money back to New Jersey, wiring cash through several bank accounts, but all of it is about to end. My mother has become the bank and is paying for some of his debt.*

*He has been complaining to my mother about a problem with his eye for some time now, so I'm taking him to our family doctor to have another look. My mother would rather not drive with him and relies on me when she feels a crisis is on the horizon. My brother is a non-compliant diabetic and with all the crap he has ingested lately, he should have stroked out by now. Either way, my feeling is that he just doesn't want to go back to work so any medical abnormality will serve its purpose.*

*I don't trust him, but I'll try to give him the benefit of the doubt medically. I have been so mad these past few months that my feelings of sadness just never seem to go away. It's true that they push me to my limit with their bickering and my mother's contradictory requests. I'm again in the middle, one player substituted for the other. I wait for the telephone of doom to ring. My nights of ceiling fan watching are every bit as distressing as before and all of my problems seem to be worse in the dark.*

When I saw her paying bills they were random, rather here and there, but it soon became painfully clear that the situation had moved to the next level, the level of alarm. I knew it would eventually go there; it had to. It was logical and I should have seen it coming. He exhausted his money train so he was about to dip into Mother's. Yeah, predictable. At that point, I realized I was all alone in this war of wills, the conflict of two against one, a fight I was born to lose. Preferences…and he wins.

> *I took him to the doctor today; soon we will see a specialist for his eyes. They bickered back and forth all day, in the car, in the waiting room, when the doctor came in, when we went to lunch. Oh God. My mother is so dreadfully hypercritical. "Fix your collar. You missed a spot shaving. It's time for a haircut. You dropped something on your pants. Where's your coat? Stop it; you know you can see," and on and on and on.*
>
> *They're both ill-mannered. I can't wait to get home; there isn't a place on my body where a knot doesn't lie. My sanity waits for no one but me but I cannot run. I vacillate between this constant anger, again growing to rage and hopelessness, and I can't hide from these unprovoked feelings as they rise in me. Of course, my wonderful man tries to divert my attention from them to anything else and I think he is becoming afraid for me but he never says.*
>
> *I can't help but feel that I have been a very unattractive wife, hassling him and pushing him to his limit. In my mind at this time he has done nothing right enough, he hasn't loved me enough, he hasn't helped me enough, and without enough, I am alone.*

I was more on task and less distracted once I started to help my brother with his affairs. I untangled his medical insurance, started juggling his bills, and then it really began…one specialist after another, one appointment and then another, next week and the next week after that. It was clear; his illnesses had been dormant for many years until recently, when the symptoms began to unfold.

We began a course of therapy, one medical condition at a time, and the specialists kept coming in and life kept evolving. Even as I tried to be kind to the office staff when scheduling his appointments, there was no denying that my fuse was becoming short. Time and again we would be delayed or denied due to an overabundance of patients or problems with his insurance and I had to use every trick in the book to get dropped onto a reasonable page in the appointment book.

## Life Is Like a Line

My frequent response was, "No, June won't do; it's only November now, blah blah blah...Terrific; thank you very much; I'll be sure to bring you a box of chocolates." Oh well, it worked; it worked every time, every fucking time.

> *Driving to the eye appointment is easy; I attempt to listen to the radio and nothing else. But it's tough, no...not tough, impossible.*
>
> *After three hours of us in one cubicle of a room, they tell us to come back in another three months and if his eye hasn't improved, he will see another specialist.*
>
> *My mother is especially critical today. The doctor ran twenty minutes late, it's snowing outside, mind your own business Cindy, find another doctor, what's with his insurance, and on and on and on. She begins picking on my brother and I have to intervene on his behalf and then I see it in her eyes: "Don't defend MY son!"*
>
> *Oh God, what a dastardly deed. While we drive home they speak only to each other; in the restaurant they speak only to each other.*
>
> *Eye contact over here, please. "Hello...I'm still sitting here," and then I am out for the day. Hot, hostile, crushed, pissed.*
>
> *Three ibuprofen five hundreds later, I'm swearing like a sailor, slamming doors, drawers, storming about, generally still wanting to smash everything in my house, and I do and say all of this in front of my very impressionable two-brown-eyes-wagging-tail little dog and I wonder, "I'm dying here; can't they see I'm fucking dying?"*

"Ring, ring," the sound I despise...

In the beginning, the telephone would ring and it was interesting to see how the situation was developing but it was not interesting anymore. Be careful what you wish for, I again warn. My brother's few weeks' respite was turning into a soap opera with much more than was originally in the script. I swear I couldn't make any of this up, and that's precisely why it was weighing on me.

All the one hundred twelve pounds of me was warned about losing any more, but I began losing my desires so my weight was the last thing on my mind. What's another one hundred and twelve for God's sake? Other than my continual edginess, I moved into a more harsh sarcasm and then lovemaking was out of the question. Lovemaking included the obvious plus hugs and handholding. Not for me; it was sit on the other couch and don't even look at me, please.

There was no doubt I was beginning to lose interest in what I enjoyed the most, my darling husband, our cherished family, our business, and life in general. I could put on the face momentarily, but it wouldn't last long.

Desperation is a horrid place to be and I began sinking more with every confrontation. The dictionary definition of hopelessness and all the symptoms it describes can never fully represent the condition of a human sinking into despair. There was no joy, I felt no inspiration, and I was filled with resentment and hatred for the life that was mine, yet I was challenged to push on.

I was disgusted with my father; he'd left me with so many loose ends and he'd chosen not to face his home life. For many years he'd run from it. He knew my mother and my brother well; he knew their weaknesses and their potential for destruction and he should have stopped them before it came to this. My mother would never allow me to help *him*; he was her family. She got defensive and my brother grew comfy and I was plain and simply screwed.

My mother's home overlooks the mesmerizing river and it's not hard to fall in love with the water when you're near it. As it rushes downstream, world-traveling freighters push upstream, heading for the locks to assist the ship home or to its waiting port around the world. So important, the water with its significant power, so combative and yet so peaceable, it is both anxious and complacent, and as the freighter's strength pushes away, the water exposes the hull.

So the power of the water parallels the intensity of man's existence. The depth of a man is seen in his beliefs, his actions, his passions, and his emotions, and all of that is his soul.

> *I must confess I have been conflicted regarding my brother. He doesn't seem well and she is beating him senselessly. It is true that once he was the enemy, but he seems pathetic now. I keep my guard up always and he is a manipulative son of a bitch overall, but I want to help him if I can.*

## Life Is Like a Line

*Sometimes I resent them, her and him. When we are together, they have each other and I have no one. I am bruised and our family is broken and I am discouraged since early in the game.*

*Vacillating is not a characteristic of mine, but this situation requires two minds. She hasn't been close to our parents, she's been angry with my mother and me for six months, she never really visited our parents even when my father was alive and ill, and she hates my brother, but she's the perfect person to run to for help; she's all about preserving the money.*

*As far as my mother goes, this couldn't be more sensitive an issue, especially when she talks from both sides of her mouth. She just makes everything harder. She has no experience in the real world and I swear to God I WILL protect her if it kills me.*

*Give him the money or not, be resentful of me and incite a fight with me, don't talk to me, threaten me, don't say thank you or I appreciate it; I don't fucking care…Ask my poor husband. My eleventh bottle of that chalky stuff…My increased doses of the purple pill and cholesterol medication and my ceiling fan and my chiropractor who practically falls on the floor with laughter when he sees me in the waiting room. I don't really care now, do I?*

You might say my sister and I had a rocky relationship. We shared good times and bad, but overall too much anger and too many harsh words and too many feelings forced us to be detached. But I was resolute; this was a critical course that perhaps we were born to take. She was going to be a beneficiary someday, so she needed to get on board right then. I took the next logical move and put aside all the harshness and I chose to forgive and forget. I added fifty or so miles to my odometer, parked my car in the driveway, and nervously walked to her front door.

"Breathe, straighten your jacket, don't be nervous, ring the doorbell, dummy." It was natural to be afraid. There was no immediate answer at the door and I slowly turned away. I was going back to my car. Relieved and disappointed both, I was going to run the hell back to the car.

Then the door swung open and there she was, looking very pretty in her pink chenille robe, and I walked in like I'd been invited, like I'd done it a hundred times before. Her face for the first time in months was not cross with me and the first look led to the first embrace and we both cried.

For all that was wrong, we are sisters and I was convinced that she would know what to do. It was true she didn't want any amount of our parents' money to be spent on him, not for any reason, not for life and not for death. As we sat and talked, I told her the unfolding tale and my worries and she was upset and we knew that our response, two against two, was necessary.

Before our goodbye, we set the date for a family meeting and promised never to separate again. I drove home on cloud nine. I was relieved that I had done the right thing and I hoped my hopelessness would leave me. So with the day and time in place, I advised my mother and she told my brother. Between my sister and me, we would get to the bottom of his plot.

All the while, my brother continued with his weaknesses on the computer, walked about the house unclothed, was worse at spilling his daily take-out food, and alternated between his own rage and version of kindness. In better days, my mother's invitation could have been stopped, but now it was too late. She didn't know what she didn't know, period. Although my brother had a lifelong career, he had spent money beyond his means and was forced to rely upon other methods of additional support. My father, guilty over their estranged relationship, had long ago established a stock account in his name, though in his lifetime he kept this a secret from my sister and me.

The problem with my brother was that he was too generous to his friends. He carried twenty credit cards in his pocket to cover his debt, but every month he came up short. He spent three hundred thousand dollars in three years, depleted his stocks, and was unable to pay for the automobile he gave his lover.

Babying him all those years did not make him responsible; on the contrary it made him less than a man and turned him into an untrustworthy liability. However, to be fair, I am certain that Mother never expected this consequence of her doing.

I must also say in fairness to my brother that they had days of happiness. Mother and son, her dream fulfilled. He bought her gifts and they dined out, lunches and dinners all around the town, popcorn at the movie theatre,

## Life Is Like a Line

visits to the mall. She simply adored him on those good days and it's all too easy to forget the bad days, especially when they're very bad, but she didn't forget, really. She just chose not to remember.

Unfortunately, neither of them could maintain a state of ceasefire for very long, especially my mother. When son would go out for most of the afternoon she would clean and be in a huff. By the time I would arrive, the ceasefire would be over and we'd be right into the criticism and quick disparaging comments with a little bickering on the side.

Bickering rips me apart. My definition of the word "bickering" is as follows: "*A very bad place; a verbal altercation between two dingbats that takes me where the hell I don't want to go; a very bad goddamn motherfucking bad place.*"

I didn't trust my brother, but I needed to learn what his motives were. Soon enough, I did. With our mother completely exposed and vulnerable, he named his price; it was in the low six figures. Extortion money to wipe him off the planet, never to return.

We confronted him, two angry sisters dressed and ready for battle, but it was during this meeting that Mother began to have a change of heart. Finally she'd had enough. Let him go! She wanted to pay him off, be done. Six fucking figures; I don't think so. My sister and I exchanged glances, my mother was lost in space and she didn't have a clue as to what was happening. There had been too much tension rising from our little circle; we'd been in a pressure cooker with no escape and it was time for its release.

> *We explain the facts of life to him and we are confrontational. His goal is to return to his East Coast apartment with a bankroll in his pocket but that is not an option. We are not going to give him any money at all.*
>
> *He says his partner is going to take up shop here, maybe stay at Mom's for awhile until they are settled.*
>
> *No fucking way. This is a joke, right? My heart is racing and my throat is tight. I want to slug him so bad I can taste it and I begin to see myself involved in a homicide. I hit him over the head with something and roll three hundred and twenty-five pounds of him down the hill, splat, right into that powerful, mesmerizing, fucking river.*
>
> *I'm sure it has plenty of garbage at the bottom; one more piece won't make a damn bit of difference. But that's not an option either, dammit. I*

*am pissed. I can barely stay in my chair. I am beyond upset if there is such a*
*place. My sister is upset too and is firm. She is not temperamental or homi-*
*cidal. "You are not getting any money. Two weeks and you're out."*

At the end of our exchange little was accomplished and he stormed out, raiding the refrigerator as he passed. I was shaking from my annoyance and my mother wouldn't let me call the police. The situation remained.

Home at night and gone during the day, we were never sure of his whereabouts. Calm and civilized; that's what my visits were without him. My newfound circumstances were exhausting. I was the referee, sick with worry, anxious about his propensity for violence. His glaring eyes, tightened lips, and contorted face showed his rage. There were no sounds, no words that hinted of his changing behavior, but I was frightened.

My mother had seen his rage, God bless her, and he no longer flashed me his silently sarcastic smile; he began to show his real self. He was no longer putting on airs, and today he was home and obviously not putting on clothes.

The problem was that he had no respect for our mother. His habits, like walking from his bedroom to the kitchen in the fucking buff, were not acceptable. I was pissed at him; no way would I accept this.

*"WHAT are you doing?"*

*He replies "W h a t?" and flashes his crooked smile. He keeps moving closer to me and then he stops.*

*"What in the hell are you doing; have you lost your goddamn mind?"*

*Silently he turns and shuffles back to his room. He stays there until I leave and my pounding heart nearly puts me in a rage. My mother, hiding in her bedroom, embarrassed, educates me…This is his usual thing.*

*My comment to him is, "Keep your 'thing' to your fucking self!"*

*It's time to leave but I am frightened. I wait for the "ring, ring" all through the night. When you're waiting for something, the night is the worst time.*

When I was a little girl, the nighttime was the scariest. There was nothing clear about the dark. It was sinister. There was a weight to the dark, something would watch me in the dark, something followed me in the dark, and

## Life Is Like a Line

the weighty "it" was everywhere the dark was. I had that feeling again, but I was no little girl.

*We're playing pool this evening in our usual way, my husband and I. It is distraction from my troubles and this is one of the few entertaining activities I care to engage in. I am a novice at this game but I win often due to my calculated lineup and smash of the ball. I am in my bathrobe, my skin against the red chenille and nothing more. I can't stay in clothes, I can't. They are binding and restricting and they press too tightly against me.*

*My husband sees me and doesn't care; he's closer to the nakedness of me, which is not my aspiration. I suppose it's about the chase and his chance look and something more. I have no wish to fulfill his desires at this time. It is not that I feel ill really but I am dreary. I am dreary and lackluster and besieged.*

*My husband has always been incredibly silent about my problems and this evening is more of the same. As he pours my cocktail and then another and then one more I've known him long enough to read him but I feel no stress from him or from the telephone that, as of yet, has not rung. He asks little of me and in my compliance I know I am living and giving a most unsatisfying existence.*

*I've had a few cocktails but I am haunted this day by a longing for that which I have forbidden myself to partake of. I am so in need. Deep in my soul, I am haunted by the pull. I am holding the mirror and I taste the rows and feel the bills. It is only in my memory. My mind, poised for future battle, whips up a fairy tale to tide me over and while I indulge myself, that narrative tempers my desires.*

*He is the first one up the stairs and I tidy up, flipping off the lights, one and then the other, and as the darkness fills the room, I feel that heaviness and it is the same old discomfort. I hear my husband filling the dishwasher. For tonight this amusement is over and once again it is time for the sleep that has been eluding me. I know the next movement will be about his desire, which for this day I will ultimately refuse.*

*My little dog has left me too; I see her lying at the top of the stairs looking down and we are making eye contact. She waits for me but she is chicken too; she has a sense about the darkness or she senses me.*

*It is very evident that I am anxious, jumpy I guess, and even the slightest surprise from out of the blue startles me and causes me to yell out. Then I get pissed. I know these fears are ridiculous but I have many reasons to feel panic and paranoia and concern. For some time now, my thoughts have been encircled by illness and worry and death and aid and helplessness and fear.*

*Fear is an element that keeps me sharp. Should my brother's boyfriend appear on my mother's front porch with his moving van in tow, I must be prepared. Should push come to shove and my mother agree to let them stay there together, I must be prepared. Should something happen to her and he decides the house is his, I must be prepared. Should I have a fucking nervous breakdown, God help me, some great psychiatrist better be prepared.*

*All this equates to being sick with worry. I have to constantly be aware, on the ball, proactive, and I am so screwed. I know one thing for sure: if his partner brings his ass into my territory, the byline in the local newspaper is going to read, "Skinny runt of a boyfriend from New Jersey is found with his head cracked opened from perhaps a lamp. It was reported he was rolling down a hill into the (fucking) river and immediately began floating downstream. Unfortunately, he was plummeted by a tree trunk and crushed by a freighter traveling to the great state of New Jersey."*

*Ah, my sweet mother fucking revenge.*

Easily provoked, edgy, and overly sensitive was nothing new for me since my brother arrived. I have been one, two, or all three of those moods and many more for quite some time. The most difficult mood to wipe out has always been my temperamental condition, and as my patience falls away from me, it is more difficult to pick and choose my victims.

A series of stressful events further lowered and altered my mood. Habitually my mother demoralized my brother and my brother then found my mother laughable or became temperamental and angry with her. Often they bickered, then were pleasant again. They'd manage to twist all the facts, she and then he, and once all was well with them, they'd turn on me.

Their codependency was deep-rooted and confusing and I found it more and more difficult to interpret the dynamics of their relationship. I only knew them from afar. I had only heard one side of the telephone conversation for thirty years; in all that time never had I seen or felt first-hand their bond. I did not understand the adoration of my mother for her son and, at the same time, her disgust and disregard for his feelings. Simultaneously, I didn't understand her defense of him or the cycle that repeated itself hour after hour, day after day.

> The lies are the most wearing for me. So if someday in the presence of my quiet I ask you to "Please leave me alone," don't be offended. I am saving you from the whispers of my hell.
>
> Don't call me with your unsolvable problems; don't ask me to do for you what in reality you will prohibit me from doing, and if I am found vacant in my robe hiding in my house, please understand that this is the day I survived.

No sooner did I think about it than it happened; the telephone rang.

> "Yes, Mom. What's wrong? Why, what's going on? What did you say? He's trying to put his pants on his head? Shit, I'll be right there."
>
> Ah, the beauty of self-employment. Feast or famine and freedom when you need it, and I took it when I could for days such as this. Driving, now speeding, I am usually doing the same going the other way. Perfect fucking irony.
>
> Going this way for this reason fills my mind with thoughts, many unkind and many concerned. I have a sense of rising hysteria.
>
> The garage door is open; I glance at the black traces of damage on the drywall and I hurry inside, not knowing what I'll find. There he is, sitting on a raised stool, leaning on the counter next to the stove, oddly enough smiling at me.
>
> "So, Mom, what happened? Please Mom, if you know something you've got to tell me; otherwise we put his health at risk. Has he taken anything… drugs…anything?" At this point I am pretty sure she is not going to tell me a damn thing.

For all the reasons she should have been, she was extremely upset and furthermore she didn't have a clue as to what had brought this on. I didn't have the heart to tell her what I was thinking. Putting your trousers on your head is fucking weird, but it was the quirky smile that worried me, his strange expression that took this from confabulation to reality. If it was a performance, he should have been in Hollywood. My hands had that familiar tremble.

> *"What's going on?" I ask my brother.*
> *He looks as if he doesn't understand me and he babbles a little.*
> *"Did you take something, maybe drugs of some kind? You can tell me;*
> *I will help you, I promise."*

He had a flat expression and no reasonable verbal response, so against my mother's wishes, I quickly searched his room. I found over-the-counter uppers, many boxes of them, and something told me my mother was feeding him my dad's meds. Halcion was the first that came to mind. My mother, frightened, wouldn't own up to anything. Maybe she didn't aid him in this way, but she was the usual suspect and she is quite experienced in the art of coverup.

We had heaven's help; our family doctor was the ER physician and he was there for three more hours. Keyed up for the trip and filled with nervous energy, my exterior was calm, cool, and collected while my insides were beginning to feel an anxious gloom. Under these conditions, my natural tendency is to entertain melancholic thoughts and then struggle through my irritability and anxiousness in an attempt to rescue, ignoring the fact that I actually need rescuing too.

Being in my parents' home under those conditions brought my father's death too close; since his passing the house had taken on a rather gloomy aura anyway. Now this new crisis only opened up those seeping wounds. My brother's brokenness was becoming apparent, and plainly I wondered about the next chapter in the story of his return.

I packed them both into the Suburban, called my husband, and raced to the hospital. While driving, I kept envisioning us there already; observing him convinced me he was in trouble. With wheelchair assistance, they were waiting for us and he was immediately seen by our own physician. I was relieved; we didn't have to go to the emergency room across the street where part of my life had died.

## Life Is Like a Line

Mentally, I prepared for the paperwork, prepared for his illness, prepared for the outcome. I was still thinking cheap entertainment, hoping against infirmity, feeling guilty for my mistrust, saddened by his bad luck. Driving under duress, every mile gave me an opportunity to get a glimpse of him and when I thought he wasn't noticing, I noticed him. Oh, God.

We passed a fast food restaurant on the way to the hospital and he gave it a long look and a babble. This was not the first time he'd wanted to stop for food while on our way to the hospital or a physician appointment.

"No, I am not going to stop for hamburgers or tacos," I told him. "No, Mom, it's not good for him. He's a diabetic; you shouldn't be feeding him chocolate anyway. Forget it, just forget it; I give up with you people. If you want to kill each other, go ahead, but please don't do it when I'm here. Goddammit."

In our twenty-minute drive, I tried to query him to assess his condition, but my mother felt it her duty to respond. With guns drawn, I began to fire upon her and I begged for her silence but she wouldn't be hushed. The result was our arrival in silence and seething hostility, both hers and mine.

In fact, all I really wanted was to ask the obvious question: "*Why couldn't this fucking brother stay in New Jersey, Goddammit!* And please, Mom, sit in the back seat and shut up!"

Finally we were there, he the village idiot, smiling weird, dumbfounded, or acting. He was quiet while Mom and I continued bickering over every little nothing that has ever been talked about since the beginning of time.

She continued throwing around insults and accusations and eventually my humiliation hit an all-time high. Then, with mood shifting from calm and compassionate to concerned and alarmed to annoyed and irritated to upset and alienated, there was nothing left but my familiar distress and loathing. It was all of us submerged in shared self-hatred. With my engine running, revved up, it was a time for pacing and sarcasm and listening and observing some more. I couldn't help but think of my poor sister, fighting morning traffic, sitting at her boring desk at work, giggling with her co-workers, having lunch, missing all this fun.

I soon realized that after fifteen months of gulping down my pride for their whims, disappearing into hidden unhappiness, and wrangling with my husband, this ER visit changed everything. Already drenched with feelings of personal failure and poor self-worth, I felt a rough and tough hatred shadowed by a sister-like weakness for him and I transitioned into a concerned sister worried sick for her goddamned brother. Still pissed that he'd come to Michigan, wishing he'd been hit by a concrete truck and flattened like a pancake on the road from New Jersey, I was frightened for him and I wanted to be of some aid to him.

I was his only hope at sanity, the only good sense at his disposal. He'd brought to my life a constant struggle. His conniving had forced a distance and severed our family relationships and I should have told him to go to hell the instant I laid eyes on him. He was a troublemaking bastard, but he at some point he'd needed the same as me. Fifty-plus years ago, that once pudgy little boy had been deprived of a basic need, our father's love. As a man, he'd constantly struggled and this had separated him emotionally from all of us.

As I looked at him in that hospital bed, pathetic and confused, I could tell he'd had a different life than us. Something had gotten totally fucked up somewhere along the line and if he wasn't acting, then he was totally screwed. I was positive this guy wouldn't reciprocate in the help department for me, but he was still my damn brother. I'd watch him like a prison guard and pray like hell.

*Emergency rooms, physicians, beds with rails, bright lights, blood tests on veins that rolled, chest x-rays, CAT scans, hurry up and wait. The smells. Look at the clock, stare at his face, his chest going up and down, count the beats, remember his oxygen level, nervous ladies' room visits, walks in the hall, and do it all over again for hours on end.*

*Try to ignore the irritable and argumentative upset of others and look beyond the criticisms of the present and just keep worrying. Worry is mind-filling, goal-setting, task-mastering; it keeps me sharp. I worry and create scenarios, play them out, analyze them, stay on the ready, and come back to the present for a taste of reality and do it again.*

*In my mother's pile of behavior, the confrontational characteristics are intensifying and diminishing with the length of time spent under this pressure. I try to remember that she is an eighty-plus-year-old woman but she*

## Life Is Like a Line

*is still very strong and still very powerful and very very demanding. As we move through the day, I try not to respond to her criticisms but I feel my annoyance mounting and my mood fluctuating with every occurrence.*

*I am fine and now I am agitated at them both and then I forget, realizing they are pathetic and I'm agitated again and now I'm fine. I get over it and then it gets over me, goddamn it. My moods are predictable, surprising, and change smoothly, naturally, normally, completely. I don't even notice them until they are drastic and uncomfortable and noticeable. When they are heightened, I am insane; I am just insane.*

*A comparison of my temperament in the worst of times and the best of times is not difficult to illustrate. I am the water; wind moves me and influences my waves. I am run by a conflicting force; I have a weakness for this energy. I am producing whitecaps. Chaotic and confused, I am volatile, a danger…dangerous. Let no craft navigate my waters, for deadly instability is at hand.*

*Transitioning, I am rising and falling, bumping up and down more smoothly, without alarm and in many directions. Slowly, intensifying, I have no foresight for what is to be and I have no reason to be alarmed. I have forgotten the storm that has come before, though I can see the remains of my brokenness. Once I am subjected to its disposition, I am powerless. I can only wait for the climax.*

*Last and most desirably, I am unruffled. I am in control. I can navigate my own life and nothing alters my course. I am well and in good temper, neither running upstream nor sinking down below. I am going with the flow, I am horizontal, and my life is running all along the line. The wind will not affect me. There is no velocity, there are no rapids, and I am at the helm.*

Families have certain behavioral characteristics. At times our family shared challenging and confrontational personalities, although some would not admit this. I was and probably still am a responder, a defender, challenging and confrontational. I would protect you from an unrighteous thumping if necessary. I'm just not the eye-rolling, smirking, bite-your-tongue or pay-no-attention sort of gal. I could never pretend, for the sake of avoidance, that dirty deeds had not been done in order to save face.

*I cannot count to ten slowly enough to keep my defenses from seeping out of every pore of my body. I cannot prevent that impulsive, reckless brain-mouth connection when I am pushed to the line, pushed up against the wall, or driven to distraction. When you beat me with your lip service, I'm coming at you with my rebuttal for your enlightenment, and if you don't appreciate my clarification, then don't press me up against the wall.*

*Listing all my negative behaviors, I aspire not to have them but I cannot deny their existence. More and more I have a short fuse, shorter than I have ever known before, and I do not wish for this. I believe I will never become a member of my mother's inner circle.*

*I know they prefer me on the outside looking in, just doing the work. I know this has brought me emotional conflict and personal sorrow and I know that I respond to them in a temperamental sort of way when I am provoked. I realize they don't see it and they don't care. Every time my buttons are pushed, I have a difficult time maintaining my calm and I have a tendency to lash out but this is my way, getting worse, but…me.*

*Since my brother is ill, I am but a consultant offering my assistance to people who are not grateful, for they are too self-important to recognize the sacrifice it takes for the task. I am being held at arms' length to prevent me from getting too close; it hits a sore spot in me. I am thinking of all these things and as I sit here it is taking me lower and I need Dad.*

*How has my life come to this? How is it that his return has dominated me and controlled my life; why has it changed so drastically? When will it end? I know they were uncooperative and scheming in their history and they know of no other way. I know I will never penetrate their bond, and though they attempt to cast me aside, I will not let them throw me away. With them I am stubborn and bullish and smiling, and in the best interests of our family, I will succumb to my own joy and my own emptiness.*

*While they examine him and prognosticate, I experience my own deep feelings of life one day at the end of the road. I have, more than once, wanted to put my life to rest but I fear my failure would bring me to his fate, a jeopardized mind in a workable body, or a living mind in a sleeping shell. I am angry and I am analyzing and I am dwelling on my destiny, poor fucking miserable me.*

## Life Is Like a Line

*As they come in and out of his hospital room, checking his vital signs and asking for signatures, they speak to us and my mother defers to me and when they leave, my face rests in my cupped hands and I close my eyes because I am overcome by my bewilderment.*

*I suppose I am hiding behind my hands, hiding from the fear of some impending doom, and in spurts my hiding from view is my shelter. I am confused and in charge and I am uneasy in these waters. Again and again they query the patient. He answers; they listen; they write. Do they believe him? Are they fucking crazy?*

*He looks unwell. He is stupefied, his head is scrambled, and no one offers hands for his face to rest in. The diagnosis: stroke, frontal...white matter...admitted to a room on the third floor.*

*He's still acting weird. He's answering questions incorrectly. He hasn't a clue as to the date or the year or even the president of the United States. I am positive that some of this new brother persona is a sham; in my mind maybe fifty percent or more of him is his newest creation.*

I have observed them in all types of circumstances and there is no doubt in my mind that their mental instability played, one off the other. Hello, world of psychosis, world of obsessions, world of the crazies who really belong on some shrink's couch. They were ill and I was perfectly crazy. My sister also thought they were nuts, so I was relieved.

I needed another sane mind for support. All along, I thought I was the one who was out of touch. Neither one of them had any common sense; they answered each other's questions incorrectly and argued incessantly if you tried to correct them, which I couldn't help but do. One player, my brother, was the stage manager who manipulated with his confusion for personal gain. The other was my mother, who would browbeat you with her condemnation in an attempt to break your spirit to gain control. Either way, you entered into a desperate condition of fuck and be fucked.

*As I stand here, I am conscious that my jaw is sore today. I have a headache, my shoulders are tight, I have heart palpitations, and my mother wants to drag me downstairs for some hospital cuisine but I am adamant about staying with my brother until the doctor arrives and she is unkind due to my refusal. She thinks my brother can get the information and relay it to us. Oh, for God's sake, is she kidding?*

*Though I am thoroughly delighted to sit here and wait it out, I can barely stay in my seat when I am within earshot of them. I don't want to be involved in their disagreements but I am. And because of that, they alter me, they change my mood, and my temper begins to flare. With them, I move from some sort of happiness to immediate hostility and never do I see the transition until I am in the well of my ugliness. They suck me in; I am their third party and habitually their critic.*

*Collectively, we are the stuff hurricanes are made of. Staying with them puts me in the eye of the storm. Inside, I can see them churning around me; I observe their behavior and watch as they destroy everything in their path. When they are all that surround me, when they are behaving tumultuously, nothing is safe, above all me.*

*So, the specialist nicked it; it is official per the neurologist. From now on our lives will be more than tied together. New Jersey will be nevermore; he will have no independence and no substantial recovery.*

*I have been pessimistic overall so this did not devastate me the way it did my mother. I am a realist; I tend to confront the issues head-on with little hope for an optimistic outcome. There will be no separation from this day forward; that is my reality and my truth. I internalize, I think, I panic, and then I call my sister.*

Much to her discredit, my mother has always shown her upset in many ways, and critical irritable argumentativeness was at the top of the list after the onset of my brother's illness. She pushed all my buttons, leading me to the same unattractiveness as her own. In my upset, I had a difficult time maintaining my self-control, and although I have never known complete calm, at least I had been calmer.

After my father's death, I was convinced that somehow my brother would bring us heartache and I was absolutely correct. Although I planned as best I could to protect our mother, there is no preparation for such shock and awe. The take-the-money-and-run scheme, six little figures for his forced departure, would have been a small price to pay in comparison with this.

## Life Is Like a Line

This fiasco was, in my mind, turning into the bizarre. The best days were spent repairing his financial quagmire and no one dared to bother me during the hunt but my mother continued to interfere. Had she paid any attention at all, she would have seen that I was changing; she might have recognized that personally I was fighting for my life.

My quick-to-snap temper and sarcastic wit were annoyances that even I was irritated by. I hoped road rage would do me in, but no such luck. As if that weren't bad enough, my husband didn't grasp what I was going through and told me that everything "would pass." He was clueless.

Very involved in the day-to-day business, his world and my world were a universe apart. My heightened unpredictable moods began to worsen to the extent that I was very sensitive, especially toward him, and I longed more for the man whose lap I had sat on as a little girl. Not knowing which way to turn, I found everything sacred to be at stake. My days of fantastic energy and my interest in life were thwarted by days of coldness and detachment. With no desire left for social fare, I hated myself and everything around me. The world was fucked and everyone was trapped…If given the opportunity, get out while you can.

Mental paralysis claimed another victim and I thought about suicide. I saw it in my head. I didn't want to die the long slow way; I'd had enough of that. No, I wanted death in an instant with no memory of me left behind.

As my brother improved, everything worsened. While in his hospital bed, he was alarmingly perplexed. His stroke had robbed him of his scheme, but in a twist of fate he would amass his riches after all: a lifetime care plan would be needed to sustain him for the rest of his days as a stroke victim and my mother would pay for it.

Now my mother knew he would never leave her. And I was the baby of the family who had adored him as a youngster. He had pulled me in the wagon and pushed me on the swing and then at some point his life had separated from ours. Now I was his unsuspecting caregiver, his court-appointed guardian and conservator. I was the resentful, sympathetic, angry, suspicious, forgiving, confrontational, concerned, and anxious sister whose crystal ball shattered right before learning the story of what was to be.

She started with him again. "John, why did you wear that shirt?"

He smiled. "They told me I should."

I tried to jump in and explain that he was lying but she pounded me with insults before I finished my sentence. She continued, "I have told you a thousand times, John, to brush your teeth."

He responded, "They told me not to; it's too soon."

I realized this was confabulation in action but my mother would never see it. "Mom, he's been sick; don't you see how he is?"

"Cindy, this is none of your concern. Don't think you are going to push me aside again; this is my son." She continued talking to him. "You need a haircut and we need to replace those front teeth." Then she needed me. "Cindy, we need to do that."

"Mom, could you please stop this? People can hear you."

"I don't care; they don't know me; you don't have to be here; you can leave."

I was starting to feel like shit and at the boiling point. "Gee, thanks a lot. You know I should be working right now; I don't really need this abuse but I think my brother needs me."

"It's always about you, isn't it Cindy?" was her response.

"AAAAAAAAHHHHHHHHH" was what I felt; "FUCK!" was what I thought.

I never realized his natural behaviors would start again so soon after his stroke, poor pitiful me. The problem was that it never was about me. I had the legal power but they seemed to make choices behind my back. Having control does not mean much when it is their intention to circumvent good sense and my mother had much experience deceiving my father. I wanted not to use my legal powers unless my mother's decisions were reckless. She asked me to be his conservator and his guardian, and because they needed help, I agreed. If she had been more guarded they would have seen me less, but they were out of control and my brother's cluttered mind still had its own agenda. He, whether intentionally or otherwise, found it necessary to aggravate my mother, and the more she doted on him, the worse their mutual behavior.

My job as the "fucking go-between" was to make excuses for them and make apologies for them and explain and clean up their messes. Neither could see the light of day nor the behavior that was most upsetting to me.

## Life Is Like a Line

During my brother's stay in the hospital, the neurologist explained that he had some clinically visible brain damage. Psychologically there were signs of confabulation; my brother gave fictitious accounts of past events, believing they were true, in order to cover a gap in the memory.

No doubt he was a pathological liar; he embellished his stories to impress people. Although "pathological liar" is not an official clinical diagnosis, most psychiatrists agree that pathological lying is often the result of a mental disorder or low self-esteem, and I believe he suffered from both.

This brings us to my mother. Her diminished capacity caused her to believe him without question and against all reason. I have learned to hate lying and confabulation and those who partake in them. Knowing his condition made it easier not to hate him, but knowing him still made my life unbearable.

> *Fighting headaches and migraines is difficult with the wrong physiology, and as my chiropractor continues to go through the motions, I am sorry. I am sorry for life's battle. I am sorry I can't be enough, that I can't be more. I am sorry I can never be more. Giving more of me makes me less of a person, and I am less than I have ever been.*

He insisted that the doctor never came in, that he'd had no food all day, that some doctor had called him on the phone asking for my mother, that he'd left the building and gone outside where his roommate was (there was no roommate; my brother enjoyed infuriating my mother), that there had been no housekeeping for days, that they were going to do major surgery on his brain tomorrow, and in the same breath he insisted he was going home tonight.

Fact or fabrication? My mother would say fact and that was a problem for me. All was confabulation, fucking pathological confabulation. Their shared dementia had me spinning and I was the one feeling insane. I learned early in the game that each incident required confirmation, and any deficiency in micromanagement eventually became detrimental. I queried the doctors and nurses and aides continually. It was the only way I could keep up.

The truth was that when I was with them, I didn't know the truth anymore; they were both convincing and when they gave an accounting of their day, the truth was a coin toss. One of us or two of us, definitely certifiable; now I see three.

He was sent to a nursing home for his recovery and there he became both healthier and wackier.

> *My father passed away one year ago and living under these conditions is such hard work. I miss him still. My spirit is tender. I am emotionally motionless and every day my fallen mind stays weak. I show no one. I have truly lost the one who smiled whenever I entered the room, who listened without interruption or judgment, someone who never cast me aside for another. I have lost the one who just loved me. I have lost the one I adored.*
>
> *I am cast in a place where no heart can be cured and where no love can penetrate. My separation has brought me to a grave place where I have yet to be rescued. I can never be rescued; I can only be reassured. I'm sorry, sorry for everything. If only I could turn back the hands of time. If only we had one more day as a family.*
>
> *As the days pass, I lose myself to further bleakness, much further than the day before. There is no real sleep for me, no real sleep, no rest for me, too much mind, too much worry, too little success, too much failure. Every day I battle for reason but I am only one leg of their triangle. I am only one part of the puzzle. I am trapped here, I can't escape, and I have lost myself in the process...I am finished. I am fucked.*
>
> *I can't stop thinking...My father was the light and now I am in darkness and they are taking me down. I am worn and I am finished. I could end this if I were stronger. Emotionally, I am too weak for suicide, too fucking weak. Goddammit. Too fucking weak.*

My emotional alarm was going off every minute my eyes were open. I hated my emotions and I hated every minute of my life. I mulled over the past and I analyzed the present, day in and day out, hour by hour, mulled and analyzed, analyzed their behavior, my situation, analyzed and administered.

> *I have had a mass of inner turmoil but I am silent. My mind desires to think in secret. Perhaps the level of determination of this newest persistence is measured by the volume of my misery and then it is used to further its*

*cause. It is emotion-driven, intertwined somewhere between my feelings of love and hatred, happiness and misery, the same damn emotions of my life, all dutiful emotions and intense passions playing me for all that I am.*

*In my heart, I am me, but my random thoughts separate me from myself. After twenty-six years of minor interference, they penetrate me now too often. I am moods and tempers. I am highs and lows. I am colors of gray and darkness. What I see now is an untimely spontaneous combustion concurrent with a strong sense of panic…a sudden thought, the overwhelming whim is…of death. Mine. I wish for it.*

*I know not from where it comes, where it originates inside me; I haven't figured out the source, the tipoff, the point of perfect perplexity that compels me to play it out inside my mind and perhaps only there.*

*When it hits, I fuel the fire with thoughts and scenes I devise to occupy my mind till near the end and then they go as quickly as they come. I am the inventor of life's most violent movies in my mind. My splendid in-living-color physical disasters have been planned with every detail in mind right down to my last breath. With each event, I am as detached as the apple fallen from a tree. When my thoughts become my determination and then reality, it will be so, and so it will be.*

*The painful walk down my path has been named for my pain, for suicide, the path of depression, the path of overwhelming desire that takes more than it gives. I am locked into my consciousness, locked into the theatre of my mind. It begins in that core place within me but not of my body alone.*

*I am engaged, mentally I am trapped, and I am seeing perfectly without my eyes. I am always astounded at my thought-provoking power to devastate myself while myself watches. If thoughts become reality, then it will be logical and fitting, given the load. No one will question my sanity; it will be reasonable and fitting.*

*Anxiety, anxiety, anxiety. With a few breaks it has been nearly constant, tiring, frightening.*

I was afraid; I just couldn't pull myself up. More of me was leaving them one day at a time. My thoughts just went there. I didn't send them; they just went. The conclusion that seemed worthy would shatter my daughters, but the weight and the strain and the test were too much. I was ill and there was too much controversy, too many angles. All sides came at me but no relief.

I was not experienced in the art of deception. I could not see clearly why there was so much criticism, so much bickering, and so many flawed hearts protecting and defending and closing up shop.

Suicide. No one knew how deep, how cutting, how powerful, how strong my weakness really was. I was believable because I wouldn't show the expressions that would fit my cerebral crime. I would instead provide humor, but I plotted my course.

How could one get help? Was there such a thing as help? Was it possible to rewind what was wound too tight? Could I go back to the womb and forward to my room? Could I find light in the world? Could I figure out what had happened to my faith?

I had lost my faith. I was empty and lonely and I had lost my faith. I felt that life was not meant for happiness; it was a sample of hell. All day sitting with them was too much. At my next visit I didn't last long; I feared me as much as them but I was not yet ready to be burned by the undertaker. So I excused myself, hopefully in time. Pathetic, complaining, quitting, hollow fucking human being, me.

# CHAPTER 13

# *Chasing Sanity*

*"Do it; misery loves company anyway."*

*I've heard my own thoughts too many times. My gynecologist is the first one presented with my problems. He is a first-class physician and a Greek, which is a plus, and I trust him. His nurses are like family. After thirty-four years with his practice, I have tenure.*

*It is my mother's annual checkup and I am preoccupied with my thoughts and I am able to listen and speak with her but I am not there; I am a million miles away. I have talked myself into something and I am afraid. I don't want to speak to him about this, but I must. I am terrified and I am embarrassed. I would rather seduce and bed him than ask this of him.*

*We exchange pleasantries and giggle a bit and then I ask and I am moved into another examination room. There is an ultrasound machine in here; it's the baby room. He comes back to me and we talk about menopause and my hot flashes and I tell him and he has that look in his eyes; I have seen it before. It's that "Are you crazy?*

## Life Is Like a Line

*You aren't crazy!" look. He doesn't believe me when I tell him. A quick office visit does not allow him a sufficient evaluation.*

*I'm not your typical frazzled suicide case, at least not right now. I don't look despondent so I must not be. But he only knows what I choose to show him in our five minutes of a relationship. I am the great pretender; I am five minutes of playful insinuation and a fun-loving tease. His ridiculous psych test, three minutes verbal, considering my body language...I know the drill; this is not my first rodeo. Then I lied and he believed me, poor man.*

*Someday I'll tell him how scary his test was and try not to hurt his feelings. The worst part is that I've already thought about suicide today and it isn't even noon. I insist upon a psych referral, adding "Just in case" to humor him. In spite of the fact that I look too good, my makeup is perfect, my deep red lips are hot, and I'm dressed to the nines with my spiked white hair fixed to perfection, I'm skinny as a rail. I'm acting quite normal, but I'm falling to pieces right before their eyes.*

*I am embarrassed to even ask for this referral, let alone be told this is all in my head. For the moment, I am disappointed in him, but I understand that for as long as he has known me, he has seen the happy, friendly, energized me. I pressure them and they pore through their collective memories until they agree and his nurse writes down the name and telephone number of an esteemed psychiatrist, a woman who practices in the vicinity.*

*I am more than relieved and the words "Thank God" keep coming to mind. The doctor makes my mother feel comfortable; he tells us a few light-hearted jokes to cool the air, and when the two-by-two piece of paper is surreptitiously handed to me, I see for the first time in a long time light at the end of the tunnel.*

*Why did I wait so long to see a psychiatrist? Much of what I experienced in my lifetime was so familiar to me. I really believed I could handle whatever came my way. It was my familial responsibility to manage my mother and her business as I promised my father. I am not a stranger to multitasking and doing what is difficult. I just didn't realize that I would be expected to deal with the impossible.*

*A two-by-two piece of paper. The difference between everything and nothing. All forty-eight years of me now rests on paper; how pathetic.*

*Remarkably, the gynecology appointment helps me forget about my awfulness but only briefly. Mornings are generally better than any other time. I fake wellness and fight an anxiety attack right after. But my good Greek doctor places his hand upon my shoulder and with his comforting eyes assures me that as soon as my family situation levels out, I "will feel fine" and I humor him once more. He is a good man and I am grateful.*

*Standing at the exit, I turn to find his smile and in the midst of all the photographs of the newborns he has delivered, I am reminded of life's preciousness. Great beginnings, those lives displayed on a wall: innocent, precious, devoted, tender, adoring, and enthusiastic souls alive with good intentions. Layers of lives of years gone by, their subsistence and their extinction, their successes and their failures never known. One's direction, a collage of life's events, and I am but the hollow of a tree.*

*Today my mother is wonderful. We laugh and reminisce but I behave poorly and there are times when I am unreasonably unkind. Regrettably, I have been this way to her before. Despite the fact that we have no brother to contend with, no controversy, no criticism, and no power struggles, I am retaliatory and argumentative and challenge her every word.*

*I am moody today. I am anxious and edgy, contrary, and in "that" state of mind. All I want to do is bitch out the world, and in doing so I hope to have some relief. Of course, my general good behavior will not allow me such a public performance so I will share it with those I love and presume it is their burden.*

*My bitching is the result of a quick mood change, I guess; it is my non-effective release of anger and hostility. My moods keep flipping back and forth, and as they do I am hard-pressed to control my frustration. There is hatred for myself when I am swinging in this way, and I surely don't wish these feelings on anyone else, nor do I want anyone to see me like this.*

*My mother is innocent today as she is on many days like this. She does not deserve company like me and I should apologize to her, but the bitterness over her choices prevents me from doing so. My hurt still festers in my heart and I am becoming detached, so with a kiss and a promise I leave her until tomorrow, and in a car of silence I head for home.*

# Life Is Like a Line

*Pacing. Should I go back and make an apology? I worry about her while I fear the unknown. Powered by a better frame of mind, my little dog and I are alone in our kitchen and I telephone to apologize for my ugliness but she doesn't hear me. She is too busy being discontented with him, and in the midst of her complaining I grasp that there is no room for my remorse.*

*My brother has monopolized her mind once more and they are tangled up in a battle for power and control and she cannot protect herself from him. I will rescue her. I cannot rescue her. My hands are tied. I am infuriated. She needs me but doesn't want me and won't let me help her. My attempt at an apology is over; I only wish to beat the hell out of my kitchen and get really drunk.*

*I do neither, but instead hold in the feelings tightly. I am caught in the fury once again. I am falling. I am failing. I am breaking down. Down, below the level line of life. Down towards the level line of death. Down far enough below to see nothing.*

The two-by-two piece of paper carried more weight than I realized. It made all the difference, though it took me days to muster up enough courage to call the number and make the appointment, only to be told I couldn't be seen for three months.

I knew I would never make it three months. I could make it to one month but never three. Dear God, not three. I felt a rising sense of hysteria. I was persistent in calling the office, even requesting that my name be added to the cancellation list they didn't maintain.

I may have sounded as desperate as I was. It was humbling to be this way, but this was the way of my fear and the way of my thoughts and the way of my secrets. It was what my mind accepted and what my mind rejected and what devoured me that created this need to be seen by a professional.

Or, simply put, I hated my life. I hated controversy, I hated my father's death, I hated this emptiness, I hated menopause, and I didn't see why life was worth living. I hated getting up in the morning; I hated going to bed at night. I recognized too that the fleck of happiness that filtered through my life was not enough and that I could not defeat the abundance of disappointment and frustration alone.

Although our recently built northern Michigan home and the reflection of the small lake provided a physical getaway, I was as gloomy as the lake was serene. During the days a cloud-filled sky would dim my summer mood, but there was no breeze to cool my fire. I was easily agitated, so my husband stayed busy and I remained transfixed alone with thoughts and a mind in full motion. Like an explosion, I began composing verse and it flowed out of me but I didn't know why. I was bleeding my thoughts and they pooled on the paper. They exposed my pain. Each word surprising within their cluster, I wavered between depression and intense energy and it was unclear in what direction I was to go. Not since my teenage years had I felt so compelled to write and so at ease in doing so. Without conscious creation, the verses began to convey an abstract of my childhood understanding, hurtful parental favorites and personal complexities built from a difficult reality. Just as if they were synchronized with my heart, they became 'the beat':

**The Beat**
voices loud, the weakest link with words of rage...the beat of life; my
    breath sustained the
turning page
life day by day with arms outstretched, events and evidence
but truths were never told and the litter of lies began to molder
and as I lived the hand that cast the mighty blow was with the one
    whose life chose isolation
still scores of years have gone with childhood memories past
instilled the thunder still remains and I am found where darkness
and ferocity subsist
although I did not see the onset of that foe
I felt it then as yours and now to calm and pause my fate
the impossibilities of holding back my own calamity
for what is mine of twists of temperament I pray cannot for all eternity
    be the soul
for paradise from this will set me free—
no more distress, a respite from this legacy

*Today a cancellation became available; it is a forty-minute drive. I shut*
*my car door and head in the direction of the office. In the parking lot I look*
*back for a retreat but I am at the point of no return and continue on the*

*path, excited and frightened and completely on my own. I feel a push from behind; maybe it's my dad giving me his best advice.*

*Once in the waiting room, I hide my self-consciousness; they make every attempt to make me feel more comfortable. I am relieved but ready to leave. I know about places like this. Male psychiatrists, mentally invasive, are voyeurs fascinated with minds filled with distressing details. As good as they may be, they aren't for women like me. Happily, this psychiatrist is a woman and by stereotype I am confident that she will be sympathetic about life in the world of hormones and men and sinking.*

*The fact that both my parents saw a shrink—enough said. This just has to be my remedy. I wait in the lobby and pretend to read a magazine. No pictures, no words penetrate my panic-stricken mind. She opens the locked door, a locked door, great…She invites me in and my mind is in collapse mode. Oh God, I am drawing a blank after hello.*

*While we walk and make small talk, I have no idea what in the hell I've just said and I'm thinking, "Is there an exit back here?" Nope, it's a short hall, here's her office, chair on the right, small couch to the left, a wall of sliding windows…Shit, there's no escape from here, not now.*

*Thank God, I really made it. I want to cry with relief but I have not cried since before my father died, not for a long while. Besides, she will never see me fucking cry; how lame would that be, slobbering like an idiot?*

*She shuts the door and I take the couch and my pounding heart is in my throat and I hope she doesn't notice that I am out of breath from my fear. Instinctively I find myself playing with my watch. This habit distracts my mind. I open and close the clasp, open and close it a few hundred times, and when it is in my hand it calms me. The watch has many parts and I feel the smoothness of the face. As I move down the band, I can feel each part of its construction. I am handling the band and it is distracting me, simply de-energizing me.*

*The doctor is a psychiatrist and I am relieved and frightened. I need help, there is shame, I have no idea what to say, it is simple unhappiness, and on some days I want to die. Simple. Voilà! What could be a better explanation than that? I have everything to live for and nothing. My life is a constant struggle. It is dread.*

*I want to ask, "Doctor, what is it that leads someone to look down at themselves slumped over their steering wheel? Are people ever too broken to mend?" I am below the line and cannot climb back up. I have a wonderful family. I am alone. I am whining. I hate to complain. I have a great life. I don't have cancer or any loss of limbs. There is a relentlessness to my being. I am its witness but it is too dangerous to perceive. I feel cold and detached, and that's just yesterday's problems. I bring to her the same issues over and over again, over and over again, over and over.*

*This, I imagine as I look around, is where the extreme meet according to the office schedule. People in the psychiatrist's office, they are the goofballs and the psychos and the knuckleheads and here I am.*

*I wonder, am I a member of the morning insanity club or am I part of the insanity wanna-bees? We shall soon see. I sit on the couch. With the wall at my back, I feel safe. The doctor's inner sanctum is small and because of that has an intimate feel. It is not decorated in a stark or medical manner. I am somewhat comfortable. The doctor immediately sits down at her desk, which is right in front of me, and I believe that we are, for the moment, sizing each other up.*

*She immediately wins; she sits in the winning chair. But her facial expression speaks about her and the tone of her voice is comforting and I feel assured that I have made the correct decision in this quest to unearth me. My mind is drifting now, conversing with itself all on its own. Then it meets hers somewhere in the middle.*

*When she asks, I give her my short history, my short tale of fucking woe, and then her icebreaker: "So tell me, why are you here?"*

*Nothing but blank thoughts. Afterwards, each subject we discuss is like a stone thrown into the water. My problems are the ripples, chaotic, multiplying, and moving one by one. Each ripple, the water's impediment, and as they move from me, the water smoothes and I find my problems lessening until the next stone is thrown.*

*I don't know if I have sadness or depression but I am physically and mentally unwell. This lowness has been with me for quite some time. I think I want to die. I really don't care about much. I have been defending and protecting and caring for others my whole life. I need help. I begin to explain my symptoms. I have repeated and unexpected panic attacks and anxiety that continue to worsen. Eventually, the doctor prescribes an antidepressant called Paroxetine.*

*Every session thereafter begins the same and I can never prethink its direction. At some point it all drizzles out. My doctor tells me that I am able to articulate my thoughts and feelings quite well, and feeling some shyness, I thank her for the compliment. I have spent hour after hour, day after day, night after night analyzing my situation and dissecting myself. There are countless details she must know before she can put the puzzle together.*

*In the recent past I have considered that my relief can only come from my brother and my mother behaving themselves, but I just don't see that happening in the near future, so the next step is to work on the state of my own existence. What that means today is that I must find a way to crawl up and out of this sinkhole that travels beneath me and work at being unearthed for awhile. I still feel like death is my outline.*

*As time goes on, my doctor analyzes and regularly prescribes. My symptoms are in full swing, and while my heart palpitations worsen, the anxiety attacks and sleeplessness shadow along behind. Unfortunately, all of my symptoms worsen on the first prescription so it is changed to Sertraline HCl.*

*The next session comes none too soon. It is more detail about my brother who came here after my father passed to steal my mother's money, yada, yada, yada. I was born, blah, blah, blah, done. I am married, I have siblings, daughters, sons, done, done. I am dying too slow a death; help me or let me go. Done, done, done fucking done.*

*Articulate perhaps, but the bottom line is there are days when I hate this and that and the other thing and I can't stand how you drive and I don't feel like eating anything so stop asking me and I am going to lie down for a while and don't you think the neighbor's grass looks like hell? Geez, don't you have an opinion about anything? I don't know why I married you; you have no mind of your own; you are like a fucking fish. Forget it; I'll sleep on the goddamn couch, and not only that but I have a headache and you have that crappy tone and I hate you and if I had one brain in my head I would divorce…Just forget it. I really hate myself. Do you want to go out for dinner or get a pizza or what? I don't really care; whatever you want to do; I'm easy.*

Pizza night reminded me of the good times long ago, of Dad and our family and pizza and Dad and pizza. He was an offender, he was a corner hog, and as he would dive into the box and begin gobbling up the corners, he would defend his actions with his broad smile, a twinkle in his eye, and his famous chuckle. "I'll eat the corners since nobody likes them anyway" he'd say, and of course we would all grunt and groan and eventually somebody else would get the last one.

Then Dad would catch hell from my mother for this blatant violation and with our exchange of glances and eyebrows raised we would carry on. This spectacle happened whenever we had pizza; oddly enough it felt like the first time every time. But my father was quite a sidewinder and he put on a perfect show no matter what. Our daughters adored him eternally; he was the teacher, they the students. Quite simply, he was a man with more spirit than will ever pass into my life again.

God, I missed him. He was the decision-maker, the guardian, the advisor, the brilliant ray of sunshine—and darkness—in the clouds. He was my silver lining. Upon his death, the torch was passed to me and it was a weighty shift that left me exposed and responsible. If I didn't say I was nervous, I'd be kidding myself. He was my sounding board; he gave me advice and always helped me through the fall. The distress is that no telephone will ever reach him.

> *What is with those scissors? I am thinking and talking so much and I hate it; I am obsessing; I have thoughts of cutting my tongue off. God, that freaks me out; that is weird. I must be a sick fuck; I must really be gone. Yes, say hello to me; I have surfaced again. No, I don't like me either, believe me. So blame it on the chemistry or the hormones and something called genes; who in the hell knows?*
>
> *Now I'm aggravated and agitated and irritable and energized and thinking on my toes and talking blah blah blah and you really don't want to listen to all of this, do you?*
>
> *"Sorry to have interrupted you again, and remember these antidepressants have killed my sex life already and please fix me up with something that won't have such an awful side effect." During certain months and*

*weeks and days my imagination could run riot forever. I think, God, if this is a test, you are really mean.*

*Then I tell her, "If I had any sense at all, I would sit in the fucking garage with the engine running and the door closed. Oh wait, hang on; I almost forgot to tell you. The other day something weird happened…I had a hallucination and I was straight, of course. I was sitting on a stool, leaning over slightly, and before my eyes I saw the air moving in front of me. It was gel-like, very thick, and I could see particles in it. As it drew me closer it was atoms and molecules moving right in front of me."*

*"No, I was not frightened. But I thought it was weird. I didn't want it to end. I remember thinking, 'Hmm, we think the air is transparent vast nothingness but it has density.' It was cool."*

*We discuss this and she makes some notes. My psychiatrist doesn't react badly when I express thoughts of suicide but I don't think she likes it particularly either. I think she has some responsibility to lock me up or something, but so far I'm still moving about the cabin, so to speak. Being the good patient that I am, I tell her not to worry. She accepts me at my word that I am to be trusted and I am hopeful that I mean it precisely and that her faith is warranted.*

We were out on the lake again. The birds continued to wake me and the stars stirred me. My mood was like the climate. It was a red-hot summer and within me there was a scorching of resentment and more disappointment. I hadn't slept more than five hours in the past three days and my doctor warned me. I did not find sleep easily. This was a new me, emotion-filled. My mother had hurt me, I loved her dearly, and though I should expect her rejection, I never saw it coming. Again verse came to me. I was nocturnal; I was alone fighting depression and melancholy. I missed my dad. Three in the morning, and this was what I had become.

### A Message to My Mother
Intelligent Design put my tiny hands in yours but vacant eyes would
     never see that miracle of life
just steps away from you lived me
        You should have loved…me

My childhood longed for more than your despair
My waking eyes learned lessons of someone else's game
　　　　　You should have loved...me
Music-laden melancholy separates the sorrowful but keeps them at their
　　breast
While others befall some symphony of despondency not like the rest
You should have loved...me
And figures exposed to battles never won but still designed would
　　horrify not glorify
While the drums beat on the message loudly passing
And when you are callous with my spirit I defend
And everything that hurts shouts out and my unwanted nature then
　　prevails
But I know that I will never cease my call and I will care for you and
　　love you even though
　　　　　You should have loved...me

*There have been so many days of emptiness and despair and this
present life doesn't feel anything like my own and though I don't feel as if I
would destroy anything pre-existent, each day is a challenge. There are days
when I am certain there are no options and the obliteration of my self by any
means seems quite desirable, the means to an end, the passing of ships on
the river of agony, the conveyor belt through the fire of cremation.*

*We're not meant to stay forever anyway, here on the planet of complete
oneness. Today I am given sleeping pills for my insomnia, Ambi something
or other. I take my dosage and fall asleep and then after three hours I wake
up and that's it; I struggle for more.*

*The Sertraline HCI dosage is now maxed out and caused me sweating
so a change is being made. Another antidepressant, Ventafaxine HCI, is prescribed today. I'm feeling quite a bit of stress over these medications and the
side effects and I am ever so anxious and edgy and swinging from the lows of
depression to something higher. Dear God, please let this one work without
all the sweating and the pacing and the paranoia and the symptoms.*

*I started before her today. "I am feeling miserable. I feel such despair
and they are killing me." Sitting in front of her, my head is hanging in my*

*hands, a sure sign of my extreme lack of hope. I sit up again. I begin with*
*that same fucking story. "My father passed away and my brother came home*
*to steal my mother's money; he is unpredictable and a confabulator." I am*
*repeating myself with each appointment. "We are self-employed so our work*
*pace is hell and though we have a new house, I fret over our income."*

*I am obsessive and now compulsive; I cannot get through the problems*
*of the past. Like musical chairs my brother and mother keep moving around*
*me, players one and two and at any time they are challenging me with their*
*lies and manipulations. Their stories have stories and I cannot keep up. I*
*am embarrassed and I am their go-between and I am their fucking police. I*
*have yet to release all that is in my memory as my medication complicates*
*me. I am worn, I am confused, I am fucked.*

*I want to pace. I can't sit for long; I am coming out of my skin. I don't*
*tell her I am thinking about suicide today. I think I have a handle on it. I*
*am rambling. "And so I continue to worry about how my brother…and my*
*mother…as they are not cooperating." As I sit in front of her, I am having a*
*strong panic attack but I am not disclosing the evilness that engulfs me.*

*"We sold my mother's house and I orchestrated her move per her request*
*to the same assisted living residence as my brother and so far the fireworks*
*have gone off every day between them. My brother wants little to do with*
*my mother and she wants everything to do with him, but he seems to be*
*acting strangely. And, oh yeah, Mother got into a car accident…There was*
*an ambulance and police for the woman she hit. No, she is fine, but…the*
*woman she hit, well, I just received paperwork for a lawsuit, and I am her*
*legal representative of course. Oh God."*

*"My brother is on the computer and it's more than 'adult.' It is boys*
*and the nurses at the residence got a glimpse of his monitor and I had to*
*intervene and the only remedy was to take it from him and I was in the hot*
*hot hot seat by my mother as well as my brother and then I had to remove*
*his phone. $500 worth of 1-900 calls in one month alone and now I can't*
*sleep and the drugs you gave me aren't helping. Shit!"*

*I don't swear too much in front of her but I am rambling on and on and*
*I want to stand up but there is nowhere to go. The last antidepressant gave*
*me profuse sweating, hallucinations, sensations, creepy sensations all over*

*me, and a kind of head pressure when I tried to withdraw. I don't understand all the side effects but they beat me.*

*I try to be patient. I know this is a difficult process, trial and error, but in the meantime I have nothing to keep me from crumbling; these drugs are supposed to be my buffer. I believe I am going insane insane insane. I am having shortness of breath and difficulty concentrating and I do not understand any of this. What began simply continues to accelerate. At the end of my appointment she asks me to be honest about the way I feel. Wanting to experiment, she gave me a small dose of a sedative, clonazepam (Klonopin), to calm me. It did the trick swimmingly.*

*Today's try is lamotrigine, an anti-convulsant medication used off-label for mood stabilization and depression. It is used for the treatment of epilepsy and an illness called bipolar disorder. She is my doctor, my psychiatrist; she will not let me fall alone.*

Disturbed, I was still racing. Tonight was just like the last, waiting for more of the same. I wrote a poem at 4:30 a.m. I had been up since 8:00 yesterday morning. I was not tired.

### This Very Heavy Load
I awakened to a state of my affairs that seemed to satisfy, then afterwards the trigger caused a chain of new events.

At that point I realized the return of my familiar theme, the overwhelming discontentment of my self.

Disobedient is my psyche, urgent words race from my feelings, colorless and abundant in the forefront of my mind.

Talkative and callous, I am speaking fast yet I am searching; nervous, my words would be much better left unsaid.

Bear witness to the dominant and inpatient me; amid the agitation I am poised once more for some impending war.

Likewise with persistent exhilaration I am struck with fascination for every situation that's in store.

I am conflicted, and as I struggle to be silent, I cannot…heart pounding, quick to comment, thinking, and the cycle comes once more.

## Life Is Like a Line

Restricted by my thoughts, a rush disturbance and I am not prepared
to edge the fall.
My acquaintances are current compound marvels but the pitfalls can be
greater than the cure.
Trial and error, disappointment by some crushing psychic failure, no
quick fix to heal the ill that is obscure.
Medical experiment at hand, repair the state that is impaired, for I am
stunned by each and every episode.
To construct my life by treatment, liberate me from the symptoms, set
me free from this very heavy load.


It was obvious that worries kept under wraps forever were deadly, and
my doctor continued to drag them out of me. Deep down, I needed her to
know and the madness had to stop; I couldn't fix it on my own. I didn't
know what was down there; I was anxious and there were cold summer
nights when I didn't know which way to turn. Some days I would feel awful
confusion; I had no experience with these circumstances and there was
constant chaos.

I was thinking about my marriage and its unavoidable difficulty under
these conditions. I had secrets. I didn't care anymore about discussing my
most personal thoughts and feelings with another human being, and she
was not an absolute stranger anymore. I told her about the perception of my
falling and the feelings of flooding concrete about to pour over the sides of
me and fill the holes that gave me breath.

After all these sessions, I knew there was no turning back. By the time she
opened me up, my heart was silently begging for more. Each session made
me anxious but I tried to look subtle at the beginning and she was smart; she
knew how to move me about exactly in the direction of my answer.

I went there in ruin. I was mentally spent and I could only see decline
in sight for us all; my behavior and feelings forced me to help myself or lose
myself. I was so depressed, and going deeper. I was fearful. I was alone. I
once had a love for people and parties. Now I was solitary.

The antidepressants for my depression either riddled me with side
effects or else they just stopped working, so we opted for another try,
again talking and talking. We kept moving up my mood stabilizer in order
to find some relief.

*We talk about the girls; they're great. She asks about my marriage. My marriage is sometimes trying; it is me, my demands, my needs, my hot head and temper. There are things about me he doesn't understand and likewise me about him. Once married, my quick temperament and quick-to-react personality worsened and if I don't get the result from him I am looking for, I become negative and belittling and then explosive. It's the typical family tradition, that bitch of a personality of irritability and irritation.*

*Good God, how did I get here? How have I become the lowest common denominator with qualities suited for the landfill of behavior? I know I haven't always been this way; I was once a sweet little kid and a peace-loving teenager and a party gal after a marriage destined for divorce. Now I am a forceful, rigid, high-strung, goal-driven warrior.*

*Then the doctor's focus goes to the other difficulties in my life. I ask her about my brother and dementia, neurologically speaking. He has had several medical appointments and I am finding him to be mentally less competent and less recognizable. My mother is really critical of him and refuses to see the situation for what it is. She is old and maybe that is the reason for her unkindness but it is difficult for me to listen to her chastise him over and over again each time we are together. God, I hate that shit. I cannot tolerate her ugliness. My neck is tight and a headache kicks in; as much as I want to, I can't even eat lunch with them. I am in their middle.*

*Last time I was getting explosive, so I left them to make a phone call, to disappear for a moment, to physically and mentally give respite to my feeble fucking mind. When I returned, they talked with each other, no eye contact for me…I don't give a shit, just eat, bicker, and let's get the hell out of here. I am in their fucking middle.*

*My brother is stable but his strokes have made him worse physically. He can barely walk, his gait is totally reflective of a stroke patient, and my mother hounds him about his "faking it." Of course I defend him and then I am on the shit list. More of the fucking middle.*

*Mentally he struggles to keep up, struggles to hide the effects, and struggles to remain the man he once was. Consequently, strangers find him believable but I know who he is, though often it is difficult to distinguish this new brother from the old. He has always been a good actor. He keeps up by letting my mother fill in the blanks, which she does instinctively very well.*

## Life Is Like a Line

*He can still manipulate our mother and his storytelling borders on per-fection. With his comedic personality, it is even more difficult to differentiate the evil, manipulative brother from the playful, bullshitting one. Me, I am the frustrated one; I go where no one dares.*

*I am irritated that I am stuck in the middle of his behavior. I am mad that my mother believes him and not me, and I am nuts for expecting that anything will ever change. I realize it's a stroke thing…It's not his fault, not entirely; I vacillate between caring about him and detesting him. I detest him. My fears are growing as he is found gallivanting in the downtown area in search of life's pleasures. Forgetting his suspenders most of the time, his pants slide down and he struggles along his way. His hair is messy. With one shoe on and the other barely, he is making his way home with an ice cream treat. I am observing him because by chance or destiny I am passing by. I pull over and park and he does not see me. He has one block to go. He leans on the buildings one by one, struggling with his gait. He is a persistent man. I worry that his deep-rooted desires and determination will bring him future problems. My mother fights me as she believes he needs to live his life with freedom in this apartment setting. She believes he should have money. "He cannot be broke, for God's sake, Cindy." In her mind he is sound and that makes me fucked. Soundness and my brother; now that is a stretch. They live with the same untruths intentionally. I am always afraid of them. There will be a price to pay, I know.*

*I am not a horrible sister; I just resent the forced searching for a wheel-chair when we are together while he hobbles alone to find his fix when we're gone. He makes it back to his building and I am free to leave but never free of him.*

*It could be worse…I realize it could be worse. My mother will never stop with the money train. I have begged her but she feels this is power over me, influence over my brother, importance for herself, whatever.*

*What they do is squelch my productivity, make me dreadfully agitated, and cause me mental exhaustion. Thank God for my psychiatrist. We dis-cuss all the latest events and my desperation and much more. I am prey to my thoughts and I have been afraid. I have an anger that feeds my tempera-mental rage. I have more; it is worse. I want to do horrible things and I am afraid of myself but I am too analytical. I hold it in. I figure it out; I think about the angles. I see a truck coming up over the horizon on a two-lane road. I am a healthy woman and I have a family…what in the hell? Same horrific sight…I have gone crazy, but it is my deep dark secret.*

*Now I see the whole truck, the driver's face. I'm on a two-lane road; I think about moving into his lane…*

*I think about destruction and drugs and disappearing, and the more they exchange blows with me, the worse they make me feel, but I cannot abandon the situation. I am not a quitter. With them, I will appear hard and then I will go home.*

*I am sad; I cannot sleep. I have nightmares about my father and I am inundated with their errands all over again. I am fighting to do my best for them but they use me. They have caused my decay and there is no drug that has been able to provide my relief and I want no longer to live in this way.*

*My moods, so much has been about my moods and how I have to fight the assortment of moods that overtake me. It has been years since my father's death; I'm worsening with every day that passes. I have spontaneous thoughts about suicide. I am afraid of the inevitability of death. I am glad. I am relieved. I will probably be relieved. Dreadfully symptomatic, I am avoiding social gatherings.*

*My doctor explains that I have obsessive thoughts and I tell her I am on the edge; I am on the fucking edge.*

*She easily takes my talking in circles and makes sense of it all. She paraphrases my plight perfectly. Thankfully, her neurological background helps me understand the effect of his strokes and the ramifications of my mother's dementia and all the other facets of my grief. In all of my ways I am dreary and dark and down. I am spiritually, physically, mentally, socially, sexually, sadly full of fear and failure. I require medications to pull me up but they are just powder in the wind. Bupropion, the antidepressant pick; lamotrigine gave me a rash that is dangerous. Any rash is potentially fatal. Give me antidepressants, more and more and more.*

*"Hi Mom; what's wrong? It's ten o'clock. Are you okay? I asked you not to give him any money. It serves you right. He's probably out buying pizza. Call me if he doesn't come home, but for God's sake, when are you going*

*to listen to me? I am sick and tired of fighting you people…I don't care; go ahead and hang u…"*

*I'll be damned; she hung up on me again. God, I want to smash something. God, goddammit, fuck! Goddammit, goddammit!*

*"Oh, it's just my stupid family…don't worry about it. I'm too upset to go to bed. Go ahead, really. I'll be fine. I have thoughts and they are not good." I send him to bed; bed is the last place for me. Too much pressure, too little interest. I am picking fights with him and I am very terse to our friends.*

*As usual, I walk past the wooden chair and sit on her couch. My stress is getting worse; I confess my thoughts. While sitting in her office, I try to present the story in chronological order so that she understands and she is remarkable; she follows my mess. While we talk, she analyzes my body language. During this appointment, I feel less fragile; anger seems to help.*

*With my two arms wrapped around her small couch pillow, it presses against my chest and does something for me; perhaps it is comforting. Perhaps it acts as the only shield available to protect me from ingesting a newer version of my pain. Perhaps I don't have a fucking clue as to the reason. I have taken it from the couch and it is mine for a long time. Mostly I am aware that I am all over her couch, uncomfortable. If not playing with my watch or holding that pillow, I'm leaning forward, holding my head in my hands, leaning on one side or the other, lying down, moving, and moving more.*

*I have lost myself to tremors, nervousness, thirst, panic, and sadness, but this time I am fixed in depression. She gives me the medical overview and then thoughts on our humanity and suggestions on how to handle my situation. She reminds and reminds again…boundaries.*

*How have I gotten here? I don't understand why this life is so turned around. I am beginning to forget life's simple things and my husband is noticing so it must be awfully bad. Generally he notices nothing, and if he does he says nothing. His silence is not necessarily a bad thing. Since I am a control freak by nature, there is a fine line between advice I need and advice I want. What I may need, I may not want.*

*I have lost money, paperwork, and a checkbook this week alone. We are self-employed; it is not helpful to lose things. Today I am discussing and experiencing my newest problems with confusion. In this phase I am overwhelmed and unable to make compound decisions.*

*This is troubling. I am not by nature confused. My mind seems to be in a constant struggle and I believe it is because of this recent influx of medical information and responsibility and I find that when pressed, my own bad behavior is more visible than before.*

*It is all difficult today and I am squirming on her couch. At home, my husband tells me that I fly off the handle easily. I think, "No doubt." Mentally I'm not better, not really. The drugs are not a panacea for me. I thought they would be…it sounded so easy at the beginning, a sort of cure, pop a pill and away we go.*

*Elicit drugs have been useful for the aches and pains in my soul, but psychiatric drugs have been non-effective overall. I have a few months of relief, but just as I begin to see the light, the medication stops working. We decide to change my antidepression medication. My white hair is turning yellow and the hot flashes are unbelievable with the Bupropion.*

*Escitalopram Oxalate, that's the script written for an antidepressant this time and oh God…I need it to work. We talk for a long time. I always feel lifted when I leave her. I might just kidnap her someday.*

*I can do nothing about my situation; it is out of my control. Just two members of my family and I am run ragged. I repeat the same subjects over and over. I have had no happiness. I am belittled and treated as if I am unnecessary to them and I put on this sham of a show so that no one will stop me from slicing my goddamn wrists open or driving into the bloody river.*

*God, I want to die. I don't want to go home…I don't want to go home today. How can they let me leave them? Don't they see me? I fight myself; fight to keep them from seeing how weak I am. Rational enough to bury the symptoms, I am frightened nonetheless.*

*Either I am not to be trusted…or I am full of shit. One or the other. I feel intense about everything and all is exaggerated. Another antidepressant? No, another seizure medication, Gabapentin, that was developed for the*

*treatment of epilepsy. Used to relieve pain, it is occasionally used off-label*
*for mood.*

I understood that people were dying every day who wanted to live. What fucking pathetic irony. For the next several months, I had to move my brother in and out of hospitals and specialized care facilities and all decisions regarding his care became my own. He was strong and stubborn like a bull and even with a damaged brain could manage to manipulate my mother to his benefit. Fortunately, he was less of a shit than before; he remembered nothing of his old life and little of his present and that helped me maneuver him in the right direction.

My mother continued as she had for so many years. I would blow up and storm out and then return five minutes later for more of the same and it would continue the next day and so on and so on. In each situation my mood would turn from accommodating to angry and my temperament from tolerant to raging. It was easy to see why I lived for my appointments with my psychiatrist. I thought I would die if she cancelled me out; I would fucking die.

*In each session she gets an accounting of the latest family episodes and how I have been affected by them. Today as I sit across from her I see that her lips are in motion and she is smiling with her eyes but I am not with her right now. I'm thinking about what I just said to her; I am watching her look back at me and I wonder if she is rolling her eyes inside her head when she is with me?*

*I tell her I am having serious and extreme mood fluctuations and I am convinced that something is happening to me. Although I still battle with my family because of my brother, my temperament does not seem to be directly connected to him anymore. My temperament, it changes; it is volatile without provocation. It is about depression and sadness and loss. Perhaps it is about delayed anger with irritability and anxiety. Either way, I am bold and intense and extreme.*

*I have never noticed anything quite like this before. On the days that I am overly sensitive, I am frantic at the same time; then I am excited with a wonderful opinion of myself and everything about me and extremely miserable at exactly the same time. I think about suicide daily. I plan it; it plans me.*

*I think about illicit affairs. I have been intensely creative but easily agitated at everything I try. There are days when I think about alcohol and drugs, about ingesting them once more, about the fearless smooth transition interested only in me, about a wonderful, nearly sexual desire that more than one visit will surely destroy.*

*I am frustrated with the failure of all my medications. My father has died, my mother is too tough, my brother is deceitful, and my sister is trying to be helpful from a distance without having to put up with the bullshit of the game. She listens to me and is the only one who really knows.*

*This balance of life is a combination of psychodrama and dark comedy and my doctor understands. The crisis I bring to her today, my own, feels all new to me with shades of prior disturbances. The chemical marvel Gabapentin, briefly my freedom from these symptoms, now ceases to benefit me at all. There is no explanation as to why all these medications fail me.*

*I sit in the waiting room quite a while, sitting and waiting and thinking, and today I think about my husband. When my mood is sound I recognize that he has a sympathetic heart for me and my problems and he never interjects or interferes. I come and go as I please and as long as he has coffee in the freezer, he seems to be tolerant of the rest.*

*After coming home from being with them, I kicked a hole in the drywall of our stairwell. He was kind enough to repair it without complaint and gave no reprimand for my actions. I am thankful for him, for his kind and quiet ways, but I have wanted to leave him many times.*

*Life together is not perfect; it is the yin and yang all over again but to a lesser degree. My psychiatrist tells me I'm hypersensitive and she is correct. I am very sensitive to his tone when he speaks to me and to his moods and quietness. For me, quietness is rejection. Most of the time I expect him to read my mind or be my alter ego. I want him to be my girlfriend and my shrink and my man and never miss a beat all at the same time.*

*He will never understand me really, especially with my newest troubles, but I wonder just how much he understands that he has never shared. I wonder how any marriage can withstand the differences of men and women. Nevertheless, I thank God for him and hope that the drugs kick in.*

*"Hi, Doctor. I'm fine; how are you?"*

*"You look great today."*

*"Thanks. You know, I'm putting on some weight. I can't take that; I just can't take it. When I first saw you, I weighed one hundred and twelve pounds…You are killing me."*

*And then her million dollar question. "So tell me, what's going on?"*

*"Well…while my brother was in the hospital his physician performed a spinal tap and they found the remnants of a once-active transmitted disease, syphilis, in the fluid of his spine. Perhaps it is contributing to his present decline; they do not know. He has another serious infection and they have tried three antibiotic medications to kill the bacterium."*

*With this news, I feel guilty and at the same time totally justified in the way I have felt about him over the years. These feelings remind me of my resentment for the way my mother made him a god when we all knew of his often deviant lifestyle.*

*While raising him up, even today, she successfully pushes aside the rest of us. I don't know why I panic for my brother, but when I am with him I feel instability and to my order there is disorder. I am in an uproar with my mother as she fights for power and control and I fear for him. Her decisions would not be prudent nor does she have any power of control. As she speaks with the nurses and doctors behind my back, I remind them of the Michigan HIPAA laws and to them I must look like a power-hungry asshole but they must understand once again that by law they shall not provide information to anyone nor may anyone other than myself authorize medical care.*

*I am the screen door and my mother is the plate glass window…decisions are hers to view but they go through me. In hospital land it seems that while the HIPAA forms must be signed and witnessed, they don't necessarily have to be followed. Every day I visit, I put out fires. They moved him from his room with no notice; he is in isolation except for seeing us because of his serious urinary tract infections as well as sepsis, a bacteria in the bloodstream or body tissue.*

*I have to beg for information about his condition. The new nurse asks questions of him and accepts his answers as true and because of this there are conflicting orders and medicines. As my mother gives opinions to the house-keeping staff and complains to the nurse, the wheel goes round and round.*

*This experience is too similar to the one I had with my father. This illness of my brother's has been encased in doubt and controversy and I am asking questions and getting…What? I walk in and out of the room, in and out, in and in and out and out of the room all day. The two of them will kill me. If I don't leave soon, I will be yelling at the top of my lungs.*

*I am fighting to be more sophisticated than them. I want so much to behave better than them, to be looked upon in a dignified way, but I can only maintain the pretense for so long before I begin to feel the fire.*

*Between them there is bickering and guesswork, a lot of guesswork. My brother says two words and my mother fills in the rest with what she believes and his sentence becomes a conversation and I want to die. I swear to God all of this cannot be real. God, I must have died and this is fucking hell.*

*Days later, they are going to release him. He is acting perfectly normal to them and health-wise they say he is much better…Good God, I feel like the circus has come to town. Bring on the clowns.*

*I take my mother home; we are silent. I leave her. I am fucking dangerous. I have been there every day all day into the night. I drive home like a complete maniac, radio thunderous on roads of desolation, and I am filled with thoughts of worthlessness. Yet I have the satisfaction of another escape, my rush into the night, to run once more and take to the air if the desire and the chance present themselves.*

*My husband smiles when I open the door and I drum up all my enthusiasm for a smile. I don't want to converse with him now; I just want to continue to be angry and hateful and full of pain. I haven't eaten—nervous stomach of course. With a message waiting for me, I return my sister's call for her daily report. I don't want to talk on the phone but I laugh and joke and cover my pain.*

*We have been through some of this together and it is her wish to help me maintain my sanity by offering to help where she is needed. Although my reasoning and decision-making skills are still intact, I am in personal danger. I am having difficulty with my moods and my temperament. I don't*

## Life Is Like a Line

*know if anyone realizes this; no one has said. Mentally, the part of my brain that is not making executive decisions is in jeopardy and on some days it feels as if it is too late. It is too late, too late to make it all stop, to turn back the clock; too late to control something I know nothing about.*

*I look to her as a future decision-maker should I become incapacitated. We have discussed this to some degree but she hasn't a clue as to what that means and she doesn't ask. I just tell her it's all too much, that they are bowling me over, that I am about to quit.*

*The next day they don't discharge him because his choking condition is worse and he stops breathing several times; he turns blue once right before discharge. I know his condition is serious. This choking issue has been a problem before. He is supposed to have his food puréed and he should turn his head to the left when he swallows but he will not comply. He fights the nurses and cheats whenever possible and my mother has promised him food at discharge.*

*Sophistication and constraint, forget it. I am cross with them in front of the others and engage in open reprimands when talking to them. Today I am the master of flying fits and I'm sure as hell not a part of their circus.*

*I ask my doctor, "What do you think we should do with this antide-pressant situation, since most of them aren't strong enough or they are not symptom-alleviating or they do not agree with my system?"*

*Medications…It's a waiting game, and if you can't wait, you're toast.*

My frustration was my doctor's, and while we changed from one medication to another, we waited and hoped. But medication alone would not help me through this long dark passageway I called the bowels of hell. It felt strange to be in this position after forty-three years of separation from psychotherapy. I couldn't help but remember the little girl sitting in the big chair talking to the nice man who sat at his large oak desk, he too wondering how I was doing.

Every week, week after week, she remembered what I forgot. Then, one after another, we changed my pills and I seemed to be getting worse. I was trading one symptom for another, one side effect for another, one family situation for another, all without a buffer. Was it situational, organic, neurological? What exactly was preventing my recovery?

My depression was bad. I couldn't fall asleep, and once I did I would wake up within a few hours and pace. I felt despondent about life. I was sorry about all of this, for my family and for our friends. I was pathetic; it was so worn, so repetitious. It was boring bullshit. People were worse off than me. Those who knew me best didn't know me at all. They would never see my pain, and I gave them no reason to know.

Incapable of freedom, that damn black cloud of depression lasted forever. Depression and rage, separated by moments of time alone. Many years and months and days of the same blackness of spirit were not easily tolerated. With my shoulders rounded and my head pushing down into my neck, I did not long to witness the enormity of life as it had become. I feared this would be my indistinguishable lifelong abnormality.

Depression is deepness; it is lethargy of the soul. I wished only to end this purposeless fate. I felt solitary; I was full of gloominess. There was nothing further to the road; there was only familiarity and desire with the ground beneath my feet.

I wanted to give up, but I had to give it another try. I had to try, but this was bullshit; after this I was going to quit. I was conflicted. It was easy to give up. I was afraid; I was possessed. My doctor knew exactly how I felt and she understood, but she was not the same defeatist as I. Watching my parents live with their own paralyzing manifestations convinced me to try once again. After all, I was their daughter.

> *"Hypersexuality is not about the act…It is about power. It is the force that takes me there. Massive confusion…internal hysteria…lasts seconds to moments in time."*
>
> *"Piece of paper. Do you have a piece of paper? Notes? I just want to write something down. I'm sorry, do you have a pen? I have something really great I need to write down."*
>
> *I can't forget it; this is good, oh God…"surge of confusion something something"…They are coming fast, my thoughts…I am writing these small notes and they are coming fast. I have saved them; my God there are so many.*
>
> *I can't remember the whole thought; there is so much of it, so complex. Ah, what was that last part? How have I stopped thinking? When did clear*

*get so muddy? What was the order of the…words…the words that were dynamite were…*

*God, that felt directed by heaven above. I store these fantastic thoughts in a pocket or in my purse for later retrieval. They will be necessary; they are needed.*

*Shit, where did I put that paper? I never noticed the enormity of these small notes; I never thought about writing them until I began finding them and reading them. They are incomplete thoughts of fantastic ideas. Here's another one in my winter coat from last year. "I hope you are my angel because that which I cannot see makes me afraid."*

*Now what in the hell was that all about? Then another. Writing again on papers. Small papers are all I have. I am taking notes while I'm driving in the car. I can barely drive for the importance of my notes; they must be preserved, remembered, saved. "But the drug is up and it'll bring me down. Chase me all around until it keeps my feet flat on the ground. I'm afraid of yesterday. Lost in me."*

*Seduction. "You're being deceived by it for it is not your friend. You are not of it, for it possesses you. When you speak of its fury your inner self is aroused but soon its mystic evidence regains and you are quieted to flavor its fury once more."*

*Small papers. They are my urgency. I save them because of the forceful need to capture on paper my profound thoughts, ideas, and mental magnifications for later retrieval. They are, at the time I write them, inner mind stimulus, persuasive and purposeful. The number I have accumulated is numerous.*

*However, upon review they are not that profound; they are incomplete thoughts written on small pieces of paper, incomplete and almost impossible to decipher through the scribbling of my hand. As I explain my frenzied small notes, my doctor nods her head affirmatively and speaks in a low voice, "Hypergraphia."*

*Hypergraphia, the overwhelming urge to write associated with temporal lobe changes in epilepsy and mania. It is also associated with the illnesses of bipolar disorder, schizophrenia, and frontotemporal dementia.*

At our next visit, it was very easy to attach something like a psychological illness to my entire family. Once my doctor gave me a medical explanation for my brother's condition and our collective lifelong behaviors, it seemed even more plausible. But each time I pointed a lone finger at him, three others pointed back at me. You might say there was something nagging at me, so I asked to read one of the books in her office and when I did, I nailed it.

When I thought about each aspect of my life from childhood forward, my heart knew. I had found a diagnosis. I had found me.

> *I'm with my doctor again. "Ah, the first item on my list, something I really need to discuss and…I really need two hours with you. Can I kidnap you and take you home? Don't laugh; I'm damn serious."*
>
> *I begin with my worst problems. I haven't slept for most of the week and my temper has been awful and I'm driving badly but otherwise life is just great. I am being sarcastic and I think she can tell.*
>
> *"I read your book on bipolar disorder, Doctor. Cover to cover." A part of every therapy session was dedicated to my family, and she was beginning to believe my brother was symptomatic of the illness called bipolar disorder, also known as manic-depressive illness. "As you know, I was hopeful that I would find information about my brother, and though I may have, each page brought a likeness to me as well."*
>
> *This session is productive. It is obvious to her that the class of medications she has been trying is of little use to me. I am a compliant patient; that is, I take my medication exactly on time each day and every day until she tells me otherwise. So submission has not been an issue. The issue is that not one medication works for everyone. I have tried one antidepressant after another and have had most of the side effects and few of the benefits. She is putting the pieces of the puzzle together slowly; all is not obvious; it is trial and error.*
>
> *My doctor explains that she would like to try a different type of medication; this experiment is a dip in the ocean of psychotropic medications. Within the psychotropics are the anesthesias, the painkillers, the psychiatrics, and recreational drugs. With six major classes of psychiatric medications ahead of me, I am hopeful time will be short. I have ingested few of the various classes but many within each class. I have taken mostly antidepressants and maxed out the dosages. It is disappointing as we add more and more and more and wean and change. It is fucking disappointing.*

# Life Is Like a Line

*While she explains which one she wants to try and why, I listen with a head full of questions and a sigh of desperation. For the moment, it is too much information. I listen with too much thought. I analyze while examining the lipstick on her lips. Where the hell is my mind?*

*I need this, the cure. I need this, the hopefulness. She tells me there will never be a cure if her diagnosis—and mine—is correct. But if no cure, then what? I find I am continuing to distance myself from the family that supports me, from my husband, my daughters, and my life. It's time to reel me in; I am drowning in the substance of life and I can't swim. I have continued allowing others to control me and manipulate me and they are sharks; they will devour me. And my behavior, my mood, my desperation, is worsening.*

*To paraphrase my mood, it is "the predominant feeling" of my life. It is everything and nothing that is emptiness and hopelessness and illness of my spirit. And so it is with urgency that we make every effort through medication to dissuade the assailing fate or face the worst of alternatives.*

*If there is no cure and she is sure, then let a triumphant handling commence so as to not lose all of me entirely to this mental ruin that today feels like failure.*

CHAPTER **14**

# *Essential Elements*

This was the turning point in my psychiatrist's strategy. Perhaps this new kind of medication would be the answer to my prayers, but I didn't like the tag that went with its success—the embarrassment of needing a psychiatrist, the monthly medications purchased at the local pharmacy where everybody knew your name, the stigma of the diagnosis that others would eventually come to know. I wanted to be a winner, but I didn't want to be considered a loser as a result. For a chance at hopefulness, I listened and I learned and I decided to try anyway.

Once begun, I had to promise to take my medication as prescribed and be diligent to prevail. This was not an antidepressant drug per se but a mood-stabilizing medication designed to be effective enough to provide an antidepressant and anti-manic result as well. My doctor was hopeful this new medication would adjust the severity of my mood swings so they would decrease in frequency and harshness and all that looked like episodes resembling an illness would be reduced.

## Life Is Like a Line

Manic. Manic. I did not understand manic, or hypomanic, or anti-manic. I did not understand any of it for a very long time. I have now spent several hundred hours learning about recurrences and brain function and stress management, and while I have hung on to every word, I have waited, if not for a cure, then for symptomatic elimination.

Dr. Emil Kraepelin, a German psychiatrist who lived from 1856-1926, stated this: "Manic patients may transitorily appear not only sad and despairing, but also quiet and inhibited. A patient goes to be moody and inhibited, suddenly wakes up with a feeling as if a veil had been drawn away from his brain, passes the day in manic (excited) delight in work, and the next morning, exhausted and with a heavy head, he again finds in himself the whole misery of his state. Or the hypomanic exultant (jubilant) patient quite unexpectedly [makes] a serious attempt at suicide."

Though it all made sense, I drew a line in the sand. I decided a manic-depressive illness was too much and that my ill was more of a nervous break-down. In spite of being poles apart from my doctor, I promised to follow her lead. Privately, I was convinced the patient was saner than the doctor, though I could not deny that every word from her lips made perfect sense.

*An illness? Illness? Excuse me? You think what? You've got to be kid-*
*ding. Hypo...Hypomania…Manic-depressive illness? M A N I C manic? Me?*
*Are you sure…?*

It was all too orbital and improbable and it was saved for the most famous of mankind, not the likes of me.

She named some names and I looked up others on the internet. Robin Williams…Patty Duke…Sting…Ben Stiller…Linda Hamilton…Jean-Claude Van Damme…Abraham Lincoln…Marilyn Monroe…Mozart.

Wasn't Edgar Allen Poe also…? Yes, and Mark Twain…Winston Churchill… Rod Steiger…Sir Isaac Newton; I love it, cosmic…Ted Turner…Vincent van Gogh…Robert Downey Jr.; I love Robert Downey Jr.…Sigmund Freud…okay, that explains it. Sigmund Freud explains everything.

I was sure she must be joking with me. She professed she was not. I thought she must be engaging in speculation. She said was not. I read more material, did the research, read, read, read, learned, learned, learned. The more I learned, the less I wanted to know. She explained bipolar as a spectrum illness that affects no two people the same way. She said it was similar to diabetes or hyper or hypothyroidism. She assured me that I was bipolar II but we discussed bipolar I just the same. She had never seen my mania side nor had I ever been hospitalized or jailed, God forbid.

> *Jailed…what in the hell is she talking about? This is all too soon and all too much. It is true that I show a severity to depression with alternating bouts of what I know to be hypomania and I can be as agitated as hell, and oh, I can fucking (sorry) swear.*

I had no basis for argument regarding my condition; I had no point of reference for my doctor's analysis. I was naturally a doomsayer, always living on a roller coaster ride of highs and lows, believing that my reactions, behaviors, and personality had simply been the living me, Type A and all that, and nothing more.

She used the words "statistically," "the research shows," "efficacy is," "diagnosis," "toxicity," "documentation," "trial studies," "observations," "frequency," "intensity," and "potentially fatal."

My words: "…I thought about suicide last week. I don't know why, exactly. It's dreamy, constant, unstoppable." I told her this new category had to work. My dreams could not be my nightmares anymore.

> *"Yesterday, maybe, no…Don't worry; I won't do it. I don't know why exactly but I feel bad right now. Sometimes I'm afraid, panicky. Some days I'm just panicky. Okay, well, I'm open to whatever you think at this point. I understand. I will. I will have it filled tonight. I understand; it will be an experiment. It has to help. Thank you; I have an appointment next week. Great. Thank you, Doctor."*

The knowledge of this possible illness of manic-depression was not freeing. A photograph of a leopard may be beautiful and perhaps you can imagine his gracefulness, but if you meet him face to face in the wild without adequate protection, you will be exposed to his aggression and hostility. Survival between you and this animal simply cannot be determined while looking at a photograph.

## Life Is Like a Line

A mood disease, manic-depression has numbers like I and II and codes for insurance company use. I was confused by the names. There were too many and they were unfamiliar to me. Initially I knew of no stigma attached to the illness because I was unfamiliar with it. I was also unfamiliar with the feeling of medical dishonor. In spite of my parents' challenges, I had lived my life without knowing or perhaps I have been ill equipped to detect mental disorders like our own. In their day, people were considered sad or moody or tempermental. We didn't think of them as having mental problems, and people kept their personal business behind closed doors.

The problem with bipolar illness, my doctor told me, is that it is the disease that sleeps. Symptoms may appear in the form of hypomania or depression and then go away for years without being seen again. It is considered a "remission."

I was told that I am not the illness; only that I had the illness. But if the illness was my behavior, then where did the illness end and I begin? It was not complicated to doubt and scrutinize and dissect myself. Bipolar. It was fascinating and deteriorating and I struggled to understand it as it evolved and evolved and evolved and the medication was changed and changed and changed.

I left her office wondering more than worrying and feeling almost broken by the news. Prior to this time, my antidepressant medication was not only unpleasant and troubling but was often distressing and harsh on my system. On the cusp of another class of medications and with my mind in a petri dish, I was fighting personal ugliness and a very severe case of depression. I had been spinning with crises and moods and medications, and as my family threw in pleasure and promises, illness and anger, my mixed bag was full.

Near fifty, never before had I been considered by anyone in the medical profession to be manic-depressive, to be mentally fucking ill. Though I'd tried numerous medications for depression, this was more gravity than that found on the moon, or in other words, I had been gravity-free for one long lifetime.

I drove home in the Corvette with the top down and the radio blasting, moving in and out, in and out of traffic, and once I neared one hundred miles per hour, manic-depression didn't matter anymore. My spirits lifted when I was flying.

Desire and my automobile, a illusive combination. Later that day, in the comfort of my own garage, I watched as the door closed behind me. My silent obsessions began to take me. Tormented by my own self-determination, it was time, and while I waited for the fumes, I analyzed and I became confused and I changed my mind.

An interesting book has been written on the subject of manic depression entitled *The Hypomanic Edge: the Link between (a Little) Craziness and (a Lot of) Success in America* by John D. Gartner, Ph.D. Dr. Gartner argues that hypomania, a genetically based mild form of mania, endows many of us with unusual energy, creativity, enthusiasm, and a propensity for taking risks. Indeed, there are some people whose success seems attributable to a perpetual state of hypomania and because they are successful, they don't come to the attention of the psychiatric profession. Gartner does point out that the constructive behaviors associated with hypomania may contribute to bipolar disorder's evolutionary survival.

Noted bipolar authority Kay Redfield Jamison at a conference in 2002 described Teddy Roosevelt as "hypomanic on a mild day." Bill Clinton, one could argue, is a walking hypomania poster boy.

The drug we tried, lithium, was something of a gold standard in the profession, an old gold standard. I learned it was a natural element, similar to the sodium in table salt, and that it is the only pure mood stabilizer available. It was discovered in the second century A.D. by a Greek physician (of course, probably a Type A himself) and rediscovered in 1949 by Dr. John Cade, an Australian psychiatrist who published a paper on it. The element lithium had been the first line of treatment for an illness called manic-depression since the 1950s, but the currently most-frequently used preparation, lithium carbonate, was not approved by the FDA until 1970.

After I researched lithium on the Internet, I drove alone to the next town and picked a drug store with a twenty-four-hour pharmacy just in case and there I had my treatment packaged. When the pharmacist called out my name, needing additional information, I cowered up to the counter where my name was repeated and I whispered information and attempted

Life Is Like a Line

to be nonchalant while my humiliation was confirmed. In the time it took to walk away from the counter, I pondered my new destiny. I noticed that my heart was pounding, and as I walked down each isle, every item looked blurred from my embarrassment.

Driving back home, inconsequential, and then at home, I asked my husband if I should and he said yes and my anxiety dove up into my throat as I swallowed the first pill that evening. The excitement was reminiscent; I was frightened and excited to take it and I waited for the outcome with the same enthusiasm I'd experienced with illegals. I took another pill twenty-four hours later as planned. I took another one at the same time the next day, and slowly I began living a more encouraging life.

There were days of moods, but they were not flip-flopping at some unbearable speed in an illegible manner. Life's aggravations were still with me, but they were not as pronounced. In other words, I began handling things better. I stopped swearing. Spontaneous thoughts of suicide lessened and then erased. My weekly report was, "I think I am better." I had a blood test to confirm what she needed to know.

"You sound better."

> Damn it, I feel spectacular in an I'm-not-an-arrogant-bitch sort of way. The pressure is different; I am not tense or overly sensitive or overtly flirtatious or overly despondent. I am me, enhanced. My mother and brother are still poorly behaved. I am forced to make changes and watch the expenditures and battle with them hand over fist, but I do it without my body shaking inside, without trembling hands, with less clenching of my teeth, and with fewer debilitating headaches at the end of the day.
>
> It took me some time to put it all together. My physiology is better. Yes, it is a remarkable change. Every moment is different, significant, and lighter, and now six months have passed; my blood shows a therapeutic level of medication in my system. It has been a consistent .08, which is far enough away from toxic to be appealing to her.
>
> Serum lithium blood levels are mandatory for those of us who use this drug, especially those who don't metabolize them very well. Routine testing is necessary to rule out the possibility of toxicity, which is easily attainable and deadly. During each appointment, I confirm that I have not felt like this

*in years, but I have noticed a diminished sex drive and my creativity has been squashed for quite some time. There are tradeoffs but I can live with them if I am willing to learn.*

*There is this water weight gain I complain about each week. My hands look gigantic; they are full of fluid. I hate that. I feel the stiffness; they are resistant to bending. My ring does not move on my finger. I'm supposed to drink ten to twelve glasses of water a day. I am sure that is a typo in the literature. There is no godly way anyone can drink that much.*

*But overall, I continue to reaffirm that my health mentally and physically has improved. I am myself again; no more symptoms. When I tell her, she looks like a kid in the candy store.*

It was literally the second day that the lithium began to alter my state. Normally it takes much longer, but for me the change was nearly instantaneous. I knew it; I felt it; I was softening. As the medication began to call me home, each therapy session was educational, and the more I knew, the more I needed to know and the less I realized I knew altogether.

In the bookstore, finding titles that matched m-d (manic-depression), slipping up and down the isles making selections, I would walk to the counter, slink up to the register, smile, be visibly friendly, and try not to look at the title. If you pick up a book on diarrhea, people think you have it. Not much has changed. Stigma.

The success of the lithium seemed to prove her theory correct. The medication kept me perfectly on the line with no spikes of mood and hopefully no chance for breakthrough episodes. Effective not only for the treatment of acute mania and acute bipolar depression, lithium also reduces the severity, duration, and frequency of manic and depressive episodes of bipolar patients. I had no idea how it actually worked in me, but it relieved my symptoms tenfold. Because I was better, my psychotherapy schedule changed from once a week to twice a month, depending upon what was happening with my brother and how the crisis affected me.

My sister, certain I had been seeing my psychiatrist for too long, came to a session; it was not fruitful but I knew how critical my doctor was, how necessary her impact in my world of disruptions, how essential her understanding when thoughts of suicide slipped me from hopeful to hopelessness.

## Life Is Like a Line

When bouncing about the line of stability, there was no embarrassment with her, no secrecy. She knew me better than I knew myself; she filled me with possibilities in a life of lost buoyancy, uncertainty, and self-doubt. As she so eloquently expressed it, each week we peeled off one layer after another, breaking down and analyzing and understanding.

> *My brother has been quite ill again, and after his hospital stay I have to move him to another facility. It is my responsibility, and as I singlehandedly move him, my only wish is to complete the task and go home, but I find that I am seething inside. I am secretly irritable and agitated and I am resentful that this is my plight. But I am not in a rage; I am merely in a hurry. I am calmer overall and when I look at my brother, confined to that bed, I forget that his condition has consumed me. I am saddened for his set of circumstances, and as I lie in the darkness of the night, I can see the many conflicts that are mine because of him.*
>
> *Disgusted and disappointed with our relationship, I have been resentful, hopeful, helpless, saddened, and relieved, and there is no more rage for him. I suppose the lithium is calming the maddening mind, the destructive mind, the angry mind, the conflicted mind, and at least on moving day, it has leveled out my weary mind.*

In addition to monitoring my serum lithium levels regularly through blood tests, my doctor continued to adjust the dosage to keep my thyroid functioning. The thyroid gland plays a major role in the body's energy regulation and it is a fact that lithium zaps your thyroid. Too little thyroid gland activity leads to sluggishness and weight gain, and too much to metabolic overdrive with a rapid pulse, nervous energy, and anxiety.

Between five and thirty-five percent of patients treated with lithium develop depression of thyroid gland functioning (hypothyroidism). When hypothyroidism develops, it seems to be able to cause an increase in mood cycling in addition to the symptoms of too little thyroid hormone (low energy, dry skin, sensitivity to heat, and puffiness around the eyes are some early signs). If your thyroid seems to "stop working," hypothyroidism should be expected.

It was clear that my thyroid needed regular attention. Not only had I forced early menopause because of my hysterectomy, I was taking a high dose of niacin for my lipids and hypercholesterolemia. Between the lithium and the niacin, my thyroid was running for its life. So far the blood test results hadn't shown that much improvement, but I continued taking the thyroid medication as prescribed. I was hopeful and I waited and life felt safe without the antidepressant disappointments of the past.

Many months brought me no relapses, and therefore the implication that the "anti-manic lithium is working" was established. I waited for a relapse; it was possible. It could come with stress, and if it did, I would appear overly exhilarated, engaging in behavior that I now understood. One at a time, my symptoms—hypomania (overcommitting), acting dangerously flirtatious or overconfident with pressured speech, engaging in risky behavior, being sexually uninhibited, driving recklessly, interrupting others, jumping from one subject to another, needing no sleep, not wanting to eat—weren't alarming. But if they began running together, sound the alarm.

Many of the symptoms Kay Redfield Jamison discusses below were states of mind I was all too familiar with. It was evident the lithium treatment approach was dead-center on because my spirits were perfectly on the line. My wellness felt like nothing short of a miracle, and there was no one who understood that better than me.

"It seems that both the quantity and quality of thoughts build during hypomania. This speed increase may range from a very mild quickening to complete psychotic incoherence. It is not yet clear what causes this qualitative change in mental processing. Nevertheless, this altered cognitive state may well facilitate the formation of unique ideas and associations. Where depression questions, ruminates, and hesitates, mania answers with vigor and certainty. The constant transitions in and out of constricted and then expansive thoughts, subdued and then violent responses, grim and then ebullient moods, withdrawn and then outgoing stances, cold and then fiery states, and the rapidity and fluidity of moves through such contrasting experiences can be painful and confusing."

Indeed, the better I felt, the more I could see just how far from normal I had strayed. There was even a period when I was too impaired to read. I

## Life Is Like a Line

didn't understand the words, I couldn't comprehend, and I didn't grasp the enormity of the problem. I felt a strong desire to read right to left rather than left to right. It was difficult to stay on page and frustrating as hell and I had no idea that simple reading or a lack thereof was connected to anything.

Each week on lithium helped me to see more clearly and behave more calmly. For too long, I had forgotten how often blessings have come my way. I had forgotten to believe and trust, and I had forgotten to pray. Once I was better, I was reminded that God had shed his light on my path. My psychiatrist told me that she believes I am a "life force" and that the strength of my convictions prevents me from *felo-de-se*, which is Latin for "felon of himself," quite literally "suicide," but I believe it is God rather than my convictions who protects me. God is the life force in me. He tests me, and when all is about to fail, he protects me.

I was managing my brother and mother well and was neither too high nor too low. I trusted my doctor and her remedy and she was right. In fact, all was so right that I made a very critical decision. I had been in remission for over six months, and I told her I strongly believed that either the medication was a miracle or that I didn't have what she thought I did, but either way, I was going to discover the truth for myself.

I know now that deciding to decrease meds is classic, just like influenza patients who want to stop taking their antibiotics once they feel well. Nearly everyone wants to taper off to determine their true need, especially when their medications are life-changing. I had to try this. I insisted, *"I've got to know one way or the other."* I told her I had to try this, that it was my experiment, and that she had to trust me and that I would be careful. I was certain I was cured, since I no longer had the symptoms. She advised against going off the lithium and I saw the look in her eyes. Eventually, it became clear to me that this was her way of proving the illness.

As agreed, I carefully discontinued my lithium and it was substituted for topiramate. Within forty-eight hours, I was becoming symptomatic and within one week I was hypomanic to the max. Things began happening to me that I could never have expected.

*Fifty-five miles an hour and the radio is blasting. It's rock and roll. I feel fantastic. This is the real me and I am elated and I want to party, really party. I feel out of this world. Symptoms? Extraordinary. Ah, screw the police but fifty-five in a thirty-five will get you arrested. Warm bed, three meals a day, and all the sex and drugs I want; how bad can it be? That's what jail means to me.*

*Joke, really. And now I say that about hospitalization, if I'm ever lucky enough to get there. I don't mean it, not really, that's a joke... THAT'S A JOKE!*

*I know fifty-five in a thirty-five is considered reckless driving but I love to drive fast. With my sunroof opened, I'm headed for home and the warm breeze is playing in my hair. The sounds of the road and the vibrations are intense. Normally I don't feel these distractions but for some reason there is a beat to the traffic, one car after another next to me and ahead of me and behind and then I am noticing the road noise and the asphalt is so worn out, so damaged. Ahead, the muffler of the truck, loud, annoying, slow old truck, pass him, I can pass that ratty old junker, plenty of room, I can pass, I do.*

*Never a drive without it, I listen to the radio but it is unable to satisfy me. I press the seek button on its face to find the exact song to fit my mood. That song is trying to change my adventure but I don't like it and I change it. There is no cry of the radio that fills me. I continue to try, rambling through the seek once and twice, ten, twenty, thirty times, pushing seek, finding nothing to satisfy my musical desires. Try a compact disc...No...No...No... No...No...No...No, radio now, station after station. It all sounds the same with no distinguishable beat.*

Many symptoms. I was impatient. I felt confused. I needed to decipher my mood, but the more I tried, the more confused I became. I was afraid; had I suffered a stroke? My mental condition was strangely a mass of twisted strands entangled in significant insignificance. I was usually into the music, playing the imaginary drums sitting in my seat, but it was not happiness music that was playing; now it was higher decibels and at the top of my energy level. This was ragtop Corvette time all over again.

Religion, lots and lots of religion spiraled in my head. Prayers never stopped, religiosity, composing prayers, blessings directly from the Lord, fantastic wonderful new blessings. Music, never getting it loud enough, the beat not vibrating enough, and I became frustrated while I drove. I ran the amber and passed two more lights. I was getting higher without the happiness. The music was evoking memories and images that I wanted to erase and the loudness and the stimulation stirred up distress. It was more than the slow burn of the illness over time; this was an instantaneous explosion of symptoms. This was the beginning of a new type of darkness and it was worse that I had ever known. With each day I lost me and became something else.

I was submerged in a medical condition that took away my ability to process thought, far away from the happiness scale. Some part of me was freaking but I was home, thank God, and hiding; finally I was home, but even at home I could not escape. There were times when I thought I was seeing things, like something moving on the floor or reflections in my mirror. Sometimes I thought I heard a noise or my name being called, but I didn't actually see anything in the house. Something felt like it was crawling in my scalp and that was weird.

*I don't care who he is or where he is; you just have to appreciate a good-looking man. Again I'm all dressed up with nowhere to go. I am by myself in the car and in my heart I am empty. At this moment I am free and elated. I am happily detached and horribly alone. I can't get to my destination fast enough but I don't want to go there. I really have nowhere to go but to them.*

*I am in traffic and I am swearing. I am anxious, I am bored, I want to be home, I am argumentative, I am a thousand miles away, and I want to party. I am on my cell phone talking to my friend and I am irritated with her kindness. With my husband, my bouts of unkindness are becoming more the usual than the unusual.*

*"I think you're just an asshole, goddamn it. I could divorce your ass in a New York minute."*

*He is aggravated; what do I expect, but in my mind it doesn't matter. I feel he will never please me. He never tries; he is only temporary.*

*Ah, geez…my phone rings and I know who it is. I should have turned the goddamn thing off. "Hello; I'll be there. I'm hurrying; I'm driving; I'm close."*

> *Goddamn it, it's just grocery shopping. What's the rush? So I'm late. What a pain in the ass; God, what a bitch. Hurry, hurry, hurry, run, run, run. What about me? My life? My time, my needs, my desires, my fantasy?*
>
> *Here's my fantasy: I will drive to the airport, pick up some hot hitch-hiker along the way, jump on a plane, and who would care? Who would even notice? My mother, that's who…She needs groceries fast before she and my brother go berserk.*
>
> *Fly away…I will go where no one else knows me, take our money, buy everything new, and leave the rest behind. Eventually I will meet someone and he will be perfect and finally I'll be happy and I will never come home.*

This was the beginning of an episode that lasted for weeks, months. It was bouts of ranting and raving and I was full of unhappiness and battling my own game of unspoken madness. My thoughts were racing, my husband couldn't follow me, and he was becoming my enemy. With each appointment, we increased the topiramate for greater relief. The medication only took the edge off. I found that I was hypomanic again, alternating with depression with symptoms of hopelessness, anger, irritation, and then back to hypersexuality.

Hypersexuality. I could have crossed the line; I was dangerously close. Hypersexuality, desire personified. I couldn't wait for my husband to return home from work, literally. It was the unquenchable thirst of sexual desire. I was submissive to its power. It was like being in another cerebral dimension and it was not about the pleasure but about the power of the act; that alone brought me satisfaction. Lovemaking…not part of the equation.

For days I was elated, euphoric, and talkative. I had enormous energy; the coverup seemed easy in small doses. I had insomnia and I was rapid cycling or mixed cycling or both.

Rapid cycling involves manic, hypomanic, or depressive symptoms that alternate as often as several times a year, several times a month, or even several times a day.

A mixed state is a condition with characteristics of both mania and depression. During a "mixed state," your thoughts may go a mile a minute but they're all angry and miserable. You may have big ideas but no energy to carry them out or plenty of energy to fuel your irritability.

A mixed state represents a distinct variety of abnormal moods separate from both depression and typical mania. A flight of ideas, excitement, and anxiety, mixed state episodes involve both depression and mania nearly every day for at least one consecutive week.

I felt personal ugliness; I was full of ugliness. The flow of current running through my head continued to be unpredictable and it changed with the intensity of my stress.

My body was not well, but my doctor didn't know what I was going through because I didn't tell her. I was appropriately paranoid. With each appointment I brought my worsening thoughts, but I only gave her the less intense version until the day I couldn't hide it anymore.

My head nestled in my hands, my sense was that my mind was like strands of twine that were coming apart. There was a freaking-out sensation, a combination of confusion and panic, an extraordinary rush of energy. It wasn't more than I have ever known, but it was more than it should have been. Energy, more and more and more and I could not stop it from coming like a cannon ball just released from the cannon. It was the energy, the energy of darkness.

I felt it was about to hit me dead center and I stayed glued to the couch. I said I was experiencing insanity and she increased the topiramate but the medication was not working; it was not enough. I stopped her from putting me back on the lithium. I wanted something else, something with fewer stigmas, something that didn't scream "bipolar," something more me, something less personality-altering. I was crazy and no one knew it. I was strong and balanced and responsible and everyone knew that, right?

On that day, there were warning signs and while she talked, I attempted to pay attention. I was glossed over but trying. I interrupted her. I was in pacing mode but I stay seated, jittery. I felt that I was noticeably florid and she must be analyzing by observation.

> *It is evening and I am pacing and I have this coming-out-of-my-skin*
> *sense. I pace. The origin of these feelings is completely unknown but they have*
> *been chasing me for quite some time now. I have never felt such vibrations. I*

*have confusion. I don't know what to do next. I am really confused and I don't know why. I am thinking of many things at once; it feels like hundreds of ideas at the same time. I can't follow them. Aggressive, in a rage, I am thinking about death. I am thinking impulsively about it and I am very nervous. I did something today, dear God, and now I live in fear. The township office. I went to the office and purchased a plot. A cemetery plot…today I purchased a cemetery plot. It is for me. No one else knows but I have purchased a fucking hole in the ground for me.*

*I think about my doctor; she is the only one who can save me. I think of her often. She is very trusting and I am lethal and I was not the same today. I wonder what is on the other side of her eyes. I should have told her. I am embarrassed. I have been living in my own world of pretense and stigma. There is no admitting defeat. I am fucking extreme. I think this is madness. I think the topiramate is worsening my situation. I think I am allergic to it.*

*Oh God, I am ill. I drive with the top down; the wind beats on my scalp. I move in and out of traffic, in and out, all the way home. I am flying. The radio is blasting. I can't find a channel, I can't find the right song, I keep pushing the buttons, the volume isn't right, the top is down, the air is on, it's too cold, I'm too hot, I'm still afraid.*

*I need to be home. I am afraid to be alone. Now I am, finally. I want to let it out, scream and run and then lie on my bed. I am in bed. I can't shut off my mind. I am only able to roll back and forth and with my husband by my side I can do nothing else. Full of anxiety, I am spilling over but how have I been filled? I want to run. I have never felt this way before to this magnitude. Is this the lithium talking back, my rude awakening?*

As the days went by, my head continued to feel different, my thoughts more jumbled, and there was this mental confusion that lasted longer under less provoking circumstances. It was as if my mind were on pause. I could see the apple dangling ahead of me but I could not move toward it. There was no mind to tell my feet to move forward. Decisions were forcefully possible only in small portions, which was all right since my mother was functioning quite well these days.

My mind was like a television with no reception, only black and white dots and that weird sound. Other senses were heightened. Easily frightened, hypersensitive, meaning I could hear the turning of every page of that news-paper of his, goddammit. The slightest morsel of stress enraged me and my thoughts were moving too fast and after all the confusion, I was at a height-ened state of consciousness. I was moving in a way with the universe; I had a connection beyond my understanding. I was sensing this mystery in another space and time right down to my core.

I told my husband and my doctor about the cemetery plot. Neither one seemed too alarmed, nor did they have any reason to be. I was fine, right? Though my husband was disappointed that I failed to purchase one for him next to mine, an alarm kept going off in my head. I started wondering how I could have done this so peacefully and began to think the whole world was crazier than I. The next day in the same manner I purchased the plot next to mine for my husband.

On a daily basis my instinct was to run and run some more, but to where? Out of my head, out of my body, out of my life, backwards and for-wards to heaven and to hell, run to where this came from, straight to hell. Who the hell was that in the mirror? I looked, but I could not find me.

> The panic attacks come constantly, anxiety constantly, run, run, my head in my hands at home on and off for hours and then days. My husband asks, "Are you okay?"
>
> Sure, fine. He believes me. They all do, but if you have to ask, I am screwed up.
>
> Frantic, that's what's happening inside of me. I can't rationalize the sensations and in the beginning I could cover them up but as the days and weeks go on, I feel more confused and more incapable of making the easiest of decisions. All I can do is care for my dependents; I have no crisis at the time, thank God.

There were days when I felt more out of my mind than in. I wondered what in the hell was happening to me. This mental state was bitter and familiar all at once. I was no longer the little girl with the two deep dimples and broad bright smile on the black and white glossies. I was not the mother who struggled to raise two beautiful daughters alone and made it, and I was certainly not the wife enjoying my life.

Even the slightest of grocery store decisions was too much, and when afforded too many choices, I walked away empty-handed, blurry-eyed with defeat. For days on end, my husband watched me bring home the same groceries of milk and juice and bread, yet there was nothing for our meal.

He should have been concerned, but he did not realize the significance. During this period, I became incapable. I was afraid while driving my automobile and I was strong and aggressive and unkind. I was compelled to be the leader of the pack but I was disorganized, could not face my work, and could not do the laundry. I was having mood swings and intense bewilderment. I pulled away from my family and desperately tried to concentrate on my brother and my mother and my responsibilities to them. We had a granddaughter and during this period I couldn't trust myself to care for her. With reasons hushed, I missed her desperately.

My mind was dangerously unhealthy and I was having trouble working. I could not make sense of the stack of paperwork, which was ridiculous. This mental sensation was frustrating and confusing. I prayed for relief. Perhaps the disturbance in my system was not from the lack of lithium in my body but from the increase of topiramate that was taking me over. I needed to discuss the increases at my next session.

> *"All of life is hard; it is just too fucking hard."*
>
> *I do not elaborate on my feelings to my husband but I am even more terrified. There are days when I feel that I am being controlled by another part of my mind, the part that is very very upset, the harsh part that I don't recognize as me.*
>
> *I believe my torment goes beyond the family affair. I find that my symptoms lessen with small bouts of distraction but then come right back. I really don't want to bother my psychiatrist after hours, but we're scared, my husband and I.*
>
> *His fear is that I am allergic to the topiramate; my fear is that I may be going mad. We decide that if she doesn't call back within thirty minutes, we're going to the ER where my old life died.*
>
> *My heart is pounding. I really can't go there. Our neighbors and friends go there and this is my secret. My mouth is bone dry and as my husband sits closely across from me, I rock back and forth in bed and I am completely alone in the universe.*

## Life Is Like a Line

In the beginning, my doctor believed my illness was either depression and/or anxiety, but our countermeasure of antidepression and anti-anxiety medications alone seemed to worsen my moods. If you are bipolar, antidepression medications can throw you into mania, bad. It became evident during my first post-lithium hypomanic then manic event that I needed the very medication I had cast aside.

This episode was more than we had bargained for, and when I look over that line where mania waited, I knew I wasn't far from crossing it. Apparently the long-term and growing stress of my family situation was intensifying my mental condition and providing a forum for more severe symptoms.

In my youth, my mood cycle seemed to be attached to something. It was a part of me and seemed to collide with opportunity or stress. My father blamed my moodiness on my menstrual cycles. Certainly my highs came more often and were more welcome, but the anger and agitation and irritation came frequently as well and were often unprovoked.

In elevation and elation I felt eager to accomplish more, lots more, and basically there wasn't anything I couldn't do. For years my mother used to say, "I want what you're taking," as if my energetic personality were injected or ingested because she saw my energy, my humor, and my high. During the days of extreme energy, I would overplan my calendar with a schedule nearly impossible to keep. Knowing it was nearly impossible exhilarated me. In hypomania, I was desirous to do everything I had never done before and more. I was filled with arrogance and self-importance too excessive and daunting for my own good.

But the days of extreme energy coupled with stress could only last so long before taking me to that place of increasing ugliness. In elation, the swell of life would provoke the mood, and once provoked, the once humorous, slightly sarcastic me would explode with the poorest of behaviors.

Psychotherapy and medication allowed me to remember things, cycles, and exhilaration, and when we put it together, it was embarrassing. Then I would realize as I drove home what I had done and said and how I must appear. I understood it so much better now, but there was so much to hate.

I was appreciative when my psychiatrist called me quickly that fateful night. As my husband sat in the chair next to our bed, I could see his eyes and a very compassionate brow drenched in fear.

"No, you talk to her; I don't know what to say…I know she's my doctor… Oh God, oh God, I'll tell her it's the pills. Oh God, what do I say?"

I stayed under the covers as I spoke with her, but my racing thoughts were preventing so much…I was guarded. "We have to change the pills or I need to go to the hospital…maybe allergic, I mean…I may be allergic or something, do you think? I need help with this medication. Aha…yes…I am freaking out, really…oh God, doctor…I don't know what to say…I can do this…pardon me? I'm sorry; I didn't exactly understand that last part."

I was scared to death; I was so embarrassed and sorry to bother her. I couldn't stop thinking. Unable to articulate my situation, stuttering, I just kept thinking. Her voice was calming, but I spoke over her and interrupted her and I should have given the phone back to my husband. I wasn't doing myself any good and I couldn't tell her precisely what was happening and I kept thinking, "Please Doctor, ask to speak with Ron," and I hoped she could read my mind but not this mind, not in this condition, not today.

I told her that I was basically okay and hoped I was passing for normal; silently I prayed she would notice my despair. My father would have told me to keep my private life private, so I fought not to sound pathetic or be visibly worse in front of my husband, but in my head I was frightfully near begging for help.

I hadn't cried for years; now I wanted to be hysterical. She told me what to do. I needed her best remedy and I was filled with anxiety and panic and too much pride and I resisted the appearance of being dramatic. Once again, her recommendation was the lithium and once again I agreed. The topiramate was stopped, thank God. It was of no benefit to me.

I swallowed three hundred milligrams of lithium immediately and went to bed. In bed there was only confusion and annoyance and a preoccupation with something that felt terribly wrong. Unfortunately, as my husband slept next to me, my mind could not eliminate the force and the awful thoughts and the nightmares that seemed to have possession of my mind, and in the depths of the night I was paralyzed with fear.

## Life Is Like a Line

Never before had such a monotonous noise filled me, and while in the bizarreness I obsessed that none of this would ever leave me. Certain this was the point of insanity, I desired to have death before I was entirely devoured. Why must I wake in the morning?

I prayed to God for his will on that night and no death came to me. I paced and I rolled and I sat and I stood; I held my head in my hands and I prayed to God. I paced and I begged and I promised and I prayed. Afraid of madness, afraid of withering, afraid of losing the battle, I prayed.

> *I am disappointed that I am being shoved down this road but I pray for the hope that does not naturally come my way. My cup is half full and I am insatiably thirsty. I fear a tennis-match life of lunacy with and without drug intervention. In the days that preceded this night, I began wildly spinning with my thoughts moving at a heightened speed until a state of confusion began to take over, but it was unrecognizable to me. It was happening for the first time all over again.*

The next morning, I felt better. That evening I took more lithium. The next morning I felt better. That night more lithium. The next morning I felt better and we kept cranking up the dose until we reached what she thought was the therapeutic dose for me, and when that evening came I experienced yet another first.

It was nearing seven and my husband, still working in the office, passed me in the hall. He hugged me and we spoke and I started feeling it. It began as excitement. Initially, excitement is not an uncommon sensation for me and when I am with my husband it can mean many things, but it only lasted a few moments before it evolved.

Alone in our living room, I began to experience my own phenomenon. It felt pure, and as it grew, my mood changed from relief to elation. Moving quickly I felt even higher, now euphoric, and finally the excitement could only be described as ecstasy.

Never having known such a natural place, I felt desperate to contain and maintain it but analytically I realized that it was over the top; this seventh heaven was probably just that. What I felt was a surge of energy like no other. It was not body energy, not "I want to run around the block" energy.

It was in my head. It was a rush. It was a head rush. It was all in my head, my head, a total soma forceful sensational unbelievable fucking rush.

In union with feeling, I knew with absolute awareness that a total change in my mental chemistry had taken place. With certainty, I experienced picks of light, sharp tapping within my brain that affected my mind. Moreover, I knew at the exact moment when the lithium began to take over. Nothing was dark, nothing was fierce, nothing was foreboding. It was pure euphoria. I was blasting forward, surging, and I can only speculate that while the lithium was being absorbed into the neurons, it was filling the emptiness that caused all that was bipolar within me. As God is my witness, the lithium was programming and reprogramming and fine-tuning my mind and I had a complete sense of it. I was a spectator during the entire process, one side of me watching from the inside out.

This deepening of chemicals over my existing chemistry came at that precise moment when all my neurons came alive at once and through some chemical synaptic transmission my nervous system was filling to capacity. Synapses allow nerve cells to communicate by converting electrical impulses into chemical signals and this is necessary for perception and thought. At that moment, this was the epitome of the extreme. Truthfully, I was higher than I have ever been straight, flying, ascending, unbelievably high, surreally, soaringly high. This euphoria was energy personified, and for a nanosecond I experienced a complete loss of self right there in our living room.

For that moment, this phenomenon made my lithium rejection worthwhile, made the mania worthwhile, made madness and lunacy and near insanity worthwhile. Lithium was now my drug of choice, my brown bottle of adulthood, and this sensation seemed to intensify over the hours, though in retrospect it actually lasted less than one hour.

It was easy to replay this sensational experience in my head and I did so over and over again. While it reverberated in my memory bank, I wanted more. Dangerously, I wondered if I could replicate that euphoric feeling by skipping a few doses of the lithium and then starting it again and then going off and on and off and on again.

I was devising my next crime. For many days, I obsessed with the idea of feeling that high again, just once more. How could I be that high just once more? Emotionally, it consumed me, and for many days thereafter I awoke to a lesser high.

My feelings were so extraordinary, I began to scribble my thoughts on paper, some illegible, some wild, some making no sense, some making perfect sense. Notes…feelings…prose on large papers, thoughts on small tiny papers, on legal and letter-sized papers, and everything in the middle. Hypergraphia was back.

Then slowly the effects of the lithium began to level out, and though my chemistry was returning to me, the words kept flowing and I continued to write. Slowly I was coming down, still feeling great, still desiring to return to that natural high, but still wondering how to get back up there, wondering if they would notice, wondering if I could go off the lithium one more time to get to that place, that manic and then euphoric place, wondering if this was cloud nine or ecstasy or paradise…I was hopeful this was what the rapture would be like.

Thinking about my stigma, about lithium and its dominance over me and my denial of it, I now pledged my trust in its ability to fill me with normalcy. I heard now and I learned; hopefully I would remember. And then the outpouring of words became the next poem.

### Salt of the Earth

You have saved me many times, yet I am anxious to abandon you
I do not see me as I am, but you are there to monitor my mix.

Working against you are the moods and manifestation of my mind's
desire
That lay me bound within my gloomy maze.

Stay with me and do not let this quirk become my naughty friend
As your vintage trust resolve the peaks and valleys that are now my
own.

My thoughts prohibit reliance for in wellness I am cured
Only to befall the endless darkness once again.

I will comply, for peace of mind cannot escape the soul, the loss too
great,

Salt of the earth, your favor and conviction, partner now be mine.

> *I'm coming down, I'm remembering the high, I'm in withdrawal, and I understand everything now…I just understand.*
>
> *She listens to me at the next appointment; she must get sick of the same bullshit I bring to her week after week after week. Eight whiny patients a day. God, if I were her I would kill myself.*
>
> *An expert in body language, here's what mine tells her: if my head is in my hands, I'm fucked. I am getting sick over my brother; he has gone from a pain-in-the-ass threat to a helpless dependent who trusts me emphatically. He has had too many strokes, loss of dignity, loss of self. He looks at me…What is he thinking? His looks tear me apart. I look back, make a joke of something random to bring a smile to his wilting face.*
>
> *His life is over. I guess he has no choice anymore. He has no bowel control; he's really blind in that left eye and I didn't believe him then but I should have…I'm such an asshole. God, how awful. How fucking awful. Today my head is in my hands. We increase my lithium…*
>
> *Eventually I ask my questions, having no idea how I've remembered them, and my doctor puts my family into perfect perspective and she understands some more. This horrible life has become more than wonderment to me but as she leads me down the path, she rescues me from danger and she makes sense of the senseless. She understands so much about the nucleus of my family that you would think she saw and heard my life just as it happened beginning with my childhood, one second at a time, up until today.*
>
> *What is my state of my mind? Am I in fact what I hoped I'd never be, sitting on her couch? Someday she'll just have to tell me; she's good at this game; she'll be gentle. She puts words to my actions, she clarifies my behavior, and she takes me from the darkness into the light. Thank God for my doctor. I seem to be in a downward spiral and I don't know why. This is a far cry from the fantastic high I once had. Today we discuss the fact that the lithium needs to go higher and we crank it up.*

Sleep came slowly and was short-lived and so I went to my computer and words came to me. I wrote about the less obvious aspects of this illness that I had not yet fully realized. I remembered now. I remembered the environment of mania, what it was to be manic. It was an unbelievable high, but the mania was not great.

I entitled this writing "When I Am in Mania" so I would remember the bipolar-driven Cindy but not be captivated by the experience of her.

### When I Am in Mania
when i am in mania

                i am in confusion
            it is strong and random
           i would rather have death at the present
      than live in mania tomorrow.
in mania,
    i am critical, and edgy, and hypersensitive.
        in mania, i am not soft.
            i am not feminine. i am not amorous. i do not feel
                pleasure. i do not smell
        my own cologne.
in mania, i am afraid. i am panicky.
    i have a window of well.
in mania, when my confusion is at its crescendo, it is only temporary
              how will i know if i'm in trouble...?

My brother was quite worn out. In the past, his behavior angered me and he fed my torrid rage. I have hated him and wished him the worst of conditions; I have ridiculed him and he has embarrassed me. But his life is now a blur, and he relied on me alone. He looked into my eyes and with the most severe of guilty hearts, I helped him. Those few years were unfamiliar and uncomfortable. I closely followed the lawsuit against my mother and every day I fought my own craving for extinction. And still with raised eyebrows they wondered, "A psychiatrist, Cindy?" Let there be no uncertainty: I lived for those psychiatric appointments. They were, they are, invaluable to me. I could never live without them; they are my breath.

*This week my psychiatrist provides me with another turn of the family wheel. I am awestruck at what she has remembered over the years and how she can take my gibberish and sort it out and relate it back to me in a fluent, clear, and logical way. She keeps up with me on the days when I can't even keep up with myself, when my thoughts are random and I feel confused.*

*And silently, when I have had enough, she fights for me. She fights with her humor and her good sense and her persistence and I don't want to disappoint her even when I have disappointed myself. Too many days I waver between the extent of my problems and depression and fear and fearlessness. Too many days I am filled with confusion and indecision and I think of all the ways to make the cycle stop. This is by far the most exhausting chase for the cure, this and my medication failure.*

*I am afraid; the lithium is not working. I am feeling no high, I am depressed, it is an impossible darkness. I cannot have an antidepressant; it could make me manic. We are talking about another classification. This week we will increase the lithium one more time before the change.*

*Lately my visits have included conversations about my father and his death and how I managed to push down my funeral grief along with every other crisis that confronts me, but truly I have faced his death quite well. My doctor tells me it is acceptable to be sad and remember and I am warm with the opportunity.*

*My sister is on the table; she is the reason for the father talk. She accuses me still of not grieving. It is evident that she knows little about my heart. I don't know if I can resolve any of this. Probably not. Each week more stupid stories and why does this shit bother me anyway?*

*My health is crap, and while I attempt to manage the depression, I am desperate to get my stomach and the headaches back in line. Being on medication has not precluded my suffering over family issues and the basket of feelings I continue to carry.*

*Melancholy; I feel melancholy. Thoughts of suicide still come to me like in the past though I don't share this with my doctor. I don't want her to have me taken away. I am straight with her except for this; I think admitting a desire to commit suicide would show a flaw in my character, and besides, there's that element of surprise. Bang.*

## Life Is Like a Line

Sessions with my psychiatrist were the only times I could focus on myself, focus on so many of the symptoms I knew nothing about. We discussed my mother and her interference at every juncture and my frustration and discouragement. I remained the referee but they still quarreled and they still took the odd man out. I was getting used to it...no, I would never get used to it.

Unable to satisfy either of them most of the time and with scores of reminders from my mother regarding my inferior status, I found myself in and out of depression, inching closer to my fear. During this period my sister tried to help me but the job required more face time than she could give. My dependents did not operate by telephone alone, they required hours of personal attention, specifically on their terms with much to be done. My commitment still intact, I kept her informed by telephone almost every night.

Everything seemed to move so quickly, and like the constant revolutions of the earth, I was dizzy from the motion. I continued to write. I seemed to be slipping deeper into depression. I would think about fatal accidents; I would see them in my head.

We were still playing with the medication. It usually takes more than one medication to make one asymptomatic, and I was on a low dose of a cocktail consisting of lithium and a playmate: carbamazepine (Tegretol, mood stabilizer), topiramate (Topomax, mood stabilizer), ziprasidone HCL (Geodon, anti-manic/psychotropic), clonazepam (Klonopin, anti-anxiety/sedative), risperidone (Risperdal, anti-manic/psychotropic), aripiprazole (Abilify, anti-manic/psychotropic), alprazolam (Niravam, anti-anxiety/sedative), or bupropion (Wellbutrin, antidepressant). My playmates kept changing with each doctor's script and so did the pharmacy, thanks to stigma.

> *Something is happening to me today. There is no forewarning. I feel slightly nauseated. I bow my head into my hands; I don't know why I do this. Everything takes place in slow motion as I close my eyes. My body movements are slow and deliberate. I see only the darkness. I realize that I am looking inside myself. It is spatially dark and deep. I am either very close or just inside my brain; it is tunnel-like.*
>
> *It is deeper than the available space in my head, infinite. What I see is infinity. I am in the universe. It is awesome, and I am struck by the elusive*

omniscient presence of our creator. It is a peaceful place. I am feeling calm and taking the enormity in stride. I am completely caught up in the experience. Time is not a factor. I have no fear. It is joy.

Once there, I want more of it; I never want to leave this place. Finally I see small specks of light within the darkness. There is a detached space larger than my own and I sense that I am connected to God in this space as well. Both are universal and connected to each other.

I begin to evaluate the possibility that I have died and I am filled with sedate elation. I begin thinking about the presence of God and acknowledge, "Yes, I knew it," and then afterwards comes the doubt. I want to explore more of the detached space; it is so much more than my own, more peaceful, more beautiful. I continue to analyze it. There are no time constraints. But I raise my head instinctively and it fades from my mind's eye.

I am completely at ease. Whether real or a dream sequence or a hallucination, it matters not to me. I am wide awake, alive still, and completely taken by its euphoria. At my next appointment, I tell my doctor. She seems concerned but I am not delusional. I am not.

I am called into combat once more. There is fire where I see smoke, but it's a fire inside me; they get to me and take me there. During my next appointment, my psychiatrist reminds me once again of "boundaries."

I have forgotten about the boundaries. There is too much to remember. I have given up on socialization; I have no desire for parties or cocktails or thoughts unspoken. I'm in a funk, still dragging, still discussing escapades, illnesses, and feelings. Every other week contemplation, recommendation, medication. The antidepressants gone, now anti-manics and psychotropics and sedatives, still one brand and then another. She is patient and consistent and when they are too overpowering, she changes them.

Truth be told, I haven't felt well for a long time and I pray that they just lock me up and get it over with. I know that life will never be right, never be the same, and I will never be back to being who I used to be. My family devoured, fucking devoured me, and I am sick…I am so sick amid the changes.

I see life as better before. Maybe that time was no better than this; maybe I just couldn't see it for myself then. I just didn't feel crazy then. I just

*didn't feel overwhelmed by the simple tasks in my life. The circumstances*
*are wearing me thin and the months and the years just fall off the calendar*
*while I fight this battle. Forgetfulness and forgiveness have saved me from*
*screaming and screaming and screaming and screami...*

As I sat directly in front of her, I was afraid to tell her of my most recent hallucination. I didn't know where she drew the line between sanity and insanity. I didn't know where the line was either.

This hallucination I called "the Fireball." We were again in the cottage. It would have been my dad's eighty-seventh birthday. I was neither numb nor emotion-filled; I was writing. My husband and I were sitting in our great room in front of the TV. By instinct I turned my head to the right. My field of vision passed Ron as he read his bookstore favorite and with the TV blaring a Hollywood find, I tuned all that is reality out. I was zooming toward something I saw coming my way. I was in a cosmic space, no longer in our home. I saw a fireball, and as it came closer I determined its size. It was enormous. It increased with each movement toward me.

I saw that the top had jagged edges but it was cylindrical, three-dimensional overall. I could see the effect the speed had on its sides as it was distorted while bursting through the air. As it came closer, it became more and more distorted, yet it maintained its perfect shape. It was glowing; it appeared to be scorching hot. It had a bright deep magnificent spectacular pure orange coloration, and for the life of me it was breathtaking.

I could see it cutting through the air. I was now outside in the space that is cosmic and I had no fear. I realized I was observing this in another layer of the atmosphere, in the stratosphere. I was in awe of the scene. It was in slow motion, coming nearer and nearer to the house, and I knew that it was about to shatter the picture window right in front of me but we have no picture window. Just as it was about to hit the glass window, I turned my head and poof...it was gone.

I told her and in response she ordered an EEG. Brain waves, tumor, cancer, crazy?

Eyes and mind completely open and aware, cosmic, the universal desires of man. I grew in awareness. I was a life force, but I struggled for mind control. I had depression, I was symptomatic, I had hallucinations, I was aggravated, and I was disgusted.

There was no sleep for me. I wrote again.

## Mind Complex

You are my disorder, and as I've grown to know you more and more, I am more afraid.

You are at the helm of my unfamiliar consciousness.

With you, I see life through eyes devoid of logic and order.

You have become my biography, the superiority of mismanagement against my will.

For when you are with me, I am needy and unprepared for all I know I cannot face.

The sudden overthrow of my reality must mean that although I struggle to remain tightly secure, I cannot.

It is then my mind complex I am bewildered and perplexed, such grave confusion.

I have been influenced by the stress in my life and this gives you access to my game but you are not as strong as you appear.

For in my madness you lead me to wild chases and to an obsession of tendencies beyond my own.

There is strangeness about me with you and there is no clear resolution to the thoughts and feelings and sensations I find.

As my thoughts divert, I am eager to oblige them even though I fear life known will then be lost.

So I struggle to keep your hypnotic and alluring disposition from my yearning memory.

Chemicals take charge with firings, confusion gone and I am high and it is clear.

It is pure euphoria and I forget about the severity of that unwelcome holiday

and I wonder, do I need the chemicals, the docs, was it that bad, can I get this high...again?

I recognize this now and it recognizes me—
The vicious cycle between episodes of sanity.

# CHAPTER 15

# *Six Pounds of Love...Lost*

Just when I thought loss was behind me, my heart was crushed. Recognition of her condition was slow, though there were signs and symptoms. Trembling at night, clammy sweats, tears in her eyes, wanting so to be with me, to sleep with me, to be held by me, but she was lower on my list than they were.

I knew in my gut that her illness was tearing her apart. She needed me, and after the doctor explained for the second time, I understood the severity of her situation. It made me ill. But decisions had to be made and the pull was toward my family 24/7.

Medications would not help; they would give her too much time to struggle in pain. Six pounds of this woman's best friend was full of cancer and I knew that soon we would not soothe each other's ache.

## Life Is Like a Line

Upon our leaving the examination room that last time, our daughter and the veterinarian injected the medication of relief that would take her from a place of misery to a place of peace.

Thirteen years of our connection ended; she left my side forevermore.

She was my little dog. She was my six pounds of selfless comfort. When I looked into her eyes, it was easy to know her thoughts. She was a soul and her soul touched mine. She saved my life many times with her selfless giving and I could not save hers.

I was dragging myself around without her and I was full of grief. Close mine, and I saw her brown eyes and I felt her. Her remains are in a box on my shelf and they will drop us in the same ground when it is my time. There is more to say and feel and honor about my little dog, but I am locked away, just as she is, in my own vault of ashes.

# CHAPTER 16

# *Fixed but Not Forgotten*

To date, I have been on more than twenty different psychotropic medications. They have mostly been antidepressants but others such as mood stabilizers, anti-manics, anticonvulsants, and psychotics have been tried. During the process of pharmaceutical trial and error, I have learned just how sensitive I am to the chemistry of these medications. It is not unusual to have side effects of one type or the other. My remission has been slowed; I have been inundated with side effects including bed sweating, dizziness, rash, nausea, immense weight gain, sleepiness, sleeplessness, and more, all that is devastating in unwellness.

*I am bloated with water and I hate that I am twenty-five pounds overweight and dying for a candy bar or two or three. I am ugly and discontented and my mind is making the rounds with my moods. I don't buy clothes. Combine bipolar with menopause, hypothyroidism, add to it our family discord and chemistry, throw in the pills and the patch or the cream and the failure upon failure, all of them. Switch on and off my mind and hear me scream.*

*I am disgusted, I am high, I am low, crushingly low. Hypomania is bullshit. I wonder if I will ever understand this disorder. More thoughts, maybe complaints, more poetry.*

*I am pissed and I will tell you so. This reflects my loathing entitled "Hypomania."*

## Hypomania

Hypomania, you have been the stimulation of my situation and the given in my life
You have betrayed me, but I never really hated you completely until now

At first a dream, uncertainties with childhood imagination, blooming unpleasant memories, no one could ever know
The early years, confusion then aversion, substances, a fresh approach to neutralize the potent flow

But hypomania, I did not know that you were waiting for me anxiously and callously again
With a hint of your existence I remember the thorny link we share

I did not know this new assault could have such endless possibilities
For when you are active in my disturbance, everything around me seems unclear

Although I can usually muster normalcy in my day, there is a hint of fury in the air
So every day the fight is on, but you are so at risk to lose control of me, the me that was and not the who I am

Hypomania, me, is stimulating, adventurous, and inspiring; neurons charging, brisk and enticing, soar with creativity and be adored
But cycle, extreme mood and disposition and decline you will, as the stress will turn your furnace into cinders

More mind embattled, the melancholy of deep depression is filled with sadness and life's bitter recollections then emerge

Misery to anguish, bleakness leads to hopelessness mournfully awake, dead to the world I am once more

With scheme in place, the unkind fate of family genes to quash the consequence of what must end

And be compliant and submissive to the course of remedy set forth by logic optimistic plan

Trial and error goes the med game, talk therapy not enough, please just forty minutes more

Explore the cycling mixed and rapid, anxiety, lethargy, and mental pain

Hypersexed with indiscretions, agitation, criticism, sensitivity, hopelessness, the episode begins

Add chemical side effects, visit the psychiatrist, no concentration, frozen in time, what's on your mind, all the highs, and suicide

Prescription and compliance, doctor's counsel, helpful family, strong determination, all is well but I'm afraid

Doc says "I'm a life force" with my strengths and healthy insight "competence" and I should make the grade

I pray to God that if by chance he'd choose to intercede, please bless the minds that are unwell and give them lives of…peace.

In this lifetime, one thousand tomorrows will not explain what has happened to me. Nor will a thousand yesterdays. The fact is that I have been on a sprint all my life, never expecting that anything this inconceivable was chasing after me. Unbeknownst to me, my other self never gave a hint of what was to be but it was by design and it was destined to catch me in my stride.

They say the longer a bipolar illness goes undiagnosed, the more difficult it is to treat and that it is the chameleon of psychiatric disorders. It is a phantom that can sneak up on its victim, cloaked in the darkness of melancholy, but then disappear for years at a time only to return in the resplendent but fiery robes of mania. Amen.

> *This is a period in which my moods are no longer frightened by the lithium in my cabinet; they have intimidated me and reduced the lithium to a near placebo and it is obvious to me that it no longer reprograms the neurons in my mind.*
>
> *I am moving from symptom to symptom and I am becoming depressed automatically and discussions with my doctor seem to move me toward the use of antidepressants once more. With each visit we increase the dose of lithium and are hopeful but I have a new phenomenon. I am seeing white flashes, disc-like shapes that come toward my eyes and seem to graze my cheeks with every move. These flashes can be seen in the light and in the dark and they are unnerving to say the least. My psychiatrist is sending me to a neuro-ophthalmologist just in case but she believes they are medication induced.*
>
> *My three-hour visit proves her right; this lithium-induced phenomenon is very typical and is called optic flashes. This visual hallucination is not harmful to me and is not accompanied by any other medical malady such as migraine headaches or seizures.*

Hallucinations caused by medication side effects are best treated by reducing dosages or discontinuing the medication, but I could not reduce the dosage of my hopeful cure, not my lifesaver, not my lifesaver. I feared its discontinuance. Lithium. Mine. I decided to work through the discs and see if they would dissipate on their own in the hopes that they would.

Though the medication wasn't working like it used to, any amount of remission was favorable. One symptom gone was a success, but I kept forgetting. Typically, when I felt it working, I would want to quit.

I still had breakthrough symptoms due to stress, and I began to freak out. I panicked and felt anxious. I could not stop talking; I could not shut up. I was full of energy and I was afraid of myself. My doctor told me every patient worries about what they might do, but it is only a worry. We tried adding an antidepressant. It was trial and error again, trial and error.

I should have exercised, but I just didn't have the energy. I vacillated back and forth between depression and hypomania. My fear...if you stand too close to the darkness, you may never return.

I was speaking with my sister but it was difficult at best. I did not blame myself for our lack of harmony but I wrote her a poem of my lament.

**My Lament**
When you feel the rhythm of your movements touch the heat from
    flames
Will the storm ever be satisfied, will nothing more remain?
When the fiery spark of raw emotion ceases to ignite
Will minds wake up hearts and move closer to the light?

When all is lost and the winds of time become too impotent to blow
Will we remember kinship solicitude for the loved ones that we know?
When for all the pain from truth the watchful mind acquired
Will the effervescence of that newness bring an end to bruised desires?

This is not the only reason for your melancholy heart—
There was resentment and uncertainty born from the start
I share your days of fickle weather events too murky to perceive
The inevitable truths repeat the secrets; you are deaf with disbelief

Where are we now, I ask, and where will this go?
Your feelings of amazement bewilder those who know
The truth you received but all it did was suffer loss
Our family shredded cannot conceive no matter what the cost

I should have considered my doctor's counsel when she advised that competent reference material warned that halting lithium may prevent its future success, a phenomenon called "lithium-discontinuation-induced refractoriness." It has been a year since I tossed out that bottle of lithium to be sure of her diagnosis, and even now we search for some pharmaceutical substitute. There were no guarantees it would have continued to work for me had I not stopped taking it, but during the past twelve months, I have been fighting the trial and error, looking for the next miracle, mentally wrestling the recurring symptoms, and coming to terms with all the thoughts of hopelessness.

I have heard words like "seductive" and "addictive" applied to bipolar disease and I am conscious of the dangers, but it is a stirring prospect just the same. The irony of bipolar is found within the winds of its storm. It is dangerous and a source of despair yet also seductive (arousing) and addictive (magnificent). When it worked at its peak, lithium carbonate prevented the highs and lows, and since I was being deprived of an addictive-like pleasurable and productive state, I insisted on taking my chances and throwing it away.

Since my father's death, I have learned about uphill battles at a snail's pace to find a diagnosis and the appropriate proprietary mix. I have swallowed trial and error, trial and error, trial and error as so many patients do until it became clear that particular medications would no longer dominate my symptoms.

At last, the doctor increased my lithium to one thousand milligrams. Seventy-two hours into the new game, it happened again. I was pharmaceutically high. It came late in the night. Naturally excitable, I couldn't sleep and I couldn't stop writing, I was euphoric; it was cool.

### Magnificent

I've turned the corner again.   Second time in three months.

My head is clear   and my mind is effervescent with thoughts
    and ideas.

I have renewed    energy.

I **never recognize the manifestations of this obsession, mania.**

**four weeks of hell.   I remember things.**   This is my rebirth.

Another chance. I am high. I am cocaine fucking high, and it is magnificent. **You must never like this.**

### Promise me   Oh foolish one

You are being fooled, oh my god this is It. . .delusion.

**MAY I have your attention please you have Successfully qualified for another episode of *bipolar land*. A genre of**

imaginative fictional events, this reality-based nightmare takes its victims through life allowing the use of improbable or impossible things with no basis in reality.

Our subjects must appear to be normal using *magic and adventure while the 'Crazy World of Arthur Brown' kicks some ass* on the radio. No problem, our very carefully selected pdoc's will most amicably provide just two chunks of this light, soft, silver-white reactive metallic chemical element with its single valence electron...And remember, when mixed with aluminum and magnesium for light-weight alloys, it can be used in batteries, some greases, some glasses, and in medicine.

I'm counting on the latter    hope against hope.

Nothing is constant. More changes. Today a lower dose of lithium, 600 milligrams due to toxicity with a blood level of 1.0. We have added valproic acid, 1000 milligrams, which is another mood stabilizer, armour thyroid, 30 milligrams for hypothyroidism, and switched from venlafaxine HCI, .25 milligrams, to escitalopram oxalate, .5 milligrams for depression. A hormone replacement compound is continued for my post-menopausal symptoms and for now all seem to be the proper cocktail, although I will accept any future changes as necessary.

How my medication cocktail works is a mystery to me, and according to my psychiatrist and pharmacologists, it has been a mystery to them as well. Scientists have discovered that abnormal levels of chemicals in the brain such as GABA (gamma-amino butyric acid) can unbalance the system and cause a chemical thunderstorm. As messages rapidly intensify and simultaneously go awry, any increase or decrease in GABA can alter systems in the brain that are involved in motivation, attention, the processing of emotion at the conscious level, and the stressful response to emotional stimuli in the environment.

## Life Is Like a Line

Finding that the GABA system is abnormal in both schizophrenia and bipolar disorder helps explain why there may be so much overlap between the clinical manifestations of the disorders. It may also help explain why antipsychotic drugs are used to treat both disorders.

It is hoped that stem cell research will eventually reveal how neurons in the brain become differentiated, how they attain their functional competence during pre- and postnatal development, and how certain populations of neurons may become dysfunctional during late adolescence and early adulthood when schizophrenia and bipolar typically begin. Scientists look to stem cell research to lead to new forms of therapy that can be applied early in the course of the illness to prevent its progression.

To my dismay, there were no fireworks once I ingested this new cocktail, no explosions in my head to signify the medications were moving in. But as they began flowing through my veins and depositing in my brain, a quiet transition began to take place, and once again the hypomania and depression peeled off to reveal a more recognizable me.

Undoubtedly bipolar disorder is challenging to diagnose because individuals can cover up symptoms of the illness or may recognize only their depression, not the manic or hypomanic phases of the disorder. Over the years, my diagnosis has changed as my illness has evolved; I have gone from clinical depression to a bipolar II rapid cycling patient to a bipolar I mixed states patient to remission and back again.

At the moment, I am saddened by the change that adds additional psychiatric diagnoses to the mix, but I understand that the condition changes as the rest of my body evolves.

*It is happening once more…I am more than unhappy, I cannot sleep, and while I lie in my bed, I am filled with worry. I am moving into depression. They are killing me and I have forgotten about boundaries. I am mournful in this life. I have pain where no pain should exist and I am blessed with a bounty of life's most precious gifts. I am lifeless. I lie here and mull over all that I have said and I am saddened that I've said too much. I have hurt peoples' feelings, I can't stop, and I am guilty once more.*

*I cannot focus. I have been taken and have not yet been returned. I cannot caress and sense with any certainty deep and profound affection.*

*My medication does not relieve me. I am simply the swaying branches on a tree, rustling with noise, making cold the air, alienating my leaves. My disconnected limbs are empty spaces as they fall victim to their death. I serve no birds a purpose. I have no strength. I am hollow. Only the woodpeckers and the squirrels engage me now.*

In times such as this, I have wanted nothing more than to end my life, and finally I have written something to address my obsession.

**Life Departed**
Why do I wish myself to be departed?
For what that is, I should not hope to be.
In secret, there is great appeal occurring—
Will it be chance, or willed by destiny?

I find in pain that music sets my senses,
The strongest tones give life no harmony.
What is the beat that drives me to this longing?
A chance escape, life's cold consistency.

The obsession of my dying is an essay of my weakness,
My aching mind romanticizes life's finality.
The battleground alone is mine covertly, secret feelings,
For any harm that would befall the knowledge I perceive.

This penchant I have for death is senseless and obscure,
It will neither solve my ills nor fill my heart.
The condition of my nature is a force that's sinking lower,
It's a helpless hopeless shadow in my dark.

Dear Lord, because of you I fight temptation,
As suicide would not my fellow be.
Great happiness would be with you and those in paradise—
Eternal rest is after life, when you take me.

So help me, Lord, to fight this mental battle,
The absurdity is craziness at best.

## Life Is Like a Line

This malady bipolar hence deceives with great disorder
For the mind in lunacy won't let you rest.

And for the souls who live with this neurosis,
Be kind to them; their minds are under siege.
Disrupt their ills with your almighty power,
Help them resist these hostile tendencies.

As I fluctuated between hell and high water, I did not see fully the nature of the ups and downs of my everyday life; I was focused mostly on the symptoms. Now, after many years of change and analysis, I see the excessiveness of the mental movement and the nature of the duration and the persistence of the adversity. Still, my feelings, my thoughts, my moods reflect a lifetime of days lived within a "personality" rather than an "illness." I had no early knowledge of this manic-depression; we are the personalities of Type As, not the illness of stigma.

> *Writing about my condition comes easily. I am disgusted; no, I am sickened. Really, I am compelled to ask, why me? Why me, why why why why why why fucking me me me me me me? I do not understand why this condition chases after me the way it does.*
>
> *There is no corner small enough, no room large enough, no thought deep enough for my escape. Medicated still, I am dumbfounded by the recurrence of this condition. We have discussed the state of my mind and the hostile disposition that possesses me. I find the more this condition is involved in my affairs, the less I am. I am in an arrangement and all I can see is the direction of my emotions on the horizon and they can go either way. If not toward the sun then into the darkness. This is an illness of my psyche, a white matter/gray matter failing fucking disturbance. Each time it returns, I retort and the wheel goes round and round.*
>
> *This condition has undressed me completely. In my mind, I am waiting for the next unprovoked experience to take place. In my skin, I am uncomfortable and I wait for another dose of the affliction. I have found myself in the coldness again and in the depths of depression. I am so pissed that this relapse has taken place and left me so unwell. Time has gotten away*

*from me. I am foggy as to what the date is and the month and the day. Medication and my mental status poke holes at my reality and have made me numb. I am changed and my life is changed and I wonder if I will ever be the same. When I took myself off my medication I did not trust that we had such an allegiance. By the same token, I did not yet accept that I had inherited this craziness.*

Though my sister assured me that this condition was only a psychiatric buzzword and that I would snap out of it, she was wrong, very very wrong, and I am so happy that she does not share this genetic affliction. I tell you now, quite honestly, this unpredictability is tiresome and each attack is like another breakdown. The situation of this condition is like opening Pandora's Box again and again and again. For without a remedial medication, then what? What treatment can there be? Insane asylum? Institutionalized? It is just a matter of time.

*My recent battle started in August; it is now January. I started writing this morning and by nightfall I am ill with severe dizziness, room-spinning, nausea-inflicting dizziness. I have moved from the shower to my bedroom floor, fearing I will fall through the glass like my brother did in New Jersey several years ago.*

*I am rolling back and forth, hands covering my face, but it is better if I try to be still. It keeps happening. I become sick in the stillness. I keep moving on the floor. The dizziness is in perfect time, perfect circles lightening fast in a perfectly fucked-up brain. I cannot make it stop; my husband calls my psychiatrist.*

*Trial and error, trial and error, trial and fucking error. This is fucking error for sure. My doctor decreases my risperidone. I am ill physically. I am not sleepy. I am frustrated and I am restless. Finally I make it to bed and several days later I write another poem.*

## Disappointment
Drugs are here to regulate my heat and keep this ill at bay
Strong force to temper mind and mood
And strength to ease my pain.

## Life Is Like a Line

A contract made from you to me to influence my charge
To make a feeling happiness
Your failures proved compliance hard
But vital still for each event, you keep me right on track
And most of all, in quality to help me to come back.

My drugs are here, conceited sorts they fail more than assure
And what they want they take from me
No excellence, no cure.

This week the fight intensified, with meds plateauing and a
Breakthrough maze
To take of mine the life I had and give me darker days
My spirit damp with heavy air alone I held the pain
But with my drugs I pray, invested I remain.

Relinquish all unbalanced sum and psychiatric ill
And give me fix with all you can in each and every pill.

It is no secret that my brother has hurt our family terribly, but to see him in this condition, deteriorating in this way, in this nursing home, oh God, it is upsetting and contributes dramatically to the thoughts that lie heavy on me.

My visits to him are at mealtimes so I can press my nose upon the glass wall that separates him from those who pass him by. I stick my tongue out at him and make horrible faces that make the other guys look away, but for my brother it just doesn't get any better than that.

All my life I have been suppressing my vacillating moods, but I believe they are more visible now than I realize. I have been caring for him for five years now, five years of constant worry. I am short-tempered. I am stressed. I am sensitive, and it takes much less than it used to for me to fly off the handle. As I strive to catch up to my own life and my own responsibilities, my mother says that he asks for me and she makes me feel like shit but I can't go there every day. I have other demands. I have other fucking demands. I am losing myself under a pile of paperwork in the office and I cannot bring myself to pass the stairs that lead me down to my desk.

My mother doesn't realize how many days I want to visit him more often and how many days I can barely drag myself about the house. It is not difficult to see which is the easier pick. Depression chooses for me but I feel at fault for my absence nonetheless.

Most days when I visit he begs me to take him to another facility, but I tell him it would be more of the same, especially since he is a dependent of Medicare and Medicaid. I have asked him to participate more in his life rather than lie in bed, but I see that he is not mentally or physically capable of the attempt. I am fucking frustrated for and because of him. I am angry most of the time. When we are all together, my mother monopolizes our time together so I visit him in secret, when I am alone.

This assisted facility is designed for those who cannot attend to their own affairs. They are not great places; they are homes of captivity where the end lies in wait. When the residents young and old make eye contact with me, I smile back into their eyes and I pray…pray for the luck of death before the clock strikes "nursing home" for me as it has for them.

Overall, I struggle to cover up feelings when I am with him and think of nothing but racing home when our visit is over. My anxiety and guilt and disappointment get me home at a hurried pace, but I am filled with this mix of moods where violence and depression reside and I do not have a sense of where it will lead. This is my pace and I am taken by it. Life is about cautious exchanges and covering up feelings and when need be I must show a callous heart. I die all the way home when I leave him and I worry and wonder about his life when I am away.

It is agony. It is agony. Agony agony agony agony agony. He is living in a state of agony and I have been given a very small percent of his life to share with him after decades of separation.

My brother and I have reconnected. I feel the crush. It is impossible to regulate my mood on these days, and when I struggle for answers and options and strength, the impossible stress begins and the guilt decays. "Dear God, I beg you for relief for myself and for him. I am selfish; I have had enough."

## Life Is Like a Line

It moved so quickly, that endless moment in time; it pressed so hard upon our souls, the needs and the desires and the jealousies of the players. While together and for reasons unknown, we became some oddity of a family.

It is with sadness that I speak of the days that came. He worsened. Within two weeks, I insisted on emergency room treatment. He was admitted, and after four more days of suffering and withering and in a near coma, our vigilance was not in vain. When we were alone, I prayed over him. I told him he could go, that his condition was worsening, and that he was not such a problem for me after all. I told him I loved him.

He was panting for two days; respiration and blood pressure were up and down and up again. When an elevated fever set in, I signed the papers. All was disconnected but left hanging as a pretense for my mother. She did not know we let nature take its course. On that day, as I stood over him stroking his head, surveying him, touching his hair, talking to him, he heard his call.

I believe what I observed during his last two calculated, unhurried breaths was the immeasurable loss of his soul. Whether it moved around me or right through me, it was simple to see the moment his body was left behind. Inches from my own, his ashen throat turned bright yellow and as the color moved up from his shoulders to the top of his head, the bright yellow became dull and he was fixed with the paralysis of death. After sixty-two years on earth, the last five being the worst for me, my brother was alive no more.

> *For the first moment, nearly evangelical in my zeal, I am certain he is heading for the very continuation of life I have so wanted for myself ever since his arrival. I am stunned and then excited and with jubilation and a turn to the heavens, I speak out that he has followed the light to paradise and isn't looking back. My unquestionable relationship with God surfaces once again. For a split second, I am jealous of his death. I wanted it more, I deserved it more, and it should have been mine, my reward for a job well done!*
>
> *Looking up toward the ceiling, I am convinced he is sticking his tongue out at me and I, unable to sneer back, wave my hands to send him on his way and then I begin to feel his absence. This familiar sensation often brings on my panic and it begins as my heart pounds and my stomach climbs into*

*my throat, and even on a psychotropic medication, the emotions of the past flood over me.*

> *We leave him with the nurses, and while my sister turns away from me in the hallway to console my mother, the momentary nurse's hug brings back to me cavernous feelings of aloneness and abandonment, both of which I have been fighting all my life.*

The hospital needed answers, so I advised them. They needed signatures, so I signed their papers, and then came the hospital finality. He was propped and wrapped and pretty in his bed; we viewed him and my mother cried and wailed and emotionally I ceased.

It was done, but for me, more of the same. I was fighting the pressure and the stress and the appearance of incapability as it was taken over by my melancholy. As his power of attorney, guardian, conservator, sister, and stupid-face-maker, my mother insisted I select his casket and flowers, make all the funeral arrangements, and contact the private golf course and arrange for the meal. All of this I arranged as requested by my mother.

Prior to his death, I was becoming symptomatic again, filling up with misery and melancholy, inefficient in memory and constantly indecisive, going deeper with every day that crawled by, deeper, going deeper and deeper, hating life, agitated, hating life, hating myself, and hating all the reasons these jobs were mine.

My doctor, paying attention to my painful preoccupations, signed for thirty more antidepressants to stop me from going any deeper.

> *I assure my mother that his soul has been forgiven. She is worried for his spirit so I reassure her. I have been symptomatic again. I have confusion and I am filled with waves of anxiety. Fortunately, Ron is with me and he is selecting my brother's new clothes, and while we both decide on one of my father's neckties, I am falsely bold and numb and exhausted.*
>
> *The funeral days seem surreal; a cluster of moments of detachment in a nearly empty room of relatives. Some of them are loving. I choke through the reading of my hand-written eulogy and although I have never really cried for my brother, I am sad for the life of separation and I pray for him.*
>
> *What I wrote for him was honest and poignant, for it was a reflection of the change in our relationship.*

# Life Is Like a Line

## Eulogy to My Intruder

When I was a small child, my preteen brother spent many hours bouncing me on his knee and taking me for long walks and all the while we laughed (I know this because I have seen us in family photographs). But as we grew, we became poles apart. It seemed as if there were hundreds of situations and thousands of reasons for me to separate my life from his. And I did just that until a warm and sunny day in May, 2001, moving day.

I dreaded the day my brother moved back home after living far away from us for over forty years. With my father's passing only two months beforehand, I did not know what to expect of his return.

I don't know why my brother came back on that day. I don't know why my brother and I were destined to share these last five years so closely. We were still poles apart and it seemed as if there were hundreds of new situations and thousands of reasons for me to want to separate my life from his again, but circumstances prevented me from running. I began as an unwilling sister forced into guardianship with a virtual stranger in his time of need, but at some point a corner was turned.

Slowly, without my knowledge, Johnny did something to me. Over the past five years, he softened my callous heart, and all the situations and all my reasons to turn away from him disappeared.

And so on this day, I thank our Lord for my brother John and for the twists and turns of my life and for all my second chances and I pray that my brother will need no other guardian but the Lord.

*My psychiatrist continues to see me on a regular basis. Nothing significant on the EEG. All results normal, but I have one more episode while lying on our bed talking with Ron.*

*Looking up at the ceiling and not paying much attention, I notice the soffit over the bay window begin to move. I tell Ron and he advises me to tell my doctor right away. Conveyor belt-like in motion, it is over as quickly as it began, but I remembered her words: "One more time and…"*

*One more time and I will be sent to the hospital for an MRI. She's had enough.*

*She is a compassionate human being whose endurance has fortified me in my days of weakness and distress. We who are treated by her are blessed. She has been my confidant, my professor, my medication authority, my friend, and she has unlocked the great mysteries of this illness and taught me about karma.*

*I am told I will be taking medication for the rest of my life, but I am stable now, though everything gives me side effects. We discuss and stay the course. Can you be "a little" bipolar? We wait and see.*

*Much later in therapy she explains that antidepressants engage the temporal lobe area of my brain, which explains my hallucinations.*

*I question the need for medication. Though this is the great temptation, there is a flatness to my personality on medication and it takes a very fine tweaking to get me where I need to be, just above the line. Manic-depression means just that— precarious highs and devastating lows and the lows last forever. Medications diminish, but when they quash what you are, they are cast aside. That is why there is so much drug and alcohol abuse with bipolar disorder. Each after their own high, we all make adjustments, illicit or otherwise, along the way.*

*The task of juggling prescription bottles to feed my mood will forever be strange and undesirable. Strange that I must, for all intents and purposes, desire to erase my high tones, my electricity, my hypomania, and all that has always been my self.*

*Strange what I must swallow so as not to endure the disobedience of my mood and my desires. How cruel to know that all that tantalizes me must be subdued. There are days when, as the milligrams rise and fall, old thoughts come back to me.*

*My psychiatrist convinces me that suicide really means escape and not death (God, let her be right), and so with that, there are days when I still think about escape. She continues to tell me that I am a life force and death from suicide is not my way.*

*But for the years of our acquaintance there is no doubt; if there is a life force in the room, it is she.*

I have slowly begun to see my sister again and in doing so I have learned that in her eyes I am not the same. Often quieter now, I am enjoying others without pressured speech, without jumping from one subject to another, without trying to convince, without giving long answers to short questions, without living life on the side of too much.

## Life Is Like a Line

In some ways I am happy to be changed. Living the highs of hypomania made me the happy person and the party girl of the family, but in hindsight I was a multitasked one who couldn't wind down until I was filled with anger and agitation. And as the family puppeteer, my skits were naturally edgy with sarcasm and sexual overtones, which I often had to battle because of the children in the house.

For my sister, it is not the fear of the illness or even the belief of its existence that is upsetting; it is simply the possibility that overmedication and perhaps the dredging up of too much in psychotherapy has taken me away.

Unfortunately, stigma will prevent her from knowing the evils I fight. As with anything in life, as one finger is pointed at me, three more point in exactly the opposite direction and it is that phenomenon no one cares to face.

In a way I am not sure it actually is the party girl or the happy person who has been lost. Lost is the woman who got too happy, for "too happy" doesn't last very long. There is a thin line between too happy and mania.

Looking back, I see that I have enjoyed two predominant moods in my life with mud in the middle.

*Recently, my mother told me I am too calm and that she is not used to me being this way. She does not like me this way. By her standards, "whatever I am on" is too much. She says she wants the old me back. I assume she is looking for the daughter of visible stress and mood changes, the engaging daughter more than warm with personality, the daughter who will not shy away from confrontation in adverse conditions. The daughter, the fighter.*

*I explain to her that today the fire-eating dragon rests, but she is not satisfied with my answer. I cannot tell my mother the words I have used to describe her in psychotherapy. I cannot explain how selecting one child over another devastates the rest. I cannot explain how medication has helped me to be less of the daughter she has always known, always trusted, always loved in her own way.*

*My mother is too old to understand or follow my lead; she does not care to analyze her place in this life nor contend with the complaints we*

*might bring to her now. I have been too much like her in too little time, and*
*although I love her, being like her is dysfunctional suicide.*

When I am writing, the words directly relate to the volatility of my mind. My writing flows within the variables of mania, and as it pours from my soul, it wakes me.

Many bipolar patients feel that a creative outlet is very helpful. As my chemistry changes, I move from one medium to another until I find the artistic outlet that satisfies me. Often medication has zapped my imaginative juices, but photography remains my desire. This is the medium where the mind's eye searches to replicate an aspiration on paper. Journaling shows the patterns in my own illness and it serves as a reminder of my feelings, my dreams, my desires, and my symptoms, which I then discuss with my psychiatrist.

This is hell outside of remission, but I feel in some way this has been my fate. I am hopeful that those who struggle shall see for themselves the commonality they share with others. There is a universal thread regarding mental illness, and although no two patients are affected the same way, the medical profession is taking notice. Findings have shown that bipolar disorder affects cultures in drastic ways, and the diagnostic system for clinical classifications throughout the world provides information to determine mental disorders. The World Health Organization Study, investigating depression in Canada, Switzerland, Iran, and Japan, found that of those studied, 76% reported cross-culturally constant symptoms—sadness, joylessness, anxiety, tension, lack of energy, loss of interest, loss of ability to concentrate, and ideas of insufficiency.

As changes in diagnosis and symptoms continue to occur, I have many dreadful days of disappointment. Expressive in frustration, I write.

**BiPolarOnEmIXEDObsessiveCoMpulsiveDisoRderGeneralAnxietyDisORDER**
You are the skull and crossbones of my life, last year's bipolar II you now
    evolve
You created a setting specifically to deceive me and simply by familiarity I
    believed
we were    one

## Life Is Like a Line

I remember you and I, those were the ultimate days…I remember you and I,
the party would ooze into my soul
I remember you and I, the high was my desire…I remember you and I,
you were always the   boss

Now I will admit that in forty-eight years, you were like steam, heavy on
    my mirror
Now I will admit that in forty-eight years, no textbook characterization
    could ever do you justice,
but I ran to keep up with what was eventually excessive
Now I will admit that in forty-eight years, I knew nothing of your
    magnetism, I knew
nothing of the penetration of my spirit or your intention of my eventual
destruction…but I ran to keep away each time the darkness reached my
    soul

But here we are, apparently at an impasse, as I struggle more to have less
    of you
The fact is that without chemical stability more of me still faithfully
    hungrily
believes that I am   yours

My psychiatrist will not allow your moody characterization of my
    personality to
destroy me, she gives me her word
My psychiatrist will not allow your cunning nature to deceive me away
    from the
spirit of medication and analysis
My psychiatrist will help to protect me from living on the jagged edge of
    your
inflicted doses of dangerous   liaisons

For each day that by some miracle you do not devour me, I am more than
    surviving
For each day that medication eradicates my symptoms, I am more than
    surviving
For each day that I have a speck of hope, I am more than surviving

For each day that I want to live, I am more than   surviving

For this is a powerful and difficult path to walk especially if it is walked
    alone
For this is a powerful and difficult path to walk laden with personal
    burden and
not easy to change…if walked alone
This is a powerful and difficult path to walk that in time may devour
    you…if walked
alone
This is a powerful and difficult path whose inescapability may be its
    finality…especially
if walked alone
5.7 million affected may not survive if walking alone…

The bipolar mind of chaos and confusion, wild agitation, suicidal tendencies, lack of clarity, depression, insomnia, elation, obsession, compulsion, paranoia, and more that infected with turbulence my post-menopausal mind is all but eliminated by remission, and now my doctor's goal is to place me back on the happiness scale.

This may be her most lofty goal; I am thankful she finds it important. As always, I pester her in wellness. I convince her of a medication dosage decrease and then struggle to keep the symptoms under wraps as they slowly begin to rise to the surface. The next two or three appointments, I am in defense mode; increase the dose and wait, and then I convince her and we do it all over again.

Reluctantly she complies because I am "very convincing." I believe she trusts me emphatically. I believe she knows I can handle whatever comes my way because I have proven myself in the worst of conditions and situations. Taking medications seems worthless to me when I'm in remission, but eventually I realize they alone keep me there.

As she leans forward, her hands clasped in her lap, her figure close to mine, she begins to weigh and advise me of the trickiness of my experiments. Mutually we worry about the ramifications of every approach. Often medications move me in a way that weakens my spirit.

## Life Is Like a Line

Though psychotherapy is an absolute necessity, it can never fully erase the highs of chemical hypomania and the natural depression that comes from the energy within. It is pharmaceuticals alone that nullify what cannot be cured. I told my psychiatrist that, without medication, I would have death or a life of insanity. It is the energy of darkness that I fear.

Mankind in lunacy, dear God, thoughts and experiences I do not wish to embrace. Funny happy comedic hypomania is not mine. This morning as I retrieve the medicine bottles, I am grateful. I separate each pill one by one from its bottle. Often I forget which one I have swallowed so I have initiated a checkoff system. Lately I have been more careful. During this period, there are five pills each morning. They are chased down. They are my maintenance as long as no trigger is activated. I will be mindful of my stress; everything and nothing has changed.

Recently I was asked to describe the pulse of a hypomanic episode. Since the query came from someone living life normally around the midline, I felt the following explanation sound:

> *Imagine you are a metronome, your life the pendulum. You feel as though your weight is at the top of the pendulum rod. You are moving slowly back and forth and you feel everything pleasantly. Your weight trigger is based on stress. No stress; today you have no stress. Your pulse is rhythmic; you can hear the "tick, tick, tick" that is the beat of your life.*
>
> *Let the pendulum rod go back and forth, back and forth, ever so gently; it's an almost poetic swaying. Now you begin to feel the pull of gravity. Feel the sound everything makes. Hear it as it gets faster, faster, "tick, tick, tick," stress begins, and more weight comes down the pendulum rod, more and then more and now more still, and then more comes at you faster.*
>
> *Now the pendulum swing is more dramatic. You have stress. God, you have stress, unrelenting, undesirable stress. You have stress. The more stress you have, the farther the weight comes down upon your core. Your pendulum is moving faster and faster to catch up. Still faster and faster, your pulse is now racing and the beat may be too fast. All becomes inaccurate. You, the metronome, can barely control the rod. Life is getting blurry but you have options.*

*You can change the measure (erase the stress), which will change your rhythm, but you don't even recognize what is happening. With all the weight upon you, your behavior may be different or your mood may be altered with a temper on your temperament. That may be noticeable. Frustrated, you stutter to speak or lash out without much provocation. You may drive your car badly. Others are awful, the world your enemy. Your mind is moving faster and your blood is racing and you're out of breath and the rod is really swinging away, exaggerating everything.*

*Metronome me—it just doesn't feel right, something's wrong, really; it's not a good feeling, this strong feeling, erratic. Now the pace. It seems too fast and now the simple task of buying bread from the market is impossible. Literally, I cannot choose. This is the beat of me today and living at this pace of mental irregularity is frightening.*

*At first it is so easy, the ticking, the pendulum rod swaying, life less chaotic. Before this I could handle it all, handle it all, handle them all. Multitask, multitask, multitask. Shock, the pendulum goes slower without provocation and then it begins again for no reason. Gravitational forces bring me down. Faster and faster, the mind is moving faster—can't keep up and now the simplest action feels like a blur.*

*Ahh, at the doc's command, pills are gleefully consumed. White, green, pink, or blue, caps or tabs, it doesn't matter, but you take them at your given time. And slowly the weight slides away from you, the pendulum rod slows and the sweep gets less and less and the tempo is more reasonable…ahh, the rhythm.*

*You're thinking more with less confusion and you remember the bread and the rest of the groceries from the list you forgot at home and with each change of the beat the "tick………tick……………tick" becomes farther apart and slower; now everything is easier. You can function again and enjoy, breathe, breathe, breathe relief.*

\* \* \*

As I reflect upon my yesterdays, I believe the power of a forceful energy has chased me. I have run from it at full speed, but the faster I ran, the more difficult it has been to manage, and as the energy grew, it began to have its way with me…against my will.

## Life Is Like a Line

Historically, there is no way to determine if the members of my family have been affected by this illness, though it would seem that genetically it's likely. Though we may share some symptoms, it is ultimately personality type, stress level, and an imbalance of brain chemicals that weaves together any bipolar connection we might share.

Right now, this instant, today, I am well. Much of the stress of the past has left me, medication seems to keep me whole, and there are days when I am so well I feel I am cured. Those lacking familiarity with bipolar symptoms will never understand the idea of "so well." Feeling so well is almost unnatural. It is a sense that you are better than you ever were before, ever. In my period of wellness, I realize that I live in change and as the world moves and evolves, so do I.

It is awful to experience the symptoms of mania along with the symptoms of major depression and/or anxiety and it is difficult for my doctor to manage them. She continues to be diligent and my medication is routinely adjusted as she watches for any recurring signs of depression or hypomania. I am currently on a cocktail consisting of three medications, lithium carbonate (mood stabilizer), Depakote ER (used for manic or mixed episodes, migraines, or epilepsy), and Lexapro (for symptoms of depression and generalized anxiety disorder). Today, my diagnosis is bipolar I, with comorbid conditions. "Comorbid" means that several disorders, including anxiety disorders, obsessive-compulsive disorder, social phobia, suicidal ideation, and substance dependence may occur simultaneously with bipolar I and II.

Since the onset of this disorder, I have been experiencing mixed mood states along with my hypomania. A mixed episode is defined by sufficient depressive and manic symptoms occurring simultaneously. The effect that this concurrency of symptoms has on the course of bipolar disorder is unclear. Some research suggests that patients with mixed episodes take longer to recover from an episode and have poorer outcomes than those who experience pure mania or hypomania. Mixed episodes are associated with an increased incidence of substance abuse and suicide ideation and attempts. In addition, manic episodes that occur in adolescence and early adulthood may be more likely to be mixed episodes. The lifetime prevalence rates of other psychiatric and medical conditions are greatly increased in patients with bipolar disorder and these comorbid conditions can make the course of the illness more difficult to treat and manage. The two most common comorbid conditions are anxiety disorder and substance abuse; the National Comorbidity Study in 1999 reported a prevalence of 93% for anxiety disorder and of 64% for substance abuse in patients with bipolar I disorder. Patients with bipolar disorder and comorbid anxiety disorder experience a more severe course of disease than those without comorbid anxiety. Patients with bipolar disorder who also have a history of substance abuse have a more complicated disease course than those with no history of substance abuse.

Every day I realize that my comorbid conditions can fluctuate at the command of my chemistry. I am vigilant with my psychotherapy appointments to monitor my symptoms. As my doctor continues to hear the things I do not say and read between the lines, she also reminds me to maintain my boundaries. Stress and sleep deprivation remain my lifelong enemies and I am fully aware that wellness requires compliance and that my chemistry is the luck of the draw. Today, I recognize hypomania for what it is…a symptom worthy of my greatest attention.

As the ebb and flow of feelings and emotions are evaluated, they often become the central dialogue. My life of late has revolved around educating myself and coping with the intensities of my moods, my symptoms, and my struggles. I have been doing research, because education is power. Fortunately, many national organizations provide informative newsletters, treatment, and referrals as well as sponsor support groups. Support groups are a wonderful place to learn and share and prepare. Whether helpful or equally vulnerable, the support group veterans are in it to win, and it is through their partnership that unendurable suffering is endured.

Looking back, I firmly believe it has been my faith in God that has prevented me from taking my own life. In and out of the Catholic Church, divorce excommunicated me but my private faith, though at times shadowy, never truly ceased to exist. Studying various Christian books, I understand more and have been able to sense God's presence in ways that have been unexplainable. Every day I am reminded of the most fundamental emotion, love. I believe, however, that this illness infiltrates and deadens the deepest part of one's soul by its darkness and deceit.

Still, in the grand scheme of things, I believe I am the luckiest person on earth. I have seen life through multiple eyes. I have felt life with my mind's eye. I have had cosmic experiences and shared the fiery grotto with those who have gone before me.

Most importantly, God has continuously given me second chances and new beginnings. Although it has been many years since I have attended an organized church with any regularity, I sense the Lord's presence and look to him for help. No suicide will keep me from being reunited with my family in paradise if I believe.

Our hearts are physiology, a hollow muscular organ that pumps blood around our bodies, sustaining life—yours and mine. But our hearts are more than that. Perhaps symbolic of affection, our hearts are the source and center of life, and only recently have the deepest and sincerest feelings become mine again.

One day, her face within inches of mine, we were fixed upon each other and the swell of purest love began to rise in me. With streaming tears, I was hopeful and joyful and felt the depth of her love.

My tears persisted and my priceless, precious, very concerned two-year-old granddaughter took my face into her hands and said, "I'm sorry, Yiayia" ("Yiayia" is Greek for "Grandma").

I was alive again. She had done nothing to warrant a request for forgiveness. If only she knew how her love penetrated my heart that day. Our brilliant toddler, so mentally uncontaminated, innately showing her tenderness, saw my frailty and responded to it.

We drove home from daycare with the sunroof opened. I told her about God and the blue sky and the white puffy clouds and the tops of the trees where the birds lived and I was so grateful to be with her. Then out of her sight down they came again, my tears. Some were for her, but most were for me. They were tears of joy, tears of joy in knowing what I have come to understand.

I have heard of happy bipolar patients, though it is too early for me to know any. I am too new at this game. I know that once overtaken with this illness, it is easy to be negative. It is easy to be negative when our minds are in constant flux. It is easy to be negative when our mouths so desperately share the tale. It is easy to feel stigma as so much of this territory is uncharted, and while everyone else can only assume my lingering cloudiness, I wait and wonder.

It is easy to be me-centered and angry and disappointed and I am all of that some of the time. It is easy to feel anxious during psychotherapy, agreeing to ingest medications, fearing the side effects, but I trust.

It is frightening to think that for severe cases, hospitalization and electroconvulsive therapy (ECT), a procedure in which a brief application of electric stimulus is used to produce a generalized seizure, are the options. As with so many other things, it is not known how or why ECT works or what the electrically stimulated seizure does to the brain.

Unfortunately, to quote Dr. Francis Mark Mondimore, M.D., "There is no cure for bipolar disorder, only treatment and management…A lifetime of stressful events (illness, death of a family member, divorce, quarrels, and family hostility) can cause 'kindling.' The 'kindling' theory asserts that people who are genetically predisposed toward bipolar disorder experience a series of stressful events, each of which lowers the threshold at which mood changes occur. Eventually, the mood episode itself is sufficient to trigger recurring difficulties, including bipolar episodes such as mania. After several episodes, kindling can take on a life of its own and mood episodes are likely to arise spontaneously. Kindling may accelerate as the patient ages or episodes may become more frequent…"

The good news is that there are options today like never before in the history of manic-depressive illness; there are more medications than ever before, more scientific research than ever before, and the general population is more aware of what this illness is and how to treat it than ever before. No longer must it be a blazing fire in your heart, for there is hope.

In the light of this day, I am well enough to fight the urge to gamble, but it gnaws at me. For me, gambling in wellness means fulfilling the desire to walk away from my psychotherapy, from my medications, and from any thoughts of being overpowered by the illness. I have no explanation as to why my mind plays tricks on me and wishes me ill. I have no explanation as to why my mind would wish success for the senseless act of living a "void of mind" condition, and yet the attraction exists.

I will call it "false wellness." The road to self-destruction is paved in it. And mind games...be wary of them. For me, they are my reminder in wellness that I am yet a patient in remission. I am playing mind games again. I thought about abandoning my medication again just yesterday. They are pure unadulterated insanity, these thoughts.

Once disappeared, the dull white saucers are flying in my face again. Today they are bright, today they are bright, they are bright again, they are bright today; they are small white oval saucers and they are back. Damn... gamble, saucers, remission, mind games...God, I hate that.

Moving forward is complicated given my fluctuating cycles, but I am supported by my wonderful family. With medication, I am able to protect them from the ugliness of me.

Over the years my husband has witnessed my varying cycles and has come to understand the ebb and flow of moods that compel me. We are perfectly matched opposites and I am blessed. He is my gift.

My daughters, raised within an earshot of my turmoil, have never ceased to be anything but helpful and kind and loving during my many years of unintentional fallen moods and temperament. I know that in many ways they have been affected by my behavior, and worse, that they remember me in all the ways I have forgotten.

Strangely enough, my mother and I have grown much closer since she has settled into her new retirement community. Although she misses my father and my brother very much, she has learned to live life without them. In addition, the slightest advancement of age-induced dementia has helped her to adjust much better than I expected. We speak not of death but of life and the road ahead.

Although she very much relies on me, she has come to understand what the past has brought to my present. With a change in medication, she is less confrontational and I am no longer defensive. Though there are days when her moods are fiery, as I sit in the middle of the embers I remain considerably calmer, cool, and collected. Unfortunately, when I am unresponsive to her anger, she retaliates. I realize that her moods are cyclical and I am always thankful when she is out of her cycle.

It is not unusual for a mother and daughter to be at odds with each other. My mother felt badly of her mother for over seventy years and could not understand the way she abandoned her younger sister while in the throes of diphtheria. She does not understand the reason for her mother's behavior and there is blame. She does not understand the rejection and the denial within the household where the parents were needed and necessary and absent, especially her mother.

Likewise, I have felt anger toward my mother for many years. She does not see the likeness she shares with her mother but I do. My mother's love for one kept back the rest. She enabled the weakest of character. As a young child, I needed warmth when she was cold. I needed her affection and love but her limited abilities were spent.

Today my mother is eighty-eight years old and she can finally demonstrate some affection for me, though it is clear that she resents me still and that I remain her scapegoat. I am the one in charge and therefore I am often blameworthy. Fortunately, it is much easier now to turn my head from her words when they are uncomfortable to digest. My ability to do so is thanks to proper management of mood medications. Ironically, my mother feels that she enjoys life more today than she once did and admits that if she'd had "I like people pills" in the old days, our father and our family would have had a better life. That is a huge commentary.

With the help of my medications, I am able to tolerate what once was intolerable with my mother. I am thankful I can be kind and calm and that I am no longer angered by her slightest fault. I have forgiven her inability to feel lasting affection for me because I understand with more certainty the facets of her own mental capabilities.

In spite of it all, I panic at the thought of losing her. I obsess and I panic. The loss of her will be another loss of me, and as my psychiatrist verbalizes her concern for this eventual outcome, I pray for a long wait.

When my mother is forgiving and courteous to almost everyone, it is a major departure from the woman who raised me, and when she verbalizes her delight like never before, it is good. Visibly I can see happiness on her face, and in my heart I am filled.

My sister and I have been traveling down a more pleasant road. I cannot deny that she has been in my thoughts, as well as a subject of many of my psychiatric sessions, for years. Though I am filled with uncertainties, I long to have a sister. There was a time when I felt reserved and hesitant when with her and I cannot deny that my altered senses have changed me. I fear her continual abandonment. It has been difficult to make eye contact with her. I have trust issues that need to be resolved and I am certain this will take time. I don't know if we will ever have our family back; it is fragmented. Dad, our glue, no longer lives to mend the broken hearts.

I have gained much and I have lost much to medication. When the first thirty pounds kicked in, I worried and I obsessed about the potential for medication obesity. None of my clothes fit, my face was puffy, and as my depression worsened, I continued with a rant and rave. My experience with a succession of hallucinations due to constantly changing antidepressant medications blew my mind. I, mother and grandmother, tripping in the living room; it was so bizarre. Bonus…all was under the care of a doctor, but it was not for me, not anymore.

Neurological withdrawal symptoms constantly kick my behind; drugs are easy going in, difficult coming off. Consistently, the withdrawal syndrome lasts for several weeks due to the half-life of the medication (in pharmacology, the half-life is the amount of time it takes for one half of the drug to metabolize in the body). Dizziness, brain zaps, sweating, irregular heart beat, anxiety, skin crawling sensations, neurological oddities, more visions. And the saucers keep coming; bob and weave for God's sake, before they strike you. My thyroid affected, adding to the mix, I am losing my faith. One pill at a time adding quantity to the combinations, remission is attained but a stressful occurrence allows for a repeat performance over and over and over again. This is what my doctor calls trial and error. I have not tested life without them altogether.

Stress…boundaries, yeah sure. My stark white hair, patches of yellow… cut it out; it's spiked already; it used to be coarse; now it's baby fine. I respect the mighty pills, you bastards. Now ingestion does not simply imply relief.

In wellness, a gastrointestinal upset begins a downward spiral where mania wakes. An extensive loss of fluid through illness can increase symptoms of bipolar disorder. I feel the rush, and as it climbs through me, it picks up speed faster and faster, higher and higher inside of me. It is in my throat. It is swirling around my chest but I remain motionless. Lasting moments like hours, the lithium has fallen below the therapeutic level; I am sure, dear God. The black energy continues to press against my body from the inside out. Anxiety and panic, irritation and agitation, and all that is this exhaust and frighten me.

It is over. In religiosity, my mind thinking fast, racing, and I am composing prayers in my head. As they come with such persistence and might, neither hand nor lips is capable of replication. Directed by hypomania or more, this is the most exciting warning sign my mind produces.

I am saddened that stability takes religiosity from me. It is like an ache in my soul. Experiencing such intense prayer and being so close to our maker must be heaven-sent and today it is all but a dream.

I am surrounded by the stained glass windows and pews of oak and my sanity consumes me as I kneel. I wonder why I am struggling in this way. Medication brings to me the very opposite of religiosity. Tonight my doctor studies my mood state during our six o'clock appointment. She believes I may be experiencing some form of over-medication, as my mind has fallen asleep. I struggle to think. I am in remission from my symptoms but I am stupefied. I am hopeful that my lack of mental perception proves her theory. We have agreed to test the waters. We are reducing my milligrams on one and increasing the other. We change them up. In the world of bipolar that is precisely what you do. We are thinking about the future and I am letting go of the past. And in doing so, I pray for answers and I will walk the uncertain path where I am led.

This book was written at the behest of my psychiatrist, Dr. Henike. On the days I brought to her and she studied closely my newest writing, analysis and discussion became her guarantee that she knew exactly where my head was. It was she who encouraged me to submit my poetry to magazines or put together a compilation of my work. Each week I became more surprised by my intense feelings, feelings derived from my senses, ink to the paper by means of the hand that waited below. Fluid, I am revealing and there is confusion, but in the fray I am in a battle and I fight back. My thoughts, journal entries built in an obsessive and compulsive world, sprinkled with hypomania and manifestations, reflect me, ill without knowing, each day of loss a spiraling mass.

> When I dream about what will happen when I am grown, I know life is going to be cool. My mom and my dad are going to grow old together. My brother and I will be close and we will see each other more. I don't know if he will ever marry but I hope so. I think my dad will love him more. Mom, well, she's feeling better. We will have our ups and our downs like any family. My sister, she still loves pink. I think she will have a big shaggy dog. She will have a husband who will be really cool and I will be an aunt and we will do stuff together and have wonderful picnics at her house. Maybe even someday I will have a dog. That would be weird and great! I suppose there will be bumps in the road but nothing that our family cannot handle. I will not like Dad or Mom getting old. I just can't think of losing them. They will always be with me because, as you know, Dad will always be my hero and I will always be at my mother's side.

Not long ago, a schizophrenia patient told me that she would not divulge certain thoughts or feelings to her psychiatrist because of her own stigma about her illness. Twelve years of therapy with the same doctor and yet stigma incapacitated her. Finally, delusions forced a 911 call where she spent a week in the hospital, days before the holidays. I encouraged her to tell her doctor everything and she promised. If you have kidney pain, tell your doctor. If you have a headache, tell your doctor. If you feel suicidal, dear God, call your doctor. If you are on medication and become physically ill, call your doctor (diarrhea will be the end of you, pardon the pun). Anything out of the ordinary, tell your doctor, tell your doctor, call your doctor. Hold back nothing, every day. And remember what my dad would say, "Don't be afraid, honey."

Standing in front of my seemingly one-dimensional mirror, I am not alone. Bipolar disorder makes me eager to know the genetics that will never be identified, but I perceive the ghosts of heredity that live within me. A small child fits into my form. I know her dimples. She walks in the shade of anxiety and depression, genetic characteristics that are mine. There are others inside of me. They are shadowy figures of sizes and sexes that are unidentified, but I sense our strong connection. It is my heredity.

> *When I grow up I will be married too. My husband will be smart and handsome and loving. He will be perfect and really tall and probably older than me. It might take a few years to find him so I might be older too. He will have a really cool car and he will be funny. We will have two girls and two boys and they will be great kids. And they will come home on holidays bringing us the grandchildren. I think we won't live in the city anymore. I like the water so maybe we will live near a lake or at least by a river. And just like Murphy's Law, anything that can happen will, but he will be strong enough to hold me in case I fall. I will try to love everyone as much as I can and I have to remember, Prince Charming, no cutting down trees, especially the climbing ones!*

Today as I sit on the little couch in front of her, I hold my head in my hands and she begins. I am not eager to expose myself; I am horribly unhappy and ready to pounce. She has endured my blabber and it seems like forever, but hallelujah, dear God; she is a saint. While I struggle to connect the dots, she speaks. My mind wanders, psychiatrist mine...mine? I never saw it coming, any of this. My constant thought: be careful with the life of your child. Chaos, stress, turmoil, are detrimental. Living is all about love. This is the illness of dark energy. This illness is an invasion of everything that ever was or could have been, but I see now, I see what this is and what I have become. I am not a wannabe, nor am I a stigma.

*I am.*

# Facts on Bipolar Disorder/ Manic-Depressive Illness

According to the National Institute of Mental Health (NIMH), approximately 5.7 million Americans have bipolar disorder, also called manic-depressive illness. This is a type of depression, and when in the depressed cycle, an individual can have any or all the symptoms of a depressive disorder.

No one really knows what causes bipolar disorder, though genes predispose people to the illness and stress can trigger an episode.

Left untreated, bipolar episodes typically become more frequent and more resistant to medication.

A *Science Daily* article from November 30, 2004, states that the Radiological Society of North America has confirmed that magnetic resonance spectroscopy may prove definitive as a diagnostic test for bipolar disorder. Using MR spectroscopy of the brain, researchers have identified significant differences between the brain chemistries of people with and without bipolar disorder.

Each year, according to the NIMH, approximately 30,000 depressed individuals commit suicide.

There is recovery through the arts. Whatever your creative outlet, it is not the medium but the act of revealing that is healing and fascinating. You may find classes in art therapy at your local college or community mental health association. While medications can impair artistic creativity, impairment does not occur in every case.

Support groups such as the Depressive and Bipolar Support Alliance (DBSA) and the National Alliance on Mental Illness (NAMI) are pivotal in wellness as they maintain regular meetings offering camaraderie and community, information, education, and support.

Living with a mood disorder means learning how to fine-tune an atypical beat of life. Maintaining regular appointments with a psychiatrist or therapist may help you to distinguish your own beat and identify symptoms when your rhythm begins to change. Even a slight change in rhythm may require an increase in medication. Be mindful that stigma is a defeatist attitude to wellness.

Anyone feeling the urge to commit suicide, whether in or out of treatment, should contact their doctor immediately or go to the nearest hospital. There are also mental health facilities or organizations that can be contacted. Or, speak with a trusted friend or relative about your feelings. No one would be better off living without you, and the people you leave behind would suffer the rest of their lives.

# Recommended Readings
# and References

Mondimore, Francis Mark, M.D. *Bipolar Disorder: A Guide for Patients and Families.* Johns Hopkins, University Press, 1999.

Jamison, Kay Redfield. *An Unquiet Mind: A Memoir of Moods and Madness.* New York: Vintage Books, 1996.

Castle, R. Lana. *Bipolar Disorder Demystified: Mastering the Tightrope of Manic Depression.* Marlowe and Company, 2003.

Duke, Patty, and Hochman, Gloria. *A Brilliant Madness, Living with Manic-Depressive Illness.* Bantam Books, 1997.

Fink, Candida, M.D., and Kraynak, Joe. *Bipolar Disorder for Dummies.* Wiley Publishing, Inc. 2005.

Lundbeck Institute: BrainExplorer.org.

Behrman, Andy. *Electroboy: A Memoir of Mania.* Random House. 2002. www.electroboy.com

Friday, Paul J., Ph.D. *Fridays Laws: How to Become Normal When You're Not and How to Stay Normal When You Are.* Bradley Oaks Publications Copyright 2002-2007. www.fridayslaws.com

**Life Is Like a Line**

## Support Organizations

National Alliance for the Mentally Ill (NAMI)
200 N. Glebe Road, Suite 1015
Arlington, VA 22203-3754
800-950-6264
http://www.nami.org/

The National Depressive and Manic-Depressive Association (NDMDA)
730 North Franklin Street
Chicago, IL 60610
800-82-NDMDA
http://www.ndmda.org/

The National Foundation for Depressive Illness, Inc.
P.O. Box 2257
New York, NY 10116
800-239-1265
http://www.depression.org/

National Mental Health Association
1021 Prince Street
Alexandria, VA 22314
800-969-NMHA
http://www.nmha.org/

National Institute of Mental Health
6001 Executive Boulevard
Bethesda, MD 20892
http://www.nimh.nih.gov/

Depression and Bipolar Support Alliance (DBSA)
http://www.dbsallance.org/
This site lists over 1,000 patient support groups across the country.

Internet Links

Accredited Health Web Site
http://www.webmd.com

Medscape (from WebMD)
http://www.medscape.com/welcome

Medline Plus
http://medlineplus.gov/

Prescribe with Precision
http://PDR.net

Bipolar Focus
http://www.moodswing.org/

U.S. Department of Health & Human Services
http://www.hhs.gov

The Federal Government Source for Women's Health Information
http://www.womenshealth.gov/

Child and Adolescent Bipolar Foundation
http://bpkids.org

Michigan Mental Health Commission
http://www.michigan.gov/mentalhealth

President's New Freedom Commission on Mental Health
http://www.mentalhealthcommission.gov

Juvenile Bipolar Research Foundation
http://bpchildresearch.org

## Bipolar Research Clinics

Massachusetts General Hospital Bipolar Clinic and Research Program
50 Staniford Street, 5th Floor
Boston, MA 02114
1-617-726-6188
http://manicdepressive.org/

University of Michigan Depression Center
Rachel Upjohn Building
4250 Plymouth Rd.
Ann Arbor, MI 48109-5763
1-734-936-4400
http://www.med.umich.edu/depression

University of Pennsylvania Behavioral Health at Penn Presbyterian
39th and Market Streets
19Philadelphia, PA 19104
1-215-662-8000
http://pennhealth.com/

Stanford School of Medicine Bipolar Disorders Clinic
401 Quarry Road
Stanford, CA 94305-5723
1-650-723-4795
http://bipolar@med.stanford.edu/

UT Southwestern Medical Center
6363 Forest Park Road, 7th Floor
Dallas, TX 75235
1-214-648-6920
http://utsouthwestern.edu/utsw/cda/dept28702/files/77996.html

## Michigan Internet Links

ACMH—Association For Children's Mental Health
http://www.acmh-mi.org/

A.D.D.A.—Anxiety Disorder Support Group of Michigan
http://www.adaa.org/

AIM—Alliance for the Mentally Ill of Oakland County
http://qww.aim-hq.org/meetgmi.html

Common Ground—Emergency Intervention
http://www.commongroundsanctuary.org

Mental Health Association in Michigan
http://www.mha-mi.org

Michigan Protection and Advocacy Service, Inc.
http://www.mpas.org/HomePage.asp

Michigan Association for Children with Emotional Disorders
http://www.michkids.org/

Mental Health Resources—University of Michigan
http://www.umich.edu/~mhealth/

Michigan Psychiatric Association
http://www.mpsonline.org/

Michigan Psychological Association (MPA)
http://www.michpsych.org/index.cfm?location=1

Michigan Mental Health Networker
http://www.mhweb.org/

**Life Is Like a Line**

National Alliance on Mental Illness—Michigan
http://mi.nami.org

Oakland County Community Mental Health Authority
http://www.occmha.org/

OCD Foundation of Michigan
http://www.ocdmich.org/

Rose Hill (Rehabilitation) Center
http://www.rosehillcenter.com/

St. Clair County Community Mental Health Agency
1011 Military Street
Port Huron, MI 48060
Phone: 810-985-8900
Access Customer Service Center: 888-225-4447 (Toll Free Hotline)
http://www.scccmh.org/

## General Listing: Internet Links

National Mental Health Association
http://www.nmha.org/

Obsessive Compulsive Foundation
http://www.ocfoundation.org/

Narsad—The Mental Health Research Association
http://www.narsad.org/

Mental Health.Net
http://www.mentalhelp.net/

Mental Health America
http://www.nmha.org/

To purchase additional copies of *Life Is Like a Line*, please contact
Silver Lining Publishing
PO Box 399
St. Clair, MI  48079-0399
www.SilverLiningPublishing.com

# NOTES

# NOTES